Cross-Cultural Behaviour in Tourism: Concepts and Analysis

Cross-Cultural Behaviour in Tourism: Concepts and Analysis

Yvette Reisinger PhD

and

Lindsay W Turner PhD

OXFORD   AMSTERDAM   BOSTON   LONDON   NEW YORK   PARIS
SAN DIEGO   SAN FRANCISCO   SINGAPORE   SYDNEY   TOKYO

Butterworth-Heinemann
An imprint of Elsevier Science Limited
Linacre House, Jordan Hill, Oxford OX2 8DP
200 Wheeler Road, Burlington MA 01803

First published 2003

British Library Cataloguing in Publication Data
A catalogue record for this book is available from the British Library

Library of Congress Cataloging in Publication Data
A catalog record for this book is available from the Library of Congress

ISBN 0 7506 56689

For information on all Butterworth-Heinemann publications visit our website at
www.bh.com

Typeset by Keyword Typesetting Services Ltd
Printed and bound in Great Britain

Contents

Foreword

In recent years the interest in cultural tourism has boomed, emerging as a large and growing segment of the tourism industry. Yet, in spite of its global and local implications, the area has not been adequately explored by tourism researchers, who first studied cultural tourism by measuring visitors to cultural attractions such as museums, festivals, fairs, exhibitions, plays, concerts, dance performances, etc. They reported on attendance, expenditure, demographics, and the economic impact of these events.

In today's global environment, however, the impact of culture must be examined in all its forms and dimensions because it has a significant impact on tourism policy, planning, development, management, and marketing. A country presents itself to visitors through many cultural factors. These can be entertainment, food, drink, work, dress, architecture, handicrafts, media, history, language, religion, education, tradition, humor, art, music, dance, hospitality, and all the other characteristics of a nation's way of life.

The deeper effects of the many aspects of national cultures on tourism need to be researched because for many countries tourism has become an important means of promoting cultural relations, international co-operation, and economic sustainability. Tourism not only promotes knowledge and understanding, but also builds a favourable image among international travellers by providing an enjoyable and comfortable experience so essential for repeat visitation. In short, tourism requires diverse cultures to understand and appreciate each other.

Successful tourism requires more than having good transportation, hotels, and resorts. It thrives on a spirit of hospitality – that particular national flavour that shares traditional ways of life and projects a favourable image to tourists purchasing goods and services.

Today, as globalization continues, diverse cultures are being brought together more and more. The Asian tourist markets are currently major sources of international outbound tourism. These culturally diverse visitors are the fastest growing market.

To date, few scholars have studied the culturally diverse visitor and the role of national cultural characteristics. Cross-cultural awareness and sensitivity to cultural differences seem to be missing in the tourism literature. Consequently, Reisinger and Turner's book *Cross-cultural Behaviour in Tourism* makes a major contribution to understanding cultural differences across nations and the impact of host and guest behaviour. The book provides insight into the concepts, definitions, and measures of cultural components that encourage tourism. It untangles the complex role of cultural behaviour and illustrates statistical tools available to analyse cross-cultural behaviour.

The book needs to find its way into the libraries and hands of government tourism public policy officials, cultural tourism professionals, tourism managers, tourism marketers, tourism scholars, and other interested individuals. Reisinger and Turner's work on this complicated and multi-dimensional subject will be invaluable to those who follow.

Charles R. Goeldner
Professor Emeritus of *Marketing and Tourism*
Editor, *Journal of Travel Research*

Preface

There is a widespread and urgent need to improve the ability of those working in the tourism industry to understand and appreciate cultural differences and to translate that understanding into effective communication and interaction, and appropriate management and marketing strategies. There is also a need to enhance the ability of students and academics to measure and analyse cultural differences in the tourism context using a scientific research approach.

Some cultural differences that are reflected in food, music, artefacts or social behaviour are visible and easily recognizable during a relatively short visitation to a foreign country. Other cultural differences such as kinship systems, social organizations and many day-to-day practices are hidden deeply in culture and require total immersion in culture, prolonged social contacts with locals and often adaptation. However, not many prospective tourists seek total immersion in a different culture and have a desire to understand the culture of others, and not many host societies seek to adapt to the needs of tourists (Robinson, M. 1999, Cultural conflicts in tourism: inevitability and inequality. In Robinson, M. and Boniface, P. (eds), *Tourism and Cultural Conflicts*, London: CABI Publishing). In tourism many of the deep cultural differences are not relevant and are not emphasized. The differences that draw the attention of most tourists are the differences in surface culture. These are often packaged and presented to tourists during their short stay without the need to learn and understand a foreign culture (Robinson, 1999).

Cultural experiences can be either satisfying or rewarding, or they can be unpleasant and generate stress and even conflict. The higher the demand for international tourism, the more opportunities there are for cross-cultural contact and the greater the potential for cultural conflict. A lessening of this potential conflict is the key to tourist satisfaction and repeat visitation. Consequently, there is a need to learn and understand the impact of cultural differences on tourist behaviour.

This book represents a timely contribution to the understanding of tourist behaviour in a cross-cultural context. An important feature of the book is that it represents a theoretical synthesis of the literature findings in the area of the impact of cultural differences on tourist behaviour rather than a critical assessment of specific findings. Evidence shows that cross-cultural differences do exist and can be observed, recorded, measured and statistically tested. The availability of sophisticated analytical techniques to measure cultural differences allows for comparability of these differences and aids in substantive theory testing. Unfortunately, appropriate methodological approaches have not been widely used or understood in tourism, marketing and management studies. The aim of this book is to overcome some of the methodological problems associated with analysing cultural differences, provide an illustration of how such research can be satisfactorily carried out and show how substantive theory can be tested.

This book focuses on quantitative research methods, which involve the collection and analysis of numerical rather than qualitative data. The aim is to present how scientific research methods can be used to identify cultural differences and similarities, confirm or reject prior hypotheses about their existence, logically interpret empirical evidence, and then make inferences and conclusions about the phenomena that may lead to the establishment of general laws for solving decision-making problems. In this way findings can be generalizable and replicable. The use of scientific methods in applied tourism research assures objectivity in gathering facts and also allows for testing creative qualitative ideas.

This book is also written under the assumption that many readers don't use quantitative methods due to their statistical complexity and user non-friendly manuals. It is anticipated that readers will appreciate receiving detailed preparation in the more complex empirical methods of scientific research, in a context of cultural differences analysis. To achieve this purpose, exposure to the material is presented in a well-ordered, logically structured and accessible way, without compromising complete coverage of the major research areas and accuracy of the statistical methods.

This book has been prepared primarily as a research reference book for tourism educators, students and practitioners looking for information relevant to the particular problem they currently face. In addition to this book, an account of Hypothesis Testing, together with a detailed Glossary and a comprehensive reference list of relevant materials which the reader might like to refer to can be found on the internet at: www.bh.com/companions/0750656689.

Although there is extensive work on tourism conducted in the German, French and Spanish languages, the literature presented in this book is mostly based on work published in English-speaking countries. We hope that readers will find it interesting and useful.

List of tables

List of figures

Page

Introduction

In recent years there has been a considerable interest in the cultural aspects of tourism. Culture in its various forms and dimensions has a significant impact on tourism planning and development, management and marketing. Unfortunately, literature that examines the impact of culture on tourism concentrates mostly on expressions of material forms of culture such as the arts, music, architecture or crafts. Researchers have neglected to analyse the deeper effects of national cultures on tourism. The elements of national cultures such as values, norms or rules have a significant impact on tourists' behaviour, their holiday expectations, experiences, satisfaction and, consequently, repeat visitation.

The examination of cultural differences is especially important to the tourism industry for several reasons. First, the tourism and travel industry has experienced a growing internationalization in the past decade. Considerable attention has been paid to the issue of cultural diversity and its relevance to tourism. The days when tourism was considered as simply confined to Westerners are gone. Contemporary tourism and increasing mobility expose people to culturally different societies. It is imperative for the industry representatives, who operate in the international business environment, to understand the influence of national cultures on their consumers, in order to compete successfully for market share. Many people visit foreign destinations to experience different ways of living, traditions and customs. Also, tourism is a service industry where people from different nationalities meet. The quality of their interaction contributes to their holiday experiences and perceptions of the visited destination.

Unfortunately, information on the nature of the cultural differences between international tourists and local hosts is not readily available. There is a need for tourism academic literature that analyses cultural

differences across nations and determines their impact on tourist behaviour. Such literature could help to identify similarities and differences
among tourists and local providers and decision-makers in different
countries. It could contribute to more adequate and effective marketing
and management strategies.

There also seems to be a failure by some researchers and tourism
practitioners to realize the importance of cultural differences for tourist
holiday experiences, satisfaction and, consequently, repeat visitation. It
is generally assumed that tourist holiday satisfaction is determined by
material and physical needs and derives from operational buying
motives such as the purchase of a product and the level of service
provision. In fact, the ability to attract and satisfy specific markets
often depends on psychological needs and is highly dependent upon
psychological buying motives such as cultural and psychological interpretation of the product purchased.

A significant part of the international tourist holiday is contact
with local hosts – people who are associated with the tourism and
travel industry such as hoteliers, restaurateurs, shop assistants, customs officials, tour guides and many others who provide services to
tourists. These people greatly contribute to the perceptions tourists
develop of the visited destination. Thus, the cultural differences,
which influence the quality of the interpersonal interaction between
tourists and hosts, can significantly add to tourist holiday experiences
and satisfaction.

The large Asian tourist markets will be the future targets of the international tourism industry. As a result, the culturally diverse tourist is the
focus of this book. A fundamental theme of this book is that holiday
satisfaction and repeat visitation of the culturally different tourist are
determined by the quality of their interpersonal experiences with culturally different hosts.

Given all of the above, it was felt that the most effective and appropriate response to the current and future international tourism needs was
to prepare a research book, which would focus on cross-cultural differences in tourist behaviour, and which would draw upon evidence from
the broad past and current literature about the present and future intercultural tourist.

The aim

The major aims of this book are as follows.

1. To review the literature on the concepts related to cross-cultural behaviour in tourism.
2. To identify and discuss the major differences between Eastern and Western national cultures and their influence on tourist and host social behaviour.
3. To show how cultural differences influence tourist holiday perceptions and satisfaction.
4. To present the fundamental quantitative methods of cross-cultural analysis.
5. To provide an in-depth analysis of five Asian cultures (Indonesian, Japanese, Korean, Chinese and Thai) in comparison with European, US and Australian cultures.

The main users

This book provides a research reference and text for university academics, students, researchers and tourism practitioners involved in all aspects of travel and tourism. It will be of use to academics and students who require an overview of the available literature on tourism in a cultural context, in a simple source combined with an associated bibliography, that will allow them to pursue more in-depth work when required.

This book can also be used as a textbook for tourism academic courses and seminars. From a course perspective, it reinforces a number of important concepts and provides the student with an integrated view of interrelated socio-cultural tourism issues. This book is most relevant for courses in tourist behaviour, cultural and social impacts of tourism, tourism marketing, tourism analysis, tourism management, and cross-cultural communication. The most suitable academic level is third year undergraduate and Masters level courses in Tourism Management.

Tourism practitioners form another readership, and in particular, tourism managers, who have a need to deal face-to-face, interact and communicate with culturally different tourists. Detailed information about the fundamental concepts of culture and an analysis of the most outstanding cultural differences between Asia, Europe, Australia and the US is given. This information is essential for improving managerial and communication skills.

Structure and content

Given the diversity of the literature on social interaction and culture, it is not surprising that a review of the literature identified several important concepts to be analysed. These concepts are presented in separate chapters of the book. Each chapter is designed to direct readers to other related chapters.

Efforts have been made to include the newest approaches to the complex aspects of the analysed concepts. However, because of the enduring nature of the subject and the diversity of the literature, some findings have been retained even though they may be regarded as dated.

Part 1

Concepts of Cross-Cultural Behaviour in Tourism

This part discusses the main general concepts in cross-cultural tourism behaviour that were identified on the basis of a very extensive and broad literature review. It has six chapters, as follows:

- **Chapter 1**, entitled Culture, has been designed to specify clearly what is meant by the concept of culture and subculture. This chapter introduces the notion of cultural differences and dimensions, and introduces the intercultural interaction model. It presents the concepts of cultural differences and, subsequently, discusses cultural differences between Asian, European, US and Australian societies.
- **Chapter 2** explores the concept of social interaction. The specific emphasis is on cultural factors and the impact of cultural differences on tourist–host interaction. This chapter discusses interaction difficulties in inter- and cross-cultural tourist–host interaction. It also introduces the concept of culture shock and methods of measuring tourist–host contact. The intent is to demonstrate and emphasize that tourist–host social interaction is a cultural phenomenon.
- **Chapter 3** provides insights into the nature of cultural values. The purpose is to demonstrate the ways in which values differentiate cultures and the role they play in cross-cultural interaction. Different types of values are discussed and their classification presented. Various cultural dimensions are presented as identified by various researchers. A measurement of values is also evaluated. The major literature findings on the differences in cultural value patterns between Asian, European, US and Australian societies are illustrated as an example of the differences between various cultures. Concepts related to cultural values such as behaviour, rules,

norms and attitudes are also briefly discussed and their interrelationships shown.

- **Chapter 4** provides an explanation of the concept of rules of social interaction. The cross-cultural differences in rules of social interaction are presented.
- **Chapter 5** examines the concept of perceptions, and their relationship to the concept of culture and social interaction. Methods of perception measurement are introduced and the literature on tourists' and hosts' perceptions for Asia, Europe, the US and Australia discussed, along with cultural stereotyping and ethnocentrism.
- **Chapter 6** of the book focuses on satisfaction. This chapter deals with various aspects of satisfaction in relation to tourist holiday experiences, including satisfaction with interpersonal relations with hosts and the service provided by hosts. Methods of satisfaction measurement are presented.

1

Culture

Objectives

After completing this chapter the reader should be able to:

- define culture, its purpose and characteristics

- identify elements of culture

- understand subculture

- identify major cultural differences and cultural dimensions

- describe the intercultural model and the influence of cultural differences on an individual and social interaction

- understand the importance of cultural differences in behaviour.

Introduction

What is the influence of culture on social interaction? The first step is to determine what is meant by the concept of culture and how it can be defined. Various definitions of culture will be discussed and a final definition written for the purposes of general research use, and the specific analysis of culture in this book. We will then look at the relationships between culture and social interaction through the various dimensions modelled in current literature that define and explain the differences between various cultures. It is the differences that make the study of culture both interesting and rewarding so we will look at the essential nature of these differences, with a close focus upon the major cultural dichotomy – the difference between the East and the West.

Concept and definitions

Culture is a complex multidimensional phenomenon that is difficult to define, and the hundreds of different definitions presented in the literature reflect this. For example, Kroeber and Kluckhohn (1985) documented that there are over 160 definitions of culture. Because culture is broad in its scope, theorists have had difficulties in arriving at one central definition of culture and have had different views about what constitutes the meaning of culture. Several scientific fields such as sociology, psychology, anthropology and intercultural communication have their own definitions of culture. These definitions range from viewing culture as an all-inclusive phenomenon ('it is everything'), to those that take a narrow view of the concept. However, despite the vast range of definitions of culture, it has been generally agreed in the literature that culture is a 'theory' (Kluckhohn, 1944), an 'abstraction' or a 'name' for a very large category of phenomena (Moore and Lewis, 1952). It has also been accepted that defining culture is difficult or even impossible (Edelstein *et al.,* 1989). 'Culture is like a black box which we know is there but not what it contains' (Hofstede, 1980, p. 13).

Let us present some definitions of culture. We choose to focus on those features of culture that contribute most to culture's influence on social interaction and to emphasize culture's multifaceted nature.

Classic definition of culture

The classic definition of culture is:

> *that complex whole which includes knowledge, beliefs, art, morals, law, customs, and any other capabilities and habits acquired by man as a member of society* (Tylor, 1924, p. 1).

This definition emphasizes the inclusive nature of the concept of culture under which many variables are included in 'a complex whole'.

Human origin of culture

Since Tylor (1924), many anthropologists have redefined the concept of culture (Kroeber and Kluckhohn, 1952; Kroeber and Parsons, 1958; Mair, 1972; Piddington, 1960; Schneider and Bonjean, 1973). All definitions commonly point to the same feature of culture: its human origin (Moore and Lewis, 1952). It was agreed that humans have created culture. Culture is broadly viewed as 'the human-made part of the environment' (Herskovits, 1948, p. 17; 1955), as holding human groups together (Benedict, cited in Kluckhohn, 1944), and 'the most complete human groups' (Hofstede, 1980, p. 26). Culture is also viewed as a way of life of a particular group of people (Harris, 1968; Harris and Moran, 1979; Kluckhohn, 1951a), a 'design for living' (Kluckhohn and Kelly, 1945), 'standards for deciding what is ... what can be ... what one feels about it, what to do about it, and ... how to go about doing it' (Goodenough, 1961, p. 522).

Behavioural anthropologists

The definitions of behavioural anthropologists indicate that culture is about human behaviour (Schusky and Culbert, 1987). Culture manifests itself in observable patterns of behaviour associated with particular groups of people (Bagby, 1953; Barnlund and Araki, 1985; Lundberg *et al.*, 1968; Merrill, 1965; Spradley, 1972). Culture determines human behaviour (Barnlund and Araki, 1985; Parsons and Shils, 1951; Peterson, 1979; Potter, 1989), is 'indispensable to any understanding of human behavior' (Nisbett, 1970, p. 223), it guides behaviour in interaction (Parsons, 1951), indicates a pattern of social interaction (Harris, 1983), and it 'guides behavior and interprets others' behavior' (Kim and Gudykunst, 1988, p. 127). However, the behavioural anthropologists' definitions of culture have been criticized for not distinguishing between patterns *for* behaviour and patterns *of* behaviour (Goodenough, 1957, 1961).

Behaviouralists argued that cultural behaviour is learned, not inherited. Culture is a collection of beliefs, habits and traditions, shared by a group of people and learned by people who enter the society (Mead, 1951). It is possible to learn new cultural behaviour and unlearn old behaviour. This means that it is possible to learn cultural traits and integrate them when generating strategic marketing (Darlington in Joynt and Warner, 1996).

Functionalists

On the other hand, the definitions of functionalists emphasize the role of culture in understanding the reasons and rules for certain behaviour. Functionalists refer to culture as a set of rules for 'fitting human beings together into a social system' (Radcliffe-Brown, 1957, p. 102). These rules allow us to better understand and predict how others will behave and why. Culture is seen as something that 'gives directions for the actors and how the actors should play their parts on the stage' (Schneider, 1972, p. 38). Some definitions restrict the concept of culture to mental rules (Harris, 1983). Others stress that culture is the socially acquired ways of feeling and thinking (Harris, 1988; Nisbett, 1970; Radcliffe-Brown, 1957), and ways of doing (Sapir, 1921). Some functionalists see culture as the means through which human needs are met (Malinowski, 1939), and values are communicated (Dodd *et al.*, 1990).

Behaviouralists and functionalists

The behaviouralists and functionalists agree that culture and behaviour are inseparable because culture not only dictates how we behave, it also helps to determine the conditions and circumstances under which the various behaviours occur; it helps to interpret and predict behaviour. In this way, interactional behaviour is largely dependent upon the culture in which the interactants have been raised. Consequently, culture is the foundation of interaction. So we can say that when cultures vary, interaction patterns also vary.

Criticism of behaviouralists and functionalists

The behaviouralist and functionalist definitions of culture have been criticized for not explaining cultural behaviour sufficiently.

- Firstly, different observers may perceive and interpret the same behaviour differently.
- Secondly, behaviour may change over time across individuals and within individuals, and may depend on situations.
- Thirdly, there may be discrepancies between what people say, what they would do and what they actually do.
- Fourthly, the interpretation of behaviour may be influenced by stereotypes.

Cognitive anthropologists

The cognitive anthropologists refer to culture as cognitive knowledge, classifications and categories, existing in the minds of people (Goodenough, 1964; Merrill, 1965; Schmidt, 1939). Hofstede (1991, p. 5) described culture as 'the collective programming of the mind, which distinguishes the members of one group or category of people from another'. This definition stresses the mental conditions that cultural experiences impose. Keesing (1974) argued that culture is a 'system of knowledge, shaped by ... the human brain' (p. 89). He criticized Schneider (1972) for comparing culture to rules indicating how the actors should play on the stage. According to Keesing (1974) rules are created by a culturally patterned mind. Hofstede (1980) argued that culture includes systems of values; and values build blocks of culture. The cognitive anthropologists have been criticized for limiting the concept of culture to knowledge, and excluding people and their emotions from the concept, whereas in fact, many other senses contribute to peoples' experiences. For instance, Cole and Scribner (1974) noted that peoples' experiences are shaped by culturally and socially defined meanings and emotions.

Symbolists

The symbolists refer to culture as a system of symbols and meanings (Kim and Gudykunst, 1988; Radcliffe-Brown, 1957; Schneider, 1976) that influence experiences. Symbols help to communicate and develop attitudes toward life (Geertz, 1973) and allow for interaction in a socially accepted manner that is understood by the group (Foster, 1962).

Although meanings cannot be observed, counted or measured (Geertz, 1973), they help to understand others' behaviour. The symbolic definition of culture has also been criticized. Levi-Strauss (1971) argued that symbols do not create culture because they are created by a culturally patterned human mind.

Culture as perceptions

Many definitions of culture indicate that culture is 'the sum of people's perceptions of themselves and of the world ...' (Urriola, 1989, p. 66). The similarity in people's perceptions indicates the existence of similar cultures and sharing and understanding of meanings (Samovar *et al.*, 1981).

Subjective culture

Triandis (1972) referred to a 'subjective culture' as a cultural characteristic way of perceiving the environment. The main elements of subjective culture are values, role perceptions, attitudes, stereotypes, beliefs, categorizations, evaluations, expectations, memories and opinions. The similarity in perceived subjective culture means similarity in perceiving all these elements. Members of a similar subjective culture have similar values, conform to similar rules and norms, develop similar perceptions, attitudes and stereotypes, use common language, or participate in similar activities (Samovar *et al.*, 1981; Triandis, 1972). Triandis (1972) emphasized the importance of understanding how the elements of subjective culture affect interpersonal interactions. He reported that the similarities in subjective culture lead to frequent interaction among members of similar cultural groups. Triandis (1972, p. 9) also noted 'when the similar behavior patterns obtained in one culture differ from the similar patterns obtained in another, we infer the existence of some differences in subjective culture'. According to Landis and Brislin (1983, p. 187), differences in subjective cultures 'are more likely to occur ... because of the differences in norms, roles, attitudes, and values between the ... cultures' that infer that 'individuals belong to different cultures'.

Culture as differences between people

Culture is about differences and cultural differences are obvious (Wallerstein, 1990). Culture can be referred to as differences between groups of people who do things differently and perceive the world differently (Potter, 1989). These differences indicate the existence of different cultures. As Triandis (1972) noted, if there were no differences, there would be no cultures. Hofstede (1980) gave evidence of the differences and similarities among cultures. In a similar way to Triandis (1972), Landis and Brislin (1983) reported the importance of understanding how the cultural differences affect interpersonal interactions. According to Landis and Brislin (1983), cultural differences can cause differences in interactional behaviours and misunderstanding in their interpretations, and thus may create conflict. In cross-cultural contact they tend to reduce interaction among members of different cultures. Therefore, the analysis of the interactional behaviour and its interpretation is critical (Albert and Triandis, 1979) for the analysis of cross-cultural contact.

Culture as information and communication

Culture has also been viewed as information (Kluckhohn and Kelly, 1945) and a communication system (Hall, 1959). Several anthropologists suggest a relationship between culture and language (Kluckhohn, 1944). Language, 'the symbolic guide to culture' (Sapir, 1964, p. 70) 'transmits values, beliefs, perceptions, norms' (Samovar *et al.*, 1981, p. 141) and facilitates man's perceptions of the world (Sapir, 1964). Cultural differences create differences in verbal communication. Differences in languages create different ways of expressing beliefs, values and perceptions.

Other definitions of culture

Culture has also been compared to social interaction, rules about behaviour, perceptions, thoughts, language and non-verbal communication. These aspects of culture affect social interactional behaviour both directly and indirectly (Argyle, 1978).

Material and non-material culture

Two different forms of culture have been distinguished: material and non-material. The material form of culture refers to the productive forces and everything necessary to support human life; the non-material or spiritual form refers to morality, tradition, and customs (Urriola,

1989). The non-material form includes cultural beliefs and values, attitudes, and perceptions. Some writers referred only to material objects and artifacts (White, 1959), while others excluded material objects from the concept of culture (Goodenough, 1971).

Cultural perspectives

Culture has been viewed from two perspectives. One perspective views culture as an ideological entity encompassing values, norms, customs and traditions (Rokeach, 1973). The other perspective views culture as a combination of ideological and material elements such as what and how people eat, what they wear and what they use (Assael, 1992; Mowen, 1993).

Tourism studies focus either on the ideological aspects of culture or a combination of ideological and material aspects of culture. For example, Pearce (1982b) analysed the social psychology of tourist behaviour. Reisinger and Turner (1997a,b; 1998a,b,c; 1999a,b) investigated cultural aspects of Asian inbound tourism to Australia as well as its perceptions of Australia's attributes as a tourism destination (Reisinger and Turner, 2000).

Tourist, host and tourism culture

Tourist culture is the culture that tourists bring on vacation. It is the culture of their own or that of their country. Tourist culture explains tourist behaviour. The host culture is the culture of the host country with which tourists are in contact (Jafari, 1987). According to Jafari (1987), the behaviour of all participants involved in the tourism process creates a distinct 'tourism culture', which is distinct from that of their routine and everyday culture. Tourists behave differently when they are away from home because they are in a different state of mind and in the 'play' mode. Hosts behave differently because they offer the tourists hospitality services. However, both groups retain a residue of their own culture when in contact. Thus, the tourist culture should be analysed in relation to 'residual culture', which explains how tourists from different cultures behave. Jafari (1987) also suggested that tourist, host and residual cultures mix together and produce a special and distinguishing type of culture at each destination, which consists of the behaviour of tourists and hosts. Further, Pizam (1999) noted that tourists of various nationalities possess simultaneously both 'touristic cultures' (i.e., the culture of group of tourists, backpackers, etc.) and 'national cultures'. He asks the question: to what extent are 'touristic cultures' free of national cultures and reflected in the behaviour of all tourists regardless of nationality?

Industry, professional, functional and corporate culture

Like nations, industries, organizations and occupational groups have their own cultures. Industries such as tourism, banking, construction, retailing or pharmaceutical have their own cultures because they share different world-views on how to manage a business. For example, the tourism industry culture is more customer-oriented than banking culture. Corporations have different cultures as well because they are influenced by the different nature of the industry, business and product (Schneider and Barsoux, 1997). Different functions in organizations – finance, production, marketing, and research and development – are also characterized by distinct cultures: they have different task requirements, time frames and customers. For example, researchers and developers tend to take a more down-to-earth approach, advertisers are more creative. In addition, distinct professions such as doctors, lawyers or engineers also have their unique cultures because they differ in their beliefs and values and have different dress codes and codes of conduct.

The focus of this book is upon the national culture rather than the cultures of businesses, occupational groups or industries. Since the majority of definitions of national culture refer to culture in psychological terms such as values, norms, rules, behaviour, perceptions, attitudes, beliefs, symbols, knowledge, ideas, meanings and thoughts (Argyle, 1978; Bennett and Kassarjian, 1972; Camilleri, 1985; Ember and Ember, 1985; Kim and Gudykunst, 1988; Leighton, 1981; Mill and Morrison, 1985; Moutinho, 1987; Peterson, 1979; Robinson and Nemetz, 1988), these definitions have been used in this book to analyse the national culture of tourists and hosts. The definition presented here

> *Culture consists of patterns, explicit and implicit, of and for behavior acquired and transmitted by symbols, constituting the distinctive achievements of human groups, including their embodiments in artifacts; the essential core of culture consists of traditional (i.e., historically derived and selected) ideas and especially their attached values; culture systems may, on the one hand, be considered as products of action, and on the other as conditioning elements of further action* (Kroeber and Kluckhohn, 1952, p. 181).

summarizes all the various interpretations of culture discussed above. This definition refers to patterns of human behaviour and people's values that determine their actions.

The above definition has been widely used by researchers recently. For example, Berthon's (1993) saw culture as the result of human actions and showed the link between the 'mental programming' and the consequences of behaviour derived from this programming. Herbig (1998) defined culture as 'the sum of a way of life, including expected behaviour, beliefs, values, language and living practices shared by members of a society. It consists of both explicit and implicit rules through which experience is interpreted' (p. 11). Similarly, Pizam (1999) referred to culture as 'an umbrella word that encompasses a whole set of implicitly, widely shared beliefs, traditions, values, and expectations that characterizes a particular group of people' (p. 393). Potter (1994) reported that the extent to which people share meanings depends on their awareness of their own held values and beliefs and their awareness of others' values and beliefs. Once they become aware of the differences in these beliefs and values, they can adjust their behaviour to enhance their abilities to work successfully with people from other cultures. According to Herbig (1998), cultural beliefs, values and customs are followed as long as they yield satisfaction. If a specific standard of conduct does not fully satisfy the members of a society, it is modified or replaced. Thus, culture continually evolves to meet the needs of society.

Purpose of culture

The purpose of culture is to teach how to do things and how to think in order to organize the world (Dodd, 1998). Its purpose is to 'establish modes of conduct, standards of performance, and ways of dealing with interpersonal and environmental relations that will reduce uncertainty, increase predictability, and thereby promote survival and growth among the members of any society' (Herbig, 1998, p. 11). Culture indicates how to live. Culture guides people through life. According to Herbig (1998), culture influences behaviour and determines which behaviour is helpful and should be rewarded, and which is harmful and should be discouraged. Culture reinforces values (Dodd, 1998). It helps to decide what is appropriate and desired, and what is unacceptable. It tells what is correct, true, valuable and important (Kraft, 1978). Culture teaches significant rules, rituals, and procedures (Dodd, 1998). It dictates what clothes to wear, what kind of food to eat, what to say, how to serve guests or what to do at a dinner party. Culture dictates ideas and sets the rules that the majority of society obeys. 'It creates a hierarchy of codes for regulating human interactions which offers order, direction and guidance' (Herbig, 1998, p. 11). Culture teaches relationships with others and aspects of forming and maintaining relationships (Dodd, 1998). Culture makes the everyday life decisions easier. Cultural rules and norms help to achieve harmony in society. Without them society would be in disarray (Jandt, 1998). Culture provides the means for satisfying physiological, personal and social needs (Herbig, 1998).

Culture also makes it possible for human society to communicate using verbal and nonverbal systems of expressive behaviour (Herbig, 1998); 'culture explains how a group filters information' (p. 12); a culture encourages a particular communication style; culture has the power to shape perception, develop feelings, images, and stereotypes (Dodd, 1998).

Culture bonds people together (Dodd, 1998) and identifies the uniqueness of the group of people. According to Leavitt and Bahrami (1988), culture identifies the uniqueness of the social unit, its values and beliefs. Members of the same culture share similar thoughts and experiences. Shared cultural norms give the members of a society a sense of their common identity (Herbig, 1998). Culture helps to define who they are (Jandt, 1998). However, few humans are consciously aware of their own culture. Only when one is exposed to foreign culture and becomes uncomfortable in it does one become aware of their home culture and the cultural differences between one's own and a foreign culture. Culture is 'the instrument by which each new generation acquires the capacity to bridge the distance that separates one life from another' (Herbig, 1998, p. 11).

Characteristics of culture

According to Herbig (1998), the following provide a set of characteristics for culture:

1. *Functional*: each culture has a function to perform; its purpose is to provide guidelines for behaviour of a group of people
2. *A social phenomenon*: human beings create culture; culture results from human interaction and is unique to human society
3. *Prescriptive*: culture prescribes rules of social behaviour
4. *Learned*: culture is not inherited and/or received by succession; it is learned from other members of the society
5. *Arbitrary*: cultural practices and behaviours are subject to judgment. Certain behaviours are acceptable in one culture and not acceptable in other cultures
6. *Value laden*: culture provides values and tells people what is right and wrong
7. *Facilitates communication*: culture facilitates verbal and nonverbal communication
8. *Adaptive/dynamic*: culture is constantly changing to adjust to new situations and environment; it changes as society changes and develops
9. *Long term*: culture developed thousands of years ago; it was accumulated by human beings in the course of time and is the sum of acquired experience and knowledge
10. *Satisfies needs*: culture helps to satisfy the needs of the members of a society by offering direction and guidance.

Subcultures

There is a distinction between dominant and variant cultures (Kluckhohn and Strodtbeck, 1961), or public and private cultures (Goodenough, 1971). Each dominant culture consists of several subcultures. Subcultures can be based on race, ethnicity, geographic region or economic or social class.

Race refers to a genetic or biological similarity among people (Lustig and Koester, 1993). For example, many western European countries include people from the Caucasian race. Race also refers to a group of people descended from the same ancestors. Race is sociohistorical in nature. It recognizes the evolution of different racial categories over time and the existence of different racial categories (e.g., white and black) in different cultures (Jandt, 1998).

Ethnicity refers to a wide variety of groups of people who share a language, history and religion and identify themselves with a common nation or cultural system (Lustig and Koester, 1993). Ethnic differences can be identified by 'colour, language, religion, or some other attribute of common origin' (Horowitz, 1985, p. 41). Since ethnic cultural traits are passed on to children, ethnicity also refers to the shared descent or heritage of a group of people (Jandt, 1998). For example, Slovaks, Croatians and Serbian represent three ethnic groups, each with their own culture, who lived as one nation in former Yugoslavia.

Geographical region refers to geographic differences within countries or similarities between countries. According to Schneider and Barsoux (1997), regional subcultures evolve due to differences in geography, history, political and economic forces, language and religion.

Economic and social class recognizes differences in the socio-economic standing of people. Regional differences evolve due to differences in people's income and wealth.

Each subculture community (e.g., racial, ethnic, economic, social or regional) exhibits characteristic patterns of behaviour that distinguish it from others within a parent culture. Each subculture provides its members with a different set of values and expectations as a result of regional differences. Therefore, the major dominant culture differs from minor variant subcultures.

Subcultures can be represented by a small group, such as a few people, or a large group such as a major religious order. People can be members of many different groups at the same time. A person might identify with being a white French-American, a Christian, and a member of the middle class. Subcultures provide their members with norms and rules that tell people how to behave, interact and think within these subcultures.

The attempt to distinguish a dominant or typical cultural pattern for any culture is extremely difficult or even impossible because of the heterogeneity of many societies. The ethnic variety can be found in all countries; for example, Australia and Canada have British, Germans, Italians, Greeks, Turks, Serbs, Croats, Polish, and many other nationalities. Some societies like the United States contain over 125 ethnic groups and nearly 1200 different religions (Samovar et al., 1998). Thus, the

15

analysis of the whole country's culture must be limited to the dominant culture of this country.

Figure 1.1 presents a model of the relationships between two sub-cultural groups. Each subculture has its own unique pattern of values, expectations, and interactions yet both groups share dominant cultural patterns. Moreover, dominant culture directs the form of public social interaction, whereas the variant minor subcultures indicate the forms of private social interaction. Therefore, interaction between people who appear to be from the same dominant culture may not be easy, because in reality they may be members of various subcultures and their backgrounds may be so different that they may not be able to relate appropriately.

Figure 1.1 Relationships between dominant cultures and minor subcultures

The focus of this book is on the dominant culture of the tourists and hosts and the public social interaction between their cultures. We concentrate on the various guidelines in dominant tourists' and hosts' cultures that affect their social interaction. The minor subcultures and private patterns of social interaction are not analysed here.

Cultural differences

Cultural differences manifest themselves in many ways. Scollon and Scollon (1995) identified numerous aspects of culture that are significant for the understanding of cultural differences (see Table 1.1).

Czinkota and Ronkainen (1993), Hofstede (1991) and Trompenaars (1993) suggested a range of elements that generate cultural differences (see Table 1.2).

Table 1.1   The aspects significant for the understanding of cultural differences (Scollon and Scollon, 1995)

Ideology *history and worldview, which includes:*	Socialization	Forms of discourse	Face systems *social organization, which includes:*
Beliefs Values Religion	Education Enculturation Acculturation	*Functions of language:* Information and relationship Negotiation and ratification Group harmony, individual welfare	Kinship
	Primary and secondary socialization	*Non-verbal communication*: Kinesics: body movement Proxemics: the use of space Concept of time	The concept of the self
	Theories of the person and of learning		Ingroup-outgroup relationships
			Gemeinschaft and *Gesselschaft*

Table 1.2   The elements that generate cultural differences (Czinkota and Ronkainen, 1993; Hofstede, 1991; Trompenaars, 1993)

Language	Social institutions Social strata or classes Family structure	Customs
Economics	Values	Material items
Religion	Attitudes	Aesthetics
Politics	Manners	Education

Cultural differences in communication

The cultural differences are reflected in communication patterns such as:

- different patterns of verbal communication (language and para-language: intonation, laughing, crying, questioning), and
- different patterns of non-verbal communication (body language such as facial expressions, head movements, gestures, use of space, use of physical distance between people) (Bochner, 1982).

Differences in *verbal communication* are related to the differences in the features of language such as:

- phonology (differences in sound)
- morphology (differences in meaning units)
- semantics (differences in meanings of words)
- syntactics (differences in the sequence of the words and their relationships to one another)
- pragmatics (differences in effects of language on perceptions) (Lustig and Koester (1993).

Whorf (1956) hypothesized that there are differences in the manner by which language influences and determines the ways in which people think, due to:

- variations in vocabulary (different words are used to express the same meaning)
- variations in linguistic grammar (due to differences in time, social hierarchy, and cultural characteristics)
- linguistic relativity and intercultural communication (differences occur due to ethnic, social class, generation, political reasons, different dialect, accent and jargon).

Differences in *non-verbal communication* occur due to differences in:

- body movements (*kinesics*)
  - emblems (gestures)
  - illustrators (visual representation of the verbal message)
  - affect displays (facial and body movements)
  - regulators (synchronizers of conversation, e.g., head nods, eye contact)
  - adaptors (body movements as a reaction to an individual's physical or psychological state)

- space (*proxemics*)
  - ○ use of personal space (intimate/personal/social/public)
  - ○ territoriality
- touch
  - ○ the meanings of touch
  - ○ differences in touch (whom, where, when)
- time
  - ○ time orientations (past/present/future)
  - ○ time systems (technical, formal/informal)
  - ○ time perceptions (long/short)
  - ○ use of time (commitment/no commitment)
- voice
  - ○ vocal communication (high/low, fast/slow, smooth/staccato, loud/ soft)
- other non-verbal codes
  - ○ chemical code system (natural body odour, tears, sweat, smells)
  - ○ dermal code system (blushing, blanching, flesh)
  - ○ physical code system (facial features, skin and hair colour, body shape)
  - ○ artifactual code system (clothing, buildings, furnishing, jewellery, lighting, cosmetics) (Lustig and Koester, 1993).

Cultural differences also occur in:

- persuasion (presentational/analogical)
- argumentation (evidence, warrants, claims, making conclusions)
- structure of conversation (topics discussed, the ways topics are presented, value of talk and silence, rules of conversations) (Lustig and Koester, 1993).

Cultural differences in social categories

Cross-cultural differences may be noticed in social categories such as role, status, class, hierarchy, attitudes towards human nature, activity, time, and relationships between individuals (Kim and Gudykunst, 1988). Cultural differences can also be found in standing, looking, touching, perceiving sense of shame, feelings of obligations, responsibility, saving face, avoidance of embarrassment, confrontation, taking initiatives, responses, and external appearance (Argyle, 1967, 1978; Damen, 1987; Dodd, 1987; Gudykunst and Kim, 1984; Hall, 1955, 1959, 1976, 1983; Taylor, 1974; Thiederman, 1989).

Cultural differences in rules of social behaviour

Cultural differences occur in rules of social behaviour (Argyle, 1967; Triandis, 1972), particularly in:

- ways of defining interpersonal relations and attributing importance to social interactions (Wagatsuma and Rosett, 1986)
- techniques of establishing and preserving relations (Argyle, 1967)
- interaction patterns such as greetings, self-presentations (Argyle, 1967)
- beginning a conversation, degree of expressiveness, showing emotions, frankness, intensity (Jensen, 1970)
- persistency and intimacy, as well as volume of interaction (Jensen, 1970)
- expressing dissatisfaction and criticism (Nomura and Barnlund, 1983)
- describing reasons and opinions (Argyle, 1978)
- exaggerations (Argyle, 1978)
- moral rules about telling the truth (Argyle, 1978)
- joking, asking personal questions, complimenting and complaining, expressing dislike, showing warmth, addressing people, apologizing, farewelling, expressing negative opinions and gift giving.

Cultural differences in service

There are also differences in understanding the concept of service. Wei *et al.* (1989) emphasized the influence of cultural differences on the interaction processes between a service provider and a visitor. 'Interacting with service personnel is a primary way in which visitors form an impression and make judgments about their hosts' (Wei *et al.*, 1989, p. 3). Poor quality service may create unpleasant encounters between tourists and hosts, low morale, and unfriendly attitudes (Wei *et al.*, 1989). Sheldon and Fox (1988) identified many cultural differences in relation to interaction patterns between guests and service providers. These differences may lead to different perceptions of what constitutes proper guests' treatment, and can shape different attitudes of hosts towards the tourists they serve (Richter, 1983). What is important for guests from the US may not be of the same level of importance for Japanese or Chinese customers. For instance, the Chinese host ignores the expectations of their guests. By escorting their guests everywhere, providing them with a very tight itinerary, and not leaving an opportunity to experience the Chinese life style privately, the Chinese hosts believe they provide their guests with a courtesy. However, American tourists may view such hospitality as an intrusion and lack of trust. Japanese hosts, on the other hand, take care of the affairs of their guests in advance and anticipate the guests' needs and even fulfil beyond needs (Befu, 1971), believing the host knows best what the guests' needs are. Such an attitude may also be frustrating for American tourists who think they know best what their needs are. American tourists may regard Japanese hospitality as uncomfortable. On the other hand, the American tradition of not anticipating the guests' needs in advance may negatively affect the Japanese tourists' satisfaction with the hospitality of the American host. As Wei *et al.* (1989, p. 3) noted, 'the cultural differences in expectations regarding service levels between hosts and visitors left many with negative impressions'.

The cultural differences listed above may be produced by regional, ethnic, religious, gender, generation and social classes differences. However, these are not discussed in this book.

Cultural problems

Cultural differences can cause problems in social interaction between participants of different cultural backgrounds. For instance, different patterns of verbal and non-verbal communications may create serious errors and lead to misinterpretation, misunderstanding and confusion (Argyle, 1967) and affect the perceptions of others (Jensen, 1970; Samovar *et al.*, 1981; Wolfgang, 1979). If the contact participants do not conform to each other's cultural patterns of interaction and expected standards, and assume that they are culturally the same or similar, they may reject each other (Argyle, 1967).

Cultural differences have particular influences on tourist–host social interaction when the tourists have a distinctly different cultural background from hosts. According to Pizam and Telisman-Kosuta (1989), in the destinations where the majority of tourists were foreigners, the residents perceived the tourists to be different from themselves in a variety of behavioural characteristics, such as attitudes or morality. However, in the destinations where the majority were domestic tourists, the differences between the tourists and the residents were perceived as only minimal (Pizam and Telisman-Kosuta, 1989). As such, these differences have marketing implications for the tourism and hospitality sector.

Cultural dimensions

The examination of cultural differences indicates that there are a very large number of elements that differ between cultural groups. The question is whether these differences can completely and adequately distinguish between all cultures. How many of the cultural elements need to be different in order to determine cultural differences? Also, the cultural elements vary in their degree of importance and impact on social behaviour. Which cultural elements have the most significant effect on social behaviour and to what degree should they be different in order to indicate cultural differences between people? Which elements should be used to successfully compare cultures?

There are many dimensions on which cultures differ (Parsons and Shils, 1951; Cattell, 1953; Hall, 1965; Mead, 1967; Inkeles and Levinson, 1969; Ackoff and Emery, 1972; Douglas, 1973, 1978). It seems that the most frequently used are the Parsons' (1951) pattern variables, Kluckhohn and Strodtbeck's (1961) value orientations, Stewart's (1971) cultural patterns, Hall's (1960, 1966, 1973, 1976/1977, 1983), Hall and Hall's (1987) cultural differentiation, Hofstede's (1980, 1984, 1991, 2001) dimensions of cultural variability, Trompenaars' (1984, 1993/1997), Hampden-Turner and Trompenaars' (1993) and Maznevski's (1994) cultural dimensions. These dimensions provide ways to understand how people's behaviour and communication differ across cultures and how they deal with social life and human relationships. They affect social interaction, the difficulties individuals have in relating to others and individual perceptions (Gudykunst *et al.*, 1988b). They can also indicate how the major cultural differences influence the cross-cultural interaction between international tourists and local hosts. Therefore, these cultural dimensions are presented below.

Parsons' (1951) pattern of variables

Parsons differentiated cultures according to the choices an individual makes prior to engaging in action:

- *Affectivity-Affective Neutrality*: the degree to which people seek gratification (immediate/self-restraint)
- *Universalism-Particularism*: modes of categorizing people or objects (general/specific)

- *Diffuseness-Specificity*: types of responses to people or objects (holistic/particular)
- *Ascription-Achievement*: ways of treating people or objects in terms of qualities ascribed to them (inherent/group qualities)
- *Instrumental-Expressive*: nature of the goals people seek in interactions with others (means to another goal/an end goal)
- *Structural Tightness*: the degree to which the norms, rules and constraints are placed on people's behaviour (tight/loose).

Kluckhohn and Strodtbeck's (1961) cultural dimensions

Kluckhohn and Strodtbeck (1961) differentiated cultures on the basis of value orientations:

- *Toward Humans*: human beings may be perceived as good, a mixture of good and evil, or evil; changeable, unchangeable
- *Toward Nature*: humans may be subjected to nature, live in harmony with nature or control nature
- *Toward Activity*: cultures may be 'being', 'being-in-becoming' or 'doing'
- *Toward Time*: past, present and future
- *Toward Relationship among People*: linear (hierarchical relationship), collateral (group relationship), individual (the individual goals take primacy over group goals)
- *Toward Space*: public, private, mixed.

Stewart's (1971) cultural patterns

The four major elements of Stewart's cultural patterns are:

- *Activity Orientation*: how people view actions and how they express themselves through activities (being/becoming/doing)
- *Social Relations Orientation*: how people relate to one another (formal/informal, direct/indirect, egalitarian/hierarchical)
- *Self-orientation*: how people view themselves, what motivates their actions, who is valued and respected (group/self-orientation, changeable/not changeable)
- *World Orientation*: how people locate themselves in relation to the spiritual world and nature (subjugation to nature/living in harmony with nature/controlling nature).

Hall's (1960, 1966, 1973) and Hall and Hall's (1987) cultural dimensions

According to Hall, cultures can be differentiated on the basis of orientation towards:

- *Human Nature*: agreements
- *Activity Orientation*: monochronic/polychronic
- *Human Relationships*: amount of space, possessions, friendship, communication
- *Relation to Time*: past/future
- *Space Orientation*: public/private.

Hall's (1976/1977, 1983) cultural dimensions

Hall also differentiated cultures in terms of:

- *Context*: the level of information included in a communication message (low/high context)
- *Space*: ways of communicating through handling of personal space (personal/physical)
- *Time*: different perceptions and orientations towards time (monochronic cultures (MTC) versus polychronic cultures (PTC))
- *Information flow*: the structure and speed of messages between individuals (covert/overt messages)
- *Language*: high context cultures (HCC) versus low context cultures (LCC).

Hofstede's (1980, 1984, 1991) cultural dimensions

According to Hofstede, cultures can be compared and contrasted with one another on five dimensions:

- *Power Distance (PD)*: the way in which interpersonal relationships develop in hierarchical society
- *Uncertainty Avoidance (UA)*: the degree to which people feel threatened by ambiguous situations
- *Individualism-Collectivism (IC)*: the degree to which individual goals and needs take primacy over group goals and needs
- *Masculinity-Femininity (MF)*: the degree to which people value work and achievement versus quality of life and harmonious human relations

- *Confucian Work Dynamism*: the extent to which the Chinese values apply in the country in which they reside (*Long-term Time Orientation*).

Adler's (1986) cultural dimensions

Adler distinguished cultures on the basis of:

- *Human activity*
- *Space*
- *Time*
- *Human nature*
- *Relationships with nature*
- *Human relationships*.

Argyle's (1986) cultural differentiation

Argyle differentiated cultures according to the degree of formality and an acceptable level of physical contact between people:

- *Formality*: formal/informal cultures
- *Touch*: contact/non-contact cultures.

Schein's (1992) cultural dimensions

Schein distinguished cultures on the basis of the following dimensions:

- *The Nature of Human Relationships*: individualism/groupism, participation and involvement, role relationships
- *The Nature of Human Activity*: doing/being/being-in-becoming, work/family/personal
- *The Nature of Human Nature*: evil/good/mixed
- *The Nature of Relations with Environment*: control/harmony/subjugation
- *The Nature of Time*: past/present/near or far-future, monochronic/polychronic, planning/development, discretionary time horizons (function/occupation/rank), temporal symmetry/pacing
- *The Nature of Reality and Truth*: external physical/social/individual reality, high/low context, moralism/pragmatism
- *The Nature of Space*: intimacy/personal/social/public, high/low status.

Trompenaars' (1984, 1993) cultural dimensions

Trompenaars compared cultures on orientation towards:

- *Human Nature*: universalism/particularism
- *Relation to Nature*: internal/external, inner/outer directed
- *Activity Orientation*: achievement/ascription, analysing/integrating
- *Human Relationships*: equality/hierarchy, individualism/collectivism and communitarianism, affective/neutral
- *Relation to Time*: sequential/synchronic, past/present/future.

Maznevski's (1994) cultural dimensions

Maznevski differentiated cultures on the basis of orientations towards:

- *Human Nature*: good/evil, changeable
- *Relation to Nature*: subjugation/mastery/ harmony
- *Activity Orientation*: doing/being, containing and controlling (thinking)
- *Human Relationships*: individual/collective, hierarchical.

The ways cultures differ on the above dimensions are discussed in Chapter 3.

Intercultural interaction model

The intercultural interaction model, which is presented below, is based on Porter and Samovar's (1988) model of the differences between three cultures and their members in an intercultural communication process. This model assists in understanding some of the consequences of culturally different people interacting together (see Figure 1.2).

Figure 1.2 illustrates the influence of culture on individuals. Three distinct squares present three distinct cultures: Culture A, B and C. Within each culture A, B, C there is an inner form, which represents the individual who is 'travelling' between the three cultures and is influenced by these cultures. The shape of the dominant culture and the shape of the individual are different. Although culture is the dominating shaping force on an individual there are also other influences besides culture that affect the individual such as social, economic, political or environmental.

Culture A

Culture B

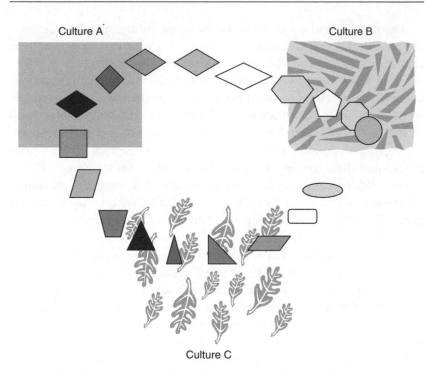

Culture C

Figure 1.2 The intercultural interaction model

The differing shadings and shapes of the individual represent the influence of different cultures on an individual. When an individual from Culture A leaves its culture and reaches Culture B, his or her behaviour changes because of the influence of a culturally different society. The individual's values, behaviour and communication style differ from those of Culture B. The degree to which culture influences an individual from Culture A and an individual from Culture B is a function of the dissimilarity of Cultures A and B.

In general, all interactions are viewed to a certain extent as *'intercultural'*, and the degree of their *'interculturalness'* depends upon the degree of heterogeneity between cultural backgrounds of the individuals involved in interactions; their patterns of beliefs, verbal and non-verbal behaviour, perceptions, and attitudes. An underlying assumption is that individuals who belong to the same culture share greater commonality than individuals who belong to different cultures.

There are variations in cultural differences during intercultural inter-action. Intercultural interactions can occur in a wide variety of situations that range from interactions between people who are members of differ-ent dominant cultures with extreme cultural differences (e.g., interactions between Western tourists and Asian hosts) to interactions between people whose differences are reflected in the values and perceptions of subcul-tures (e.g., interactions between American tourists and British hosts). This supports Sutton's (1967) theory of various degrees of differences in cultural backgrounds of the contact participants. Samovar and Porter (1991) presented these differences along a minimum-maximum dimension and reported that the degree of difference between cultural groups depends on the comparison of their cultural dissimilarity.

The maximum difference was found between Asian and Western cul-tures (Samovar and Porter, 1991) (see Figure 1.3). The members of cul-tural groups with minimal differences had more in common than members of groups at the middle or maximum end of the scale. The members of similar cultural groups spoke the same language, shared the same religion, experiences and perceptions and saw their worlds as similar. However, it was noted that although these groups were similar, they were also culturally dissimilar to some extent and had divergent beliefs, values and attitudes and, therefore, might also differ significantly.

Samovar and Porter's (1991) scale allows us to examine cultural dif-ferences between nations and gain insights into the influence of these differences on social interactions in a cross-cultural context. Examples of the cultural differences between nations and, in particular, between Asia, Europe, the US and Australia are discussed in Chapters 3–6.

Importance of understanding the cross-cultural differences in behaviour

Members of the American, European, Asian and Australian societies have opposite cultural orientations and expectations due to social interaction. The cultural differences between the members of these societies can have a direct impact on their social interaction in the tourism environment. Due to cultural differences Asian, European, US and Australian societies may have a different understanding of what constitutes appropriate behaviour. Qualities such as being yourself, open, friendly, direct,

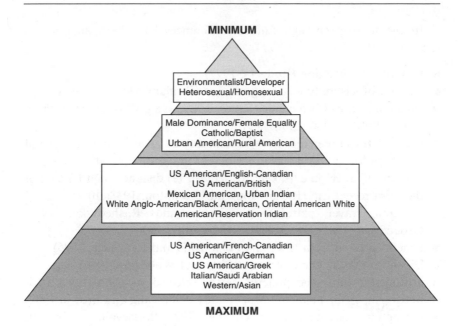

Figure 1.3 Cultural differences among cultures and subcultures according to Samovar and Porter, 1991

confident, outspoken and informal, truthful in interpersonal relations that are admired in the American culture are not admired in Asian societies that view Americans as aggressive, lacking grace, manners and cleverness. What one culture regards as normal and acceptable behaviour the other one may regard as insulting and irritating. Therefore, it is important to analyse the cultural differences in behaviour and understand which of these differences have the most detrimental effects.

Tourism cross-cultural studies

The role of cultural differences in determining tourist behaviour has not been paid much attention in tourism research (Pizam, 1999). This is unfortunate because cultural differences are especially relevant to the tourism industry. The tourism industry is increasingly experiencing globalization, cultural characteristics represent an attractive element of the tourism product itself, and tourism is a service industry where people from different cultures can meet (Pizam, 1999).

In the tourism context, cultural differences have been analysed in the:

- patterns of recreation (Rodgers, 1977)
- amount of leisure time among nations (Ibrahim, 1991, Szalai, 1972)
- leisure and travel behaviour (Ritter, 1987, 1989; Cho, 1991; *Business Korea*, 1991; Barham, 1989)
- vacation travel preferences: (a) availability of vacation time and use of that time for vacation travel; (b) actual amount of vacation time; (c) amount of travel undertaken; (d) length; (e) distance; and (f) cost of the most recent trip (Richardson and Crompton, 1988a,b)
- vacation travel patterns (Sussmann and Rashcovsky, 1997; Groetzbach, 1981, 1988; Chadee and Cutler, 1996)
- benefits derived from travelling (Woodside and Lawrence, 1985)
- leisure/recreation choice criteria (Pitts and Woodside, 1986)
- attitudes towards and preferences for selected vacation travel attributes (Ah, 1993; Yuan and McDonald, 1990; Yang and Brown, 1992)
- perceptions/stereotypes/image (Brewer, 1978; Boissevain and Inglott, 1979; McLellan and Foushee, 1983; Pi-Sunyer, 1978; Pizam and Telisman-Kosuta, 1989; Pizam and Sussmann, 1995; Pizam and Reichel, 1996; Pizam and Jeong, 1996; Pizam *et al.*, 1997; Pizam *et al.*, 1994; Reisinger and Waryszak, 1994a,b, c; Wagner, 1977; Wee *et al.*, 1986)
- vacation travel in the US (Goodrich, 1985)
- awareness of, and visitation to, selected attractions (Couturier and Mills, 1984)
- values, rules of social interaction, service perceptions, satisfaction with interaction between Asian tourists and Australian values (Reisinger and Turner, 1997a,b; 1998a,b, c; 1999a,b; Reisinger and Turner, 2002a,b)
- motivation (Lee, 2000; Mattila, 1999)
- destination image (Chaudhary, 2000; Baloglu and Mangaloglu, 2001)
- contents of tour packages (Enoch, 1996)
- tourists' role preferences (Yiannakis *et al.*, 1991)
- importance of food and foodservice preferences (Sheldon and Fox, 1988)
- service quality (Armstrong *et al.*, 1997), and many others.

These and other studies are described in more detail in further chapters. The major finding of these studies is that national cultures influence tourist and host behaviour. Therefore, national culture of tourists warrants more detailed examination.

Culture and tourism marketing management

One of the most important aspects of successful international tourism development is to understand the cultural differences between international tourists and a host society. These differences are particularly related to cultural values and the needs and perceptions of international tourists and hosts. Hosts can regard tourism products and services as being satisfying for domestic tourists within a cultural context of a host society. However, international tourists might not regard the same products and services as adequate and satisfying. The aim of tourism marketing is to satisfy the needs and wants of various groups of international tourists. Successful international tourism marketing depends upon the understanding of the cultural background of tourists whom marketers attempt to target, and how this background determines the expectations of these tourists. If the tourism products or services do not adequately satisfy international tourists' needs and fail to address adequately the cultural values of the tourist society, tourism marketers and managers must revise and/or adjust their product offerings.

It is not suggested here that the total tourism product should be adjusted to match the international tourists' expectations. Many international tourists travel overseas to experience culture of a host destination and learn about the cultural differences in traditions, food or dance. Many travellers are motivated by the cultural uniqueness of the foreign tourism product. Rather it is suggested that marketers need to address a potential tourist market from a cultural point of view prior to marketing to it.

Cross-cultural differences are not only limited to language, food or dance, but are also experienced in a variety of human interactions between international tourists and local hosts, including their non-verbal behaviour, religious beliefs, time orientation, attitude to privacy, their manners, customs, forms of address, body language or gestures. These cultural elements are potential grounds for cultural misunderstanding and conflict between international tourists and locals. They can induce fear often accompanied by stress and generate tourist dissatisfaction with a tourism product. These experiences and feelings are culturally conditioned, subjective and dependent upon time and space. Marketers and managers must study them to be able to learn about others and one's own, recognize the differences, understand how cultural factors influence the others' behaviour, and implement strategies that would successfully target the particular cultural group.

Summary

Culture is a multivariate concept. There are many definitions of culture. These definitions are complex, unclear and there is no consensus definition that can be widely accepted. The majority refer to culture in psychological terms. There is a dominant culture that influences the majority of people, and there are subcultures with regional differences. Any group of people is characterized by various cultures. Members of the same culture share the same cultural orientation. Cultures differ on a variety of cultural elements. The maximum cultural differences were found between Asian and Western societies. Cultures can be distinguished on the basis of cultural dimensions. Cultural differences are especially relevant to the tourism industry. There have been studies done, which identify cultural differences in the tourism context. Tourism marketers and managers must be aware of the cultural differences between international tourists and local hosts to be able to provide an adequate and satisfying product to tourists.

Discussion points and questions

1. Explain what culture is and what are its major elements.
2. Does culture have a purpose?
3. Can cultural elements completely distinguish between different cultural groups?
4. How many of the cultural variables need to be different in order to assess cultural differences? Since they vary in their degree of importance and impact on the interaction patterns, to what degree should these variables be different to indicate cultural differences in social interaction?
5. Are there any transcultural variables by which cultures could be successfully compared?
6. Why is the examination of cultural differences especially relevant to the tourism industry?
7. Give examples showing the differences in social behaviour between international tourists and local residents.
8. Is the assessment of cultural differences between international tourists and hosts always easy and possible?

9. Can one claim that national culture determines tourist behaviour?
10. How important is the understanding of cultural differences for tourism marketers and managers?

Further reading

Asante, M. W. (1989) *Handbook of International and Intercultural Communication*. Newbury Park, CA: Sage Publications.
Brislin, R. (1993) *Understanding Culture's Influence on Behavior*. Orlando: Harcourt Brace Jovanovich.
Jandt, F. (1998) *Intercultural Communication: An Introduction*. Thousands Oaks, CA: Sage Publications.
Kroeber, A. and Kluckhohn, C. (1985) *Culture: A Critical Review of Concepts and Definitions*. New York: Random House.
Samovar, L., Porter, R. and Stefani, L. (1998) *Communication Between Cultures*. Belmont, CA: Wadsworth Publishing Company.
Schein, E. (1992) *Organizational Culture and Leadership*. San Francisco, CA: Jossey-Bass Inc.

2

Social contact

Objectives

After completing this chapter the reader should be able to:

- define the concept of social contact, its purpose and characteristics

- understand social contact in tourism

- identify forms and characteristics of tourist–host contact

- explain the contact hypothesis and its outcomes

- identify determinants of tourist–host contact

- identify types of intercultural tourist–host contact

- understand the interaction difficulties in inter- and cross-cultural tourist–host contact

- understand the concept of culture shock, its types, symptoms and stages

- identify measurement techniques of social contact and measurement problems.

Introduction

This chapter introduces the concept of social contact with specific emphasis on tourist–host contact. The factors that determine tourist–host contact are discussed along with the impact of cultural differences on tourist–host contact in a cross-cultural setting. The outcomes of tourist–host contact and the concept of culture shock are presented since they are ultimate results of the interrelationships between cultural background and social contact. The measurement of tourist–host contact is also discussed. For the purpose of this book, *contact* and *interaction* are used interchangeably.

Concept and definitions

Most studies on social contact have been conducted in the United States. The concept is complex and there are many definitions of social contact (Cook and Sellitz, 1955). Social contact may refer to the:

Social contact can refer to a multitude of different experiences (Cook and Sellitz, 1955). In past studies the term contact has referred to a very brief trip as well as long-term friendships. Social contact can take place in a multitude of different situations (Cook and Sellitz, 1955). Further, past studies show that social contact takes place within the work situation, the residential neighbourhood and between children, adults, college students, and so forth. According to Bochner (1982), each social contact is personal, always occurs between a minimum of two people, and is often referred to as an interpersonal encounter. Murphy (2000) defined social contact as the everyday encounter with other people. Each social contact has the potential to be positive, negative or superficial (Fridgen, 1991).

> 'Personal association taking place under certain circumstances; or to the interaction which covers a wide range of behaviors from observation of members of the other group without any communication, to prolonged intimate association' (Cook and Sellitz, 1955, pp. 52–53).

Two levels of social contact have been identified: co-presence and focused interaction (Murphy (2000) cites Gahagan (1984) and Goffman (1967)). Co-presence contact refers to the minimum level of social interaction, which occurs 'when two or more individuals signal (through their bodily and facial movements, and the use of space) their awareness of one another's presence and their accessibility to one another'. Focused-inter-action occurs 'when people gather together and cooperate to sustain a single focus of attention as in conversation, games, and transaction in shops'. 'The co-presence may or may not lead to focused interaction in the form of conversation' (p. 51).

An important framework, which helps to analyse social contact, is Analysis of Social Situations (Argyle *et al.*, 1981) theory. This theory identifies nine core components that influence any social interaction (see Table 2.1).

Table 2.1.   Major components that influence social interaction

Analysis of Social Situations theory

Nine features of social interactions have been identified (Argyle, Furnham and Graham, 1981):

- Goals, which are the purposes that direct and motivate social interaction
- Rules, which are shared beliefs that regulate social interaction and generate actions so that the goals can be achieved
- Roles, which include the duties, obligations or rights of the social position of the contact participants
- Repertoire of elements, which is the sum of verbal and non-verbal behaviour appropriate to the situation
- Sequences of behaviour, which is the specific order of actions needed to behave effectively
- Concepts, which are elements that individuals need to possess to behave effectively in the social situations and attain situational goals
- Environmental setting, which is the setting in which the encounter occurs and consists of spaces, modifiers, boundaries
- Language and speech that make individuals understand how to behave in the interaction, e.g., vocabulary, grammar, codes, voice tone and situation-specific variations in language
- Difficulties and skills, which are social situations that require perceptual, motor, memory or linguistic skills in order to be successfully understood

Pearce (1980b) emphasized the importance of skills that are needed for individuals to engage in social interaction and determine the degree of difficulty the participant has in social interaction. Those who are skilled socially can interact smoothly.

Social contact in tourism

The concept of social contact can be applied in a tourism context. Social contact with tourists can be:

- Tourist–host
- Tourist–tourist
- Tourist–potential tourist
- Tourist–provider contacts (Fridgen, 1991).

The focus of this book is on the tourist–host contact, which can be defined as the personal encounter that takes place between a tourist and a host.

Ambiguity in defining tourists and hosts

There is ambiguity in defining tourists and hosts. Many researchers do not distinguish between different categories of tourists. They refer to tourists as sojourners or guests and to tourist–host contact as guest-host contact (e.g., Nozawa, 1991). Hosts are defined either as (a) local residents; (b) people of the visited country; or (c) those employed in the tourism industry who provide a service to tourists.

Nominal definition of a tourist

The nominal definition defines a tourist as a temporary visitor staying at least 24 hours in the region visited for the purpose of leisure (holiday, sport, study, recreation), business, family (visiting friends and relatives), or meeting and conferences (McIntosh and Goeldner, 1997). The term tourist has a range of meanings that differ by the degree of institutional-ization, type of encounter exchange, form of travel, traveller's status and so forth. The definition of a tourist is further accentuated when one starts crossing cultural borders. For example, in many parts of the South Pacific tourists are treated as 'guests' rather than tourists (Vusoniwailala, 1980).

Operational definition of a tourist

The operational definition indicates that the tourist is a culturally differ-ent temporary overseas visitor, arriving at a holiday destination for a minimum of 24 hours and maximum 12 months for the purpose of holiday, business, study, family, sport, or conference. This definition is used for the purpose of this book.

Definition of a host

The host is a national of the visited country who is employed in the tourism industry and provides a service to tourists such as hotelier, front office employee, waiter, shop assistant, custom official, tour guide, tour manager, taxi and bus driver. Nettekoven (1979) referred to this type of host as a 'professional host'.

Physical setting of a tourist–host contact

Tourist–host contact occurs in a wide variety of settings, for example as the tourist travels in planes and buses, stays in hotels, dines in restaurants, visits tourist attractions, goes shopping or to nightclubs, talks to tour guides, watches local street life or observes local dances.

Forms of tourist–host contact

Tourist–host contact may take different forms. It may consist either of business transactions at shops, enquiries in the tourist information centres or at the front office, or just friendly greetings on a street. Three major contact situations between tourists and hosts have been identified:

- when tourists purchase goods and services from residents
- when tourists and residents find themselves side by side at an attraction, and
- when the two parties come face to face during the process of information exchange (DeKadt, 1979).

Contact between tourists and hosts of different cultural backgrounds

Contact between tourists and hosts of different cultural backgrounds refers to the direct face-to-face encounter between tourists and hosts who are members of different cultural groups This type of contact is experienced by tourists when they travel from a home culture to the host culture, and by hosts when they serve tourists from a foreign culture. When the interaction occurs between tourists and hosts from two different cultures this type of contact is referred to as intercultural contact, whereas when the interaction occurs between tourists and hosts from more than two cultural groups it refers to cross-cultural contact. An example of intercultural contact is the interaction between two cultural groups such as American hosts and Asian tourists. Since both populations represent several distinct cultural groups, their interaction can also be of a cross-cultural nature.

Contact hypothesis

Several theories related to social contact between individuals from different cultural groups have been developed. One theory, which is related to the social contact between people from different cultures, is the 'contact hypothesis'. Several reviews of the literature on the contact hypothesis have been published (e.g., Allport, 1954; Cook, 1962; Rose, 1948; Saenger, 1953; Williams, 1947). The contact hypothesis suggests that contact between people of different cultural backgrounds may result in positive as well as negative outcomes.

Positive and negative outcomes of the contact between people from different cultures

The contact hypothesis states that social contact between individuals from different cultures results in mutual appreciation, understanding, respect, tolerance and liking (Bochner, 1982; Fulbright, 1976), develops positive attitudes (Fisher and Price, 1991), reduces ethnic prejudices, stereotypes, and racial tension (Cohen, 1971; Mann, 1959; Robinson and Preston, 1976) and improves the social interactions between individuals. It also contributes to cultural enrichment and learning about others (Li and Yu, 1974; Nunez, 1963; UNESCO, 1976; Vogt, 1977). However, the same contact may also develop negative attitudes, stereotypes, prejudices and increase tension, hostility, suspicion and often violent attacks (Bloom, 1971; Bochner, 1982; Mitchell, 1968; Pi-Sunyer, 1978; Tajfel and Dawson, 1965). Differences in national origin, cultural values (Feather, 1976, 1980a, 1980c, 1986a, 1986b) and cultural gaps (Jackson, 1989) generate clashes of values, conflict, and disharmonies (Biddlecomb, 1981; Boissevain, 1979; Choy, 1984; Cooke, 1982; DeKadt, 1979; Hall, 1984; Ngunjiri, 1985; Peck and Lepie, 1977; Petit-Skinner, 1977; Pi-Sunyer, 1982; Reiter, 1977; Urbanowicz, 1977; Wood, 1984; Young, 1973).

It was strongly argued that contact between people from different cultural backgrounds leads to tension, misunderstanding and stereotyping (Albers and James, 1983, 1988; Bochner, 1982; Brewer, 1984; Cohen, 1982; Din, 1982; Evans-Pritchard, 1989; Jordan, 1980; Macnaught, 1982; Mohamed, 1988; Sutton, 1967); exclusion from mutual activities, feeling the sense of a social barrier, difficulty of forming personal friendships (Asar, 1952; Peterson and Neumeyer, 1948; Rathore, 1958; Schmoker, 1954); formality of contact (Taft, 1977); development of superficial relationships (Watson and Lippitt, 1955); problems of adjustment and language barriers (Arjona, 1956); feelings of inferiority, self-rejection (Bettelheim, 1943; Lewin, 1941); resentment (Jordan, 1980); irritation (Doxey, 1976); frustration and stress (Holmes and Rahe, 1967; Rogers, 1968; Taft, 1977). This contact creates communication problems (Argyle et al., 1981; Klineberg, 1980; Porter, 1972), leads to the loss of a sense of security and emotional well being (Lynch, 1960), ethnocentrism and stereotyping (Triandis and Vassiliou, 1967). When there are differences in subjective cultures (Taft, 1977; Triandis, 1972) social contact can even be a threatening experience, participants may feel like outsiders, intruding, undermining values of the other culture (Bochner, 1982). Such contact may inhibit social interaction (Selltie et al., 1956) and future contact may even be lost (Kamal and Maruyama, 1990). It has been argued that the more frequent the social contact is between people of different cultural backgrounds, the more negative the feelings that may develop (Anant, 1971).

Contact hypothesis in a tourism context: the positive view

The contact hypothesis can be applied in a tourism context. Although the application of the contact hypothesis to tourism has been criticized (Turner and Ash, 1975), the theory is still popular as it demonstrates tourism's potential for fostering understanding between nations and peace. For example, in the study of social and cultural impacts of tourism policy in Tunisia (Bleasdale and Tapsell, 1999) it was noted that where tourists were friendly and respectful and demonstrated an interest in Tunisia beyond the beaches, local residents perceived tourists as guests, developed pride in their Tunisian culture, socialized with tourists and learned and used other languages. Contact with tourists and knowledge of each other was seen as being important. Thus, the contact between tourists and hosts from different cultures can lead to enhancement of tourists' and hosts' attitudes toward each other and give them an opportunity to learn about the others' culture and foster social interaction (Bochner, 1982). Tourist–host contact results in a positive attitude change toward hosts (Pearce, 1982b). For instance, Israelis' negative pre-holiday attitudes toward Egyptians changed after holidaying in Egypt (Amir and Ben-Ari, 1985) and Australians developed positive attitudes towards Israelis (Taft, 1979). It was noted that the higher the intensity of the social interaction between hosts and working tourists, the more positive was the change in attitudes towards hosts (Pizam, Uriely and Reichel, 2000). Those who had longer contact also developed more favourable attitudes to each other (Li and Yu, 1974). For instance, those Australians and Papua New Guineans who had more time to interact, and became familiar with each other, had more positive attitudes (Feather, 1981). Tourist–host contact may also result in exchange of correspondence and gifts (Smith, 1957), the development of an intense personal relationship that persists for years (Smith, 1957), the development of friendships with hosts (Boissevain, 1979; Pearce, 1988) and psychological satisfaction (e.g., Stringer, 1981). It was found that working tourists who intensively interacted with their hosts reported high satisfaction with their stay at the destination (Pizam et al., 2000).

Contact hypothesis in a tourism context: the negative view

It has been argued that the development of positive attitudes is not possible since the tourist–host contact is superficial. According to Hofstede (1997), contact between tourists and hosts of different cultural backgrounds is 'the most superficial form of cultural encounter' (p. 215). Tourists' and hosts' perceptions of each other are highly distorted. Hosts develop their perceptions of tourists on the basis of symbols such as clothing or music (Hofstede, 1997). Tourists develop their opinions of hosts on the basis of host work status, responsibilities and the outcomes of their mutual commercial exchange. These perceptions are superficial and may create communication problems. In fact, tourist–host contact may result in a negative change of attitudes (Anastasopoulos, 1992; Bloom, 1971; Brewer, 1984). Several studies show that the encounter between two groups does not contribute to a significant positive attitude change (Milman et al., 1990; Pizam et al., 1991). Journeys to historically unfriendly destinations such as travel by Americans to the USSR (Pizam et al., 1991) and Israelis to Egypt (Milman et al., 1990) can result in only minor changes in attitude of the tourists towards their hosts, with the majority of these changes in the negative direction. The results of the encounter between working tourists and the hosts are less likely to be positive since their relationships are mainly based on economic exchange, which may add extra tension to their encounter (Uriely and Reichel, 2000). The encounter between tourists and hosts only confirms previous attitudes toward each other, regardless of whether these attitudes are positive or negative (Pearce, 1988). Also, the specific character of tourist–host contact may lead to pressure to develop stereotypes rather than broaden people's horizons. Most tourists are just 'passing through' rather than emerging themselves in the life of the host society (MacCannell, 1976).

In addition, tourist–host contact generates clashes of values. For instance, since tourists have begun visiting Tahiti to see beautiful women, the Tahitian male has been forced into subservient roles, which contrasted with the traditional values of Tahitian society where men are dominant (Petit-Skinner, 1977). Due to the pursuit by tourists of certain liberal values, which can affront the Islamic religion, host attitudes toward tourists became negative (Din, 1989). The hosts of Arab states were not pleased having non-Islamic tourists, because the woman's dress, the use of alcohol and the mixing of the sexes were areas where tourists broke domestic social rules (Ritter, 1975). Tunisian women found the tourists' dress offensive and often referred to other negative aspects of tourist behaviour such as rudeness, drunkenness and disrespect for Tunisian culture (Bleasdale and Tapsell, 1999). It was also strongly suggested that tourist–host contact leads to tourist isolation, separation and segregation from the host community (Bochner, 1982; Pearce, 1982b, Pi-Sunyer, 1973; Smith, 1977) and stress. Tourists also experience victimization and harassment while on holiday. For instance, British tourists can experience considerably higher rates of victimization (theft, burglary, violence, threats) than they were likely to experience while at home (Brunt et al., 2000). Tourists visiting Barbados experienced harassment (verbal and physical abuse, sexual harassment) at the beach, in the streets and while shopping (Albuquerque and McElroy, 2001).

Further, the contact between tourists and hosts from different cultures can create communication problems due to linguistic, gesture, spatial, time and status differences (Pearce, 1982b). It can generate orientation, luggage organization, safety, and health problems (Downs and Stea, 1977; Harmon et al., 1970; Pearce, 1977b). Under such circumstances the tourist–host contact creates only disappointment, feelings of discouragement and dissatisfaction (Pearce, 1982b).

However, the literature suggests that despite all the negative outcomes, the advantages of tourist–host contact outweigh the disadvantages. Tourist–host contact can break the isolation of cultural groups, create awareness of each group and provide an opportunity to learn each other's language and history. It can be a starting point for more fundamental intercultural encounters (Hofstede, 1997).

Tourist–host contact in less developed countries

In less developed countries where cultural differences between tourists and hosts are greater than in more developed countries, the negative effect of direct tourist–host contact is increased (Biddlecomb, 1981; Boissevain, 1979; DeKadt, 1979; Milman, 1990; Pearce, 1982b). Rich tourists who visit Third World countries have little respect for local values (Din, 1989). Tourists are often perceived as aggressive and insensitive (Lind and Lind, 1986). The tourist–host contact often generates exploitation, assault, victimization (Pearce, 1982b, 1988; Farrell, 1982) and numerous social problems. Pearce (1982b) suggested that while all of these processes need not be present at once, they occur due to large cultural differences that are important elements shaping tourists' and hosts' perceptions of each other.

Determinants of tourist–host contact

The lack of agreement as to the outcomes of the contact between tourists and hosts raises the possibility of different factors that determine the results of the tourist–host contact. The literature points to four major groups of factors that influence tourist–host contact:

- temporal (e.g., time, different roles played by a tourist and a host)
- spatial (e.g., physical such as distance, and social such as social positions of a tourist and a host, social rules they have to conform to)
- communication (e.g., different language and non-verbal behaviour)
- cultural (e.g., different values, perceptions, attitudes) (Evans, 1978; Fridgen, 1991).

43

Temporal and spatial factors

■ The 'nature of the tourist–host contact' and the social situation in which this contact occurs determines its outcomes. Literature suggests that tourist–host contact is:

1. *brief* (Fridgen, 1991)
2. *temporary and non-repetitive* (Sutton, 1967)
3. *open to deceit, exploitation and mistrust* because tourists and hosts do not have to take into account the consequences of their behaviour such as dishonesty, hostility and cheating (Van den Berghe, 1980)
4. *asymmetric* in terms of meanings for both sides (Hoivik and Heiberg, 1980), different roles and goals (Sutton, 1967), different situation status (Din, 1989; Shamir, 1978; Van den Berghe and Keyes, 1984; Mittelberg, 1988), different motivations and behaviour (Cohen and Cooper, 1986), different access to wealth and information (Van den Berghe and Keyes, 1984), different commitment and responsibilities (Cohen and Cooper, 1986; Hoivik and Heiberg, 1980), different socio-economic position and cultural identity (Din, 1989; Jafari, 1989)
5. *unbalanced* (Fridgen, 1991)
6. *superficial* (Cohen and Cooper, 1986)
7. *not intensive* (Hoivik and Heiberg, 1980)
8. *lacking spontaneity* (Fridgen, 1991)
9. *commercial,* limited only to business transactions (Fridgen, 1991), transformed into a source for economic gain (DeKadt, 1979)
10. *requiring friendliness and strong concern for quality of service* from service providers (Fridgen, 1991) for the purpose of profit (Cohen and Cooper, 1986; Jafari, 1989)
11. *formal* (DeKadt, 1979) depending on the situation: (a) tourists buy goods or services; (b) meet together at the place of tourist attraction that both use, for example, beach, golf-course; (c) meet together during the exchange of information and ideas when the contact is the least formal
12. *competitive* (Din, 1989)
13. *involving an element of dreams and admiration* (Hoivik and Heiberg, 1980)
14. *demanding new experiences* (Sutton, 1967) that may be positive, for example, when hosts are professional in offering product, or

negative when hosts are not capable of meeting tourist demands, lack product knowledge, choices available, and so forth, and

15. *ambiguous* (Hoivik and Heiberg, 1980).

- The *opportunity for contact* determines the occurrence of the contact (Amir, 1969; Stouffer *et al.*, 1949). The opportunity for contact allows participants to get to know and understand one another (Cook, 1962). If no opportunity exists, no contact occurs. The differences in opportunities for contact are important (Kelman, 1962; Sellitz and Cook, 1962). Different opportunities for contact provide different chances for interaction (Schild, 1962). Crompton (1979a) found that social contact is positively related to the opportunity to interact with people. If opportunities for contact are provided, the contact may even develop positive attitudes and encourage future contact. Otherwise it may create negative attitudes (Kelman, 1962). Sharpley (1994) argued that tourism as a social process brings people together in the form of social interaction. However, Brunt and Courtney (1999) disagree suggesting that only the first situation when tourists purchase goods and services from residents (DeKadt, 1979) can generate some interaction. Due to its specific nature and the unfavourable conditions under which it takes place tourist–host contact provides little opportunity for deep social interaction between tourists and hosts (Evans, 1978; Fridgen, 1991). 'Any contact which is transitory, superficial or unequal is a primary ground for deceit, exploitation, mistrust, dishonesty and stereotype formation' (MacCannell, 1984, pp. 384–388).
- The *place*, in which the tourist–host contact occurs, decides about the opportunity for the tourist–host contact. Nettekoven (1979) argued that since tourists are highly concentrated in places of tourist attractions, and are isolated in the 'tourist ghettos' that employ most of the 'professional hosts', these places offer the maximum opportunities for tourist–host encounters. Therefore, most tourists' encounters are with 'professional hosts'. However, it was also argued that an intensive interaction is more likely to develop between tourists and tourists. It is even less likely to develop between tourists and 'professional hosts'.
- The *interpersonal attraction* of the contact participants to each other determines social interaction (Triandis, 1977b). Kim (1991) suggested that attraction is determined by perceived similarity in attitudes. The greater the similarity, the more likely the contact participants are to agree with each other's views and beliefs, and the more likely they are to interact. Culture influences the level of attraction (Byrne *et al.*, 1971) and perceived similarity.

- The *attributes* of the contact participants influence the social contact (Sutton, 1967). Examples of personal attributes are tolerance, enthusiasm, interests, or generosity. The hosts' welcoming attitudes toward tourists, efforts to understand tourists' needs, and the tourists' willingness to understand and respect the hosts' culture increase the chances for their mutual interaction. On the other hand, hosts' resentment of tourists, lack of appreciation of the tourists' cultural background, arrogant behaviour toward tourists, sense of superiority and the tourists' lack of respect of the host's culture decrease the chances for their interaction (Nozawa, 1991).

- Social contact is positively related to *social motivators* such as the desire to interact with people of the host community (Cohen, 1971, 1972; Robinson and Preston, 1976; Crompton, 1979a; Schul and Crompton, 1983; Fisher and Price, 1991). However, many tourists and hosts may encounter each other with no desire to interact at all. Also, some tourists may prefer to interact with fellow tourists of the same national background rather than with foreign hosts (Brislin, 1981). Others may prefer to engage in conversations with foreign hosts in shops or restaurants and exchange information about their own countries, but without committing themselves to follow-through (Schuchat, 1983). Some may prefer participation but without an assimilation with the locals (Jacobsen, 2000). Only some tourists may like to interact, engage in deep and long interactions, know each other better, share personal experiences, and develop long-term friendships. The motivation to interact socially with other people is influenced by the cultural orientation towards social relationships.

- The *touristic orientation* may determine tourist–host relations (Uriely and Reichel, 2000). When the relationships between tourists and hosts are based on economic exchange personal relations are not emphasized (Uriely and Reichel, 2000). In fact, the relationships between working tourists and hosts based on the employee-employer relationships may even involve elements of tension and conflict and, thus, the contact can suffer. Consequently, those who are engaged in paid work as part of their touristic experiences are more likely to be disappointed with these encounters and avoid social contact with hosts. However, since they also hold fewer expectations about their encounter with hosts than those who perceive it as part of their tourist experience, they may also be less exposed to disappointment from the tourist–host contact and be more positive about it (Uriely and Reichel, 2000).

- *Rules of social behaviour* determine the variance of behaviour in many social interactions (Triandis, 1977b). These rules concern introductions, greetings and farewells, names and titles, behaviour in public places, parties and so forth. These rules provide guidelines for social interactions and they differ between cultures.

- The *status* of the participants is important for the development of social interaction (Kelman, 1962; Kramer, 1950; Morris, 1956; Sellitz and Cook, 1962; Triandis and Vassiliou, 1967). If one participant's status is lowered, then hatred may develop (Amir, 1969). Social contact also depends on the degree to which the participants share mutual 'interests', 'activities', have common 'goals' (Sellitz and Cook, 1962) and are 'cooperative' (Allport, 1954; Williams, 1947). Social contact will develop when:

1. contact participants have equal status
2. contact occurs between members of a majority group and higher status members of a minority group
3. there is a favourable social climate that promotes interaction
4. contact is intimate rather than casual or superficial
5. contact is pleasant and mutually rewarding rather than stressful
6. contact participants share common activities, interests and goals of higher importance with the group rather than the individuals
7. contact participants cooperate rather than compete, and
8. contact participants share the same philosophies (Amir, 1969; Bochner, 1982; Robinson and Preston, 1976; Triandis and Vassiliou, 1967).

Perceived status, casualness, intimacy or co-operation varies across cultures.

- The *perceived costs and benefits* determine whether or not the interaction is perceived as rewarding; the social interaction increases when it is perceived as rewarding (Triandis, 1977b). If the perceived costs outweigh benefits, the contact is perceived negatively and achieves negative outcomes. However, if the perceived benefits outweigh costs, the perceptions of contact are positive, despite initial negative perceptions (Ap, 1992) and contact can be perceived as rewarding. The greater the rewards received from the interaction, and the fewer the costs, the more likely the interaction will take place in the future. Since tourist–host contact can be compared to a social exchange (Sutton, 1967), the social interaction between tourists and hosts can be assessed in terms of perceived costs and benefits. Unfortunately, tourist–host contact is often perceived negatively because there is often an imbalance of benefits and costs for tourists and hosts in terms of psychological rewards from their mutual contact. The assessment of the perceived costs and benefits depends upon the cultural similarity and differences between participants. The more similar interactants are, the more likely they perceive their interaction as rewarding. The more different interactants are, the more likely they perceive their interaction as being costly for them.

■ The *resources that are exchanged* determine social interaction (Triandis, 1977b). Six kinds of resources of exchange in an interaction have been identified, comprising money, goods, services, love, status and information (Foa and Foa, 1974). Foa and Foa (1974) argued that the natural reaction of the receiver of certain resources is to return a resource of the same kind. The perceived value and significance of the exchanged resources depends upon cultural beliefs. As Triandis (1977b) noted, the appropriateness of certain exchanges in response to another's behaviour is governed by culturally determined social rules and norms. For example, in Polynesia, hospitality is reciprocated by gifts, food, crafts; a financial contribution to the hosts; and/or by hosting in return (Berno, 1999). Western tourists do not expect such long-lasting consequences as a result of their transactions (Van den Berghe, 1994).

Cultural factors

Tourist–host contact is determined by cultural factors (Amir, 1969; Sutton, 1967; Taft, 1977). However, not much has been done on cultural variables that determine tourist–host contact. Amir (1969) noted that the influence of cultural variables is very important for the explanation of social contact. It is particularly important for analysing tourist–host contact where tourists and hosts are members of different cultural groups, speak different languages, and have different values and perceptions of the world (Bochner, 1982; Sutton, 1967).

■ *Cultural values* are of importance because they determine tourist–host contact (Sutton, 1967; Taft, 1977). Differences in cultural values create differences in perceptions of status, common goals (Amir, 1969), interests, activities, and willingness to cooperate or compete. Culture determines the value of the interpersonal cues for the perceived, and the extent to which the perceiver considers them to be important (Triandis, 1977b). Cues are more likely to be perceived as having value if they are familiar to the perceiver. The cultural environment determines the extent to which stimuli are familiar (Gibson, 1969). For example, much social interaction in the South Pacific is based on the concepts of social obligation, including reciprocity and generosity (Berno, 1999). Generosity in a Polynesian context is about investment in human relationships and establishing an obligation, which will be reciprocated in the future. The Western style of profit accumulation and financial motivation conflict with the Polynesian collective sharing and reciprocity (Berno, 1999). Consequently, financial gains are not perceived as having value by the Polynesian hosts, and reciprocation is not regarded as being important by Western hosts. In Western societies the products and services provided to tourists have been commercialized, the social interactions have been transformed into a source of economic gain, and the proportion of non-economic relationships decreased (DeKadt, 1979).

■ *Attitudes* towards each other determine the development of social contact of those interacting (Smith, 1955, 1957). Stouffer *et al.* (1949) found that American soldiers who had more positive attitudes toward Germans had more contact with German civilians. Also, the intensity of attitudes plays an important role in the development of social contact (Amir, 1969; Guttman and Foa, 1951). Festinger and Kelly (1951) reported that those with more positive attitudes tended to be more active in social relations, and those with less positive attitudes tended to be less active. Negative attitudes prevented the development of interactions between the guests and the hosts because they created reservation, suspicion, dissatisfaction and lack of understanding (Sapir, 1951). The attitudes within charter tours in the Mediterranean precluded social interaction with the locals. The anti-tourists and travellers made new acquaintances during their tour predominantly with fellow vacationers (Jacobsen, 2000). Levine (1979) called for greater consideration of the hosts' attitudes, especially positive attitudes that determine whether the contact will occur. He also agreed that negative attitudes either jeopardize development of contact, or create an antagonistic relationship. Williams (1964) noticed that the more prejudiced a person is, the less likely the person is to be involved in interaction. However, prejudice does not mean avoidance of contact. Even highly prejudiced people seek contact with others, for personal advantage (Williams, 1964).

In tourism, the development of attitudes is possible only when tourists purchase goods and services from residents who deal frequently with tourists in their work. These attitudes mostly represent a mixture of positive and negative attitudes depending on both parties' motivation and status.

- *Perceptions* of each other determine social contact between interactants. Culture encourages the development of different perceptions and guides the perception of interpersonal cues. When a person evaluates another positively, he or she is likely to be evaluated by the other positively, and vice versa (Triandis, 1977b). Positive perceptions enhance social interaction, and negative perceptions reduce it.
- The *cultural familiarity and similarity* facilitates interactions because it reduces uncertainty (Berger and Calabrese, 1975) and anxiety (Stephan and Stephan, 1985). Rokeach (1960) argued that the major factor in the social distance between two people is the degree of the perceived similarity. According to Pogrebin (1987), people develop social relations with those who are relatively similar to members of their own culture and ethnic group. Triandis (1977b) reported that people who know each other, or who belong to the same race or tribe are more likely to interact than people who do not know each other or belong to different tribes. Weingrod (1965) reported that Iraqi settlers rarely visited the Moroccans, Tunisians and Hungarians who lived near them, but visited other Iraqi settlers who lived miles away. It appears that people prefer to develop social contact with their own national group, or those with a similar background, who speak the same language even if they are not their friends, rather than with people from different countries. Therefore, although the opportunities for tourist–host contact may exist, tourists and hosts may develop social contact with those of similar backgrounds only. It is the cultural similarity between tourists and hosts that promotes tourist–host contact (Obot, 1988; Sutton, 1967).

Further, perceived cultural similarity in values is positively related to positive perceptions and the extent of the social contact (Feather, 1980b). Those with similar values are perceived more positively than those with dissimilar values. Those who perceive their values to be similar are also likely to interact more socially than those who perceive their values to be dissimilar (Feather, 1980b). Large differences in the perceived value system inhibit interaction (Feather, 1980b). Perceived cultural similarity is also positively related to mutual attraction, liking, decrease in social distance, and increase in familiarity between the contact participants (Brewer and Campbell, 1976).

However, the similarity in values and beliefs become the most critical factors only when the relations continue and the interaction intensifies. Also, cultural similarity does not facilitate friendship formation, which requires similarity in interests and attitudes (Rokeach *et al.*, 1960). Further, Knapp (1978) noted that when the social interaction is brief and superficial, the differences are few, and the chance of being rejected is small. Under such conditions dissimilarity could also attract people to each other. Blau (1977) argued even further, suggesting that although the rate of social contact between people with different characteristics decreases as population increases in heterogeneity, at a critical point increasing heterogeneity and dissimilarity results in reduction in social barriers and increases the chances of social contact between people who differ. When differentiation increases, people begin to associate with out-groups rather than to have no associates at all, thus, social contacts are enhanced.

Communication

■ Cultural similarity facilitates the *effectiveness of communication* between people. People enter social interactions with those who they can communicate with in a similar way. As Rogers and Bhownik (1971) noted, the communication between people who are similar is more effective than communication between dissimilar people. Consequently, social interaction depends upon the effectiveness of communication. One reason why individuals do not enter social contacts with members of other cultural groups is that their initial interactions with culturally different people are superficial and often result in ineffective communication. Since this communication is not as effective as one would wish, people did not try to have contacts with strangers (Gudykunst and Kim, 1997). However, Simons *et al.* (1970) argued that moderate similarities between people might lead to the most effective communication and satisfying interaction.

In summary, the potential for social interaction and effectiveness of communication between tourists and hosts depend upon the cultural knowledge they have of each other. The more cultural knowledge people have, the more they know about other cultural groups, the better they can predict their behaviour (Honeycutt *et al.*, 1983). Consequently, the easier it is to enter social relationships.

There are other factors that should be taken into account when analysing the tourist–host contact. Knox (1985) listed 20 factors, which include language, norms of friendliness, or crowding. Others noted that the tourist–host contact varies depending on:

- different types of tourists and hosts
- different types of travel arrangements (Nozawa, 1991; Sutton, 1967; Var *et al.*, 1994)
- the role of the culture broker (e.g., tour guide) (Nozawa, 1991)
- the stage of tourism development and the number of tourists and hosts at the destination visited (Husbands, 1986; Nozawa, 1991)
- the amount of information about each other (Nozawa, 1991) and
- types of tourism.

For example, Cohen's (1972) drifters, Vogt's (1976) wanderers, Riley's (1988) long-term budget travellers, or working tourists (Mittelberg, 1988; Uriely and Reichel, 2000) have more opportunity for direct and more meaningful encounters with hosts than institutionalized mass tourists who travel in organized tours, are taken care of by tour guides and are surrounded by an atmosphere familiar to them.

However, the factors listed above are not discussed, since their discussion exceeds the scope of this book. Nevertheless, they should be examined in future cross-cultural tourist–host studies.

Types of intercultural tourist–host contact

Different types of intercultural tourist–host contact have been identified depending on the degree of interculturalness between tourists and hosts.

Interculturalness

The critical variable that determines the tourist–host contact is the degree of 'interculturalness' in the encounter or the extent of similarity and differences between participants (Levine, 1979). Encounters in which individuals are very similar to one another are the least intercultural, whereas those encounters in which the individuals are very different from one another are the most intercultural (Lustig and Koester, 1993). However, it is not just the presence or absence of cultural differences, but the degree of difference between the individuals that influence their interaction (Kim and Gudykunst, 1988). The degree of difference might range from very small to extreme. As the degree of difference increases, the level of interculturalness increases (Sarbaugh, 1988).

Types of intercultural encounters

The degree of interculturalness allowed distinguishing between three major types of intercultural encounters (Sutton, 1967), depending on the similarities and differences in cultural backgrounds of the individuals:

A. where the cultural background of individuals is the same, or similar
B. where the cultural background of individuals is different, but the differences are small and supplementary
C. where the cultural background of individuals is different, and the differences are large and incompatible.

In the first two types of contact (A and B) individuals are not separated by cultural differences. They have similar backgrounds and they share cultural commonalities. The level of interculturalness in their contact is low, and they understand each other accurately. Their social contact is most effective. In the third type of contact (C) participants are separated by large cultural differences (Sutton, 1967). They have fewer cultural commonalities, their interaction is more difficult and less efficient. As the differences among the culturally different participants increase, their encounter leads to friction, misunderstanding and misinterpretation (Sutton, 1967), and consequently, inhibits interaction. According to Triandis (1977b), when people belong to different cultures, the more dissimilar they think they are, the more likely it is that they distort the meaning of each other's behaviour. Similarly Sutton (1967, p. 227) stated: 'the greater the differences among the two cultures, the greater the probability that encounters ... will lead to friction and misunderstanding', and misinterpretation. As the degree of intercultural differences between two or more people become wider, communication is less likely to occur and information exchange is less likely to be effective (Rogers and Steinfatt, 1999).

The types of intercultural encounters presented above can be applied in a tourism context to tourist–host contact. The larger degree of difference between tourists and hosts, which distort their behaviour and create dissimilar interpretation of this behaviour, the more intercultural is their contact, and vice versa. According to Pizam and Telisma-Kosuta (1989), in the destination where the majority of tourists were foreigners, the residents perceived the tourists to be different from themselves in a variety of behavioural characteristics. However, in the destinations where the majority were domestic tourists, the differences between the tourists and the residents were perceived as only minimal.

Interaction difficulties in inter- and cross-cultural tourist–host contact

In inter- and cross-cultural tourist–host contact, tourists and hosts are '... confronted with a culture different from their own in terms of customs, values, standards and expectations' (Mishler, 1965, p. 555). Many situations are unfamiliar to them. They do not know how to interact and respond to each other. As Brislin (1981) indicated, the behaviour that is regarded as desirable in one culture may be inappropriate in another. The cultural differences between tourists and hosts create tourist–host friction (Bryden, 1973), misunderstanding and even hostility (Bochner, 1982). Therefore, when there is a meeting of tourists and hosts from cultures that differ in interpersonal conduct, difficulties can occur with the tourist–host contact. According to Pearce (1982b), tourists always experience interaction difficulties in contact with hosts due to the cultural differences between tourists and hosts. The main interaction difficulties created by differences in culture were found to be:

- interpersonal communication and behaviour (e.g., language fluency, polite language usage, expressing attitudes, feelings, emotions);
- non-verbal signals (e.g., facial expressions, eye gaze, spatial behaviour, touching, posture, gesture); and
- rules and patterns of interpersonal interaction (e.g., greetings, self-disclosure, making or refusing requests) (Bochner, 1982).

All of these elements vary across cultures (Furnham, 1979; Hall, 1959) and are likely to cause misunderstanding.

Communication difficulties

Pearce (1982b) reported that cultural differences between tourists and hosts create substantial communication difficulties that occur due to lack of experience with the foreign culture. However, although verbal and non-verbal communication skills play a very important role in effectively dealing with members of other cultures (Kim and Gudykunst, 1988; Spitzberg and Cupach, 1984), the specific behaviour that reflects these skills varies across cultures (Ruben, 1976). For instance, Asian women believe that revealing personal feelings violates cultural rules of politeness and respect. It is the role of friends and family members to sense that the other person is hurt or angry, without a person having to express these negative feelings (Marshall, 1979).

Rules of social interaction

Most inter- and cross-cultural tourist–host contacts are characterized by interaction difficulties caused by cultural differences in rules of social interaction. Each culture has its specific rules of proper introduction, expression of opinions, showing respect and so forth. For instance, Bochner (1982) found that the most difficult social situation encountered by foreign travellers in Britain was developing personal interactions. Stringer (1981) reported that in bed-and-breakfast establishments even different customs of handling cutlery and eating habits caused irritations, and were grounds for interaction difficulties between tourists and hosts.

Further, cultural differences in rules of social interaction influence mutual perceptions of tourists and hosts. The same rules of social inter-action may create negative or positive perceptions. Tourists and hosts, who are skilled socially in rules of their own culture may be socially unskilled in the rules of a foreign culture because they do not have the skills to interact smoothly in that culture (Pearce, 1980b). Therefore, they may feel inadequate, frustrated or embarrassed (Bochner, 1982) and develop negative perceptions of the nationals of a foreign culture. According to Pearce (1982b) and Sutton (1967), cultural differences are very important factors that influence interaction difficulties and shape perceptions of tourists. However, it can be argued that social interaction between tourists and hosts does not have to be characterized by difficul-ties. These difficulties may be significantly minimized or even eliminated when tourists and hosts are aware of the differences in their cultural backgrounds. Therefore, the understanding of cultural differences in background is the key feature for identification of interaction difficulties.

An important theory, which facilitates the analysis of difficulties in cross-cultural interaction between tourists and hosts, is a Coordinated Management of Meaning (CMM) theory (Cronen and Shuter, 1983). The CMM is a theory of human communication that deals with intercultural communication and comparative patterns of communication. The CMM places cross-cultural interaction at six different levels of complexity (see Table 2.2).

The CMM theory suggests that the six levels of cross-cultural difficul-ties that may occur in tourist–host encounters need attention in order to solve the problem for the interacting parties of different cultural back-grounds (Pearce et al., 1998). For the cross-cultural interaction to be

Table 2.2   Levels of cross-cultural interaction (Cronen and Shuter, 1983)

Coordinated Management of Meaning (CMM)

Six levels of complexity of cross-cultural interaction have been identified (Cronen and Shuter, 1983):

- Verbal and non-verbal behaviour: how clearly people understand one another's speech, gestures, posture or signals
- Speech acts: the way meaning is attached to forms of address such as status or level of formality
- Episodes: sequence of behaviour, rituals, arrangements for eating, sightseeing, tipping, gift giving, etc.
- Relationship: nature of social relationships, rights and expectations, formation of friendships
- Life script: the way people perceive themselves in their behaviour, their relationship to others and physical environment
- Cultural pattern: the way the larger community is defined, what is perceived as honesty, justice, reality, truth or equity within a society

successful and satisfactory it needs to achieve a degree of understanding in the exchange of messages at various levels. When the CMM theory is combined with the Analysis of Social Situations theory 'it is possible to analyse any single element of difficulty between tourists and hosts according to the level of encounter in CMM theory and the key social features in the Analysis of Social Situations' (Pearce *et al.*, 1998, p. 354).

Culture shock

Culture shock is one of the most recognized difficulties encountered by travellers to foreign cultures (Adler, 1975; Bochner, 1982; Lysgaard, 1955; Oberg, 1960; Taft, 1977). Initially, the concept was used for analysing the experiences of sojourners who lived for a significant period of time (longer than 12 months) in another culture, for example, diplomats or army officers.

Definition

Culture shock is experienced by an individual who encounters a different culture. This is a shock caused by an inability to cope in a new cultural environment, being overloaded with unfamiliar stimuli one cannot comprehend, confronted with different ways of life and doing things, inability to ask questions and understand the answers, or recognize food (Rogers and Steinfatt, 1999). Culture shock was defined as '... the reaction of sojourners to problems encountered in their dealings with host members' (Bochner, 1982, p. 172), and 'the loss of equilibrium' due to 'loss of familiar signs and symbols of social intercourse' because they 'encounter ... differences in an alien culture' (Craig, 1979, p. 159), lack of familiar cues about how to behave in a new culture (Oberg, 1960); 'reaction to unsuccessful attempts to adjust to new surroundings and people' (Lundstedt, 1963, p. 8).

Symptoms of culture shock

Hofstede (1997) noted that the visitor in a foreign culture adopts a mentality of a child and 'learns the simplest things over again', often with difficulties. This normally 'leads to feelings of distress, of helplessness ... and hostility towards the new environment' (p. 209). Many symptoms of culture shock have been reported such as strain, sense of loss arising from being removed from one's familiar environment, a feeling of impotence from being unable to deal competently within the new environment, embarrassment, humiliation, depression, feelings of being rejected by the members of the new environment, confusion about one's own values, identity, incompetence, frustration, negative feelings toward hosts, refusing to learn a new language, increase in irritation, fatigue, criticism, decline in initiatives, even preoccupation with cleanliness and worries (Bochner, 1982; Brislin and Pedersen, 1976; Oberg, 1960; Taft, 1977; Textor, 1966). Oberg (1960) reported that common symptoms of culture shock is an excessive washing of hands, extreme concern over drinking the water, eating local food and the cleanliness of bedding, an absent-minded and far-away stare, loss of appetite, an over dependence on being with one's own nationals, sudden anger over minor problems, great concern over minor skin irritation and slight pains, and a terrible longing to be back home. Jandt (1998) identified two types of symptoms of culture shock. Physical symptoms include stress on health and safety, fear of physical contact with anyone in the new country, craving, use of alcohol and drugs, over concern about cleanliness, and a decline in work quality. Psychological symptoms include insomnia, fatigue, isolation, loneliness, disorientation, frustration, criticism of the new country, nervousness, self-doubt, irritability, depression, anger, and emotional and intellectual withdrawal. Hofstede (1997) noted that many visitors to a foreign country can become physically or mentally ill, commit suicide, or remain so homesick that they have to return home quickly.

Culture shock and social interaction

Culture shock has an adverse effect on intercultural interaction because such communication becomes less effective. Participants of intercultural interaction may interpret their anger and frustration as hostility or hate. The larger the degree of cultural differences between the contact participants, the larger culture shock they may experience, the less information is exchanged and the less effective is their interaction.

Types of culture shock

Several types of culture shock have been distinguished. Byrnes (1966) identified *role shock,* which occurs due to lack of knowledge about the rules of behaviour. Smalley (1963) recognized *language shock,* which occurs due to problems with an unfamiliar language and an inability to communicate properly. Guthrie (1975) and Taft (1977) distinguished *culture fatigue* – tiredness, which occurs due to constant adjustment to a new cultural environment. Bennett (1977) identified *transition shock* – negative reaction to change and adjustment to a new cultural environment, inability to interact effectively within a new environment. The concept of culture shock and transition shock has been further extended to include *re-entry shock* (Gullahorn and Gullahorn, 1963), which refers to the emotional and physiological difficulties experienced upon returning home from overseas.

Culture shock in tourism

Many tourists experience culture shock when they travel to a foreign culture. Encounters with taxi drivers, hotel staff, receptionists, shop assistants, and customs officials may be stressful due to differences between the tourist culture and the culture visited. Tourists do not know what to expect from their hosts and hosts often behave in ways that are strange to tourists. The same behaviour may be considered appropriate in one culture, and inappropriate or even rude in another. Tourists often do not know how to greet others in a foreign culture, what is appropriate to say in conversation or even when and how much to tip the waiter. There are many situations that are confusing and make the trip difficult. Therefore, tourists might have to adapt to new local values, rules and customs in order to interact successfully with the hosts of a foreign society.

Unfortunately, it has been argued that tourists experience culture shock to a lesser degree than diplomats or business people. However, 'this is not always the case and many reactions of tourists are not markedly different from those of foreigners' (Pearce et al., 1998, p. 350). Pearce et al. (1998) also suggested that not only tourists experience culture shock, but the host population also suffers from the same shock. The encounters may be stressful for both because they are confronted with new values and behaviour. The socio-cultural and psychological impact of tourists on hosts is greater when the host population had limited exposure to other cultures (Pearce, 1982b).

Stages of culture shock

When experiencing a new culture each traveller has to go through several stages of culture shock (Bochner, 1982). Oberg (1960) identified four stages of culture shock: (1) a 'honeymoon' stage characterized by fascination and optimism; (2) a 'hostility' stage characterized by negative attitudes toward the host society and increased contact with fellow sojourners; (3) a 'recovery' stage characterized by an increased ability to cope in the new environment; and (4) an 'adjustment' stage characterized by acceptance and enjoyment of the new cultural environment.

Gullahorn and Gullahorn (1963) proposed a U-curve of cultural adjustment or satisfaction with sojourn: initial optimism, the subsequent disappointment, adaptation and the gradual recovery. The U-curve has been extended to the W-curve (Gullahorn and Gullahorn, 1963; Trifonovitch, 1977). An additional stage of a re-entry (return home) has been adopted. In the first stage, 'honeymoon', when the travellers prepare themselves for travel, they are excited about going to a new culture and their expectations are high. In the second stage, 'hostility', travellers arrive in a new culture and start experiencing culture shock. They discover cultural differences between the host and a home culture, feel frustrated and unable to solve problems in familiar ways, reject the new culture and seek out people from the home culture. In the third stage, 'humour', visitors adjust to the host culture, begin to appreciate the new culture, interact with locals, learn the local language, and even joke in a foreign language. They spend less time with people of the home country, accept differences, and become adjusted to the host culture. In the fourth stage, 'at home', individuals look forward to returning home, regret they have to leave the new culture and become happy about returning home. In the fifth stage, 'reverse culture shock', travellers experience re-entry shock upon return to the home culture. They feel that the home culture has changed and does not match reality, they can't find familiar cues in the home environment, feel confused, alienated, unable to fit into their own culture, and become depressed. In the sixth 'readjustment' stage, tourists learn to cope with the problems at home (see Figure 2.1).

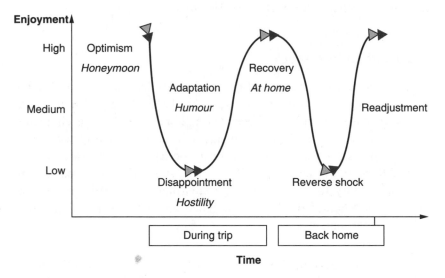

Figure 2.1 The U-curve and W-curve of cultural change, adaptation and adjustment over time

Hofstede (1997) presented an acculturation curve of a change in sojourner's feelings over time. In a short phase 1 'euphoria', individuals experience the excitement of travelling to and seeing new places. In the longer phase 2 'culture shock', individuals experience the different way of living and customs in the new environment. In the longest phase 3 'acculturation', the individuals learn about local customs and values, become more confident to function in a new cultural environment and develop social relationships. In phase 4, the 'stable state', the individuals reach psychological stability. They may either: (a) maintain negative attitudes towards a foreign environment and continue feeling isolated; (b) adjust to a new environment, feel the same as at home and become biculturally adapted; or (c) develop more positive attitudes towards a foreign than home environment and behave like 'natives'.

Similar patterns of culture shock and adjustment were proposed by Adler (1975), Smalley (1963), Brein and David (1971) and Jandt (1998) (see Table 2.3).

Both culture shock and reverse shock show that culture is an extremely important influence on human behaviour (Rogers and Steinfatt, 1999). However, it can also be a very useful learning experience. An individual can gain important understanding about cultural relativism and become better aware of cultural differences and better prepared for a next sojourning experience (Rogers and Steinfatt, 1999).

Intensity and duration of culture shock

The intensity of the feelings in each stage and duration of culture shock depends on the degree of cultural differences between the foreigners and the receiving culture (Porter, 1972; Stewart, 1966), the cultural knowledge of the individual, the ability to adjust, the length of stay in the foreign country, frequency of overseas travel, number of friends in a host community, type of tourist, type of travel arrangements and many others. For example, the greater the degree of the cultural differences between tourists and hosts the more intense could be culture shock. Some tourists may experience culture shock, limited to the initial stage only (Gullahorn and Gullahorn, 1963; Taft, 1977). Some may never leave the 'honeymoon stage' (Gullahorn and Gullahorn, 1963) or 'enthusiasm and excitement' stage (Brein and David, 1971), particularly when their stay in a new culture is very short. Instead of being frustrated tourists may feel excited about new experiences in the foreign culture fulfilling their motivations (Mehrabian and Russell, 1974). Others may find themselves in a constant stage of confusion. Some others may try to learn about the foreign culture and realize 'the weightlessness that comes when your sense of cultural gravity is knocked out' (Bohannan and Van der Elst, 1998, p. 54). Those who are more familiar with the foreign culture and/or have a better knowledge of it can cope better. Also, those who have better social skills can adjust quicker. However, even those who are highly skilled in adjust-

61

Table 2.3. Patterns of culture shock and adjustment

	1 stage	2 stage	3 stage	4 stage	5 stage	6 stage
Oberg (1960)	Honeymoon	Hostility	Recovery	Adjustment		
Gullahorn and Gullahorn (1963)	Honeymoon	Hostility	Humour	At home	Reverse culture shock	Readjustment
Brein and David (1971)	Optimism	Experience of difficulties, frustration	Learning to cope	Feeling lost at home		
Hofstede (1997)	Euphoria	Culture shock	Acculturation	Stable state		
Jandt (1998)	Initial euphoria	Irritation and hostility	Gradual adjustment	Adaptation		

ment to new environments in their own culture may find it difficult to cope and adjust to foreign culture.

Further, individuals who stay in a foreign culture for only a short period of time (e.g., 1–3 months) can still experience all stages of culture shock. Others who stay longer (e.g., several years) may experience each stage of culture shock over a year or more before acculturation occurs. Taft (1977) argued that tourists who visit a large number of cultures in a short time could be in constant shock because they have little chance to adapt to each new culture. Also, those travellers who have at least one close friend from a host community experience less culture shock than those with no friends from the host community (Sellitz and Cook, 1962). It has been argued further that not every type of tourist has to experience culture shock. Mass tourism offers only limited opportunities for tourist–host interaction. The short stay, organized in advanced pre-purchased packaged and guided tours, provide an environmental bubble which protects mass tourists from direct contact with a new culture and foreign hosts, stress and anxiety.

Shortcomings of the U-curve and W-curve

The patterns of culture shock have been described in 'curves' that indicate the patterns of adaptive change over time. The U-curve and W-curve patterns have not always been observed in empirical research. Church (1982) noted that support for the U-curve hypothesis is weak, inconclusive and overgeneralized. Not all studies have reported that sojourners begin their cross-cultural experiences with optimism (Klineberg and Hull, 1979). Even those who supported the U-curve pattern noted its significant dependence upon time and questioned its usefulness. The W-shaped curve has been criticized for being inaccurate, given the complexity of traveller types and individual differences and experiences, and lacking in evidence (Klineberg and Hull, 1979).

Measurement of tourist–host contact

The literature review indicates that there are a very large number of variables that can be used to measure social contact in general. Allport (1954) indicated 30 variables that can measure social contact

including area of contact, social atmosphere, status of the participants, and the culture of the individuals who are in contact. Cook
(1962) suggested measuring social contact by analysing such aspects
as the characteristics of the contact situation, contact participants,
their attitudes, requirements and expectations from the interpersonal
interaction, and the influence of rules and norms. Cook (1962) called
for the measurement of contact for different subjects for different
characteristics. There are suggestions that social contact should
be measured by the number of people encountered and the status
of individuals (Chadwick-Jones, 1962), nationalities (Triandis and
Vassiliou, 1967), the degree of intimacy (Goldsen *et al.*, 1956), or
number of friends made (Vassiliou *et al.*, 1972). The measurement
of cross-cultural contact is difficult because of the differences in
cultural meanings of the measuring variables such as status, intimacy,
friendship and so forth.

The best-known measurement techniques of social contact are:

Bale's measurement

Bales (1950) based his measurement of social contact on observation
of interactions. However, this method, although useful, was assessed
as difficult to apply in order to examine all possible types of interactions.

Triandis and Triandis' Social Distance Scale

A Social Distance Scale developed by Triandis and Triandis (1960) was
rejected as an invalid indirect measure of social contact between people of
different cultural backgrounds due to the differences in social distance
across cultures.

Hall's Social Distance Zones

Hall (1966) measured social contact by four physical social distance
zones: intimate, personal, social, and public. He observed the dependence of social distance zones on cultural background. Little (1968)
noticed that different cultural groups prefer different social distance.
The distance that is considered intimate in one culture may be considered more casual in another (Triandis, 1975). McAllister and Moore

(1991) found that the social distance between Australians and Asian groups was greater than between Australians and Europeans. The greatest social distance was observed between Australians and the Vietnamese group.

Vassiliou *et al.*'s measures

Vassiliou *et al.* (1972) measured social contact by the number of intimate friends made:

- *Maximum contact* was established with those who had several intimate friends
- *Some contact* was established with those who had no intimate, but few close acquaintance, and many remote acquaintance, and
- *No contact* was established with those who had no intimate friends and no close or remote acquaintances.

Gudykunst's measures

Gudykunst (1979) analysed cross-cultural contact by developing:

- *The Cross-Cultural Interaction Index,* which measured the amount and type of social interaction inferring a level of 'difficulty' in interacting with people from different cultures
- *The Potential for Cross-Cultural Interaction Index,* which measured the proportion of free time spent with people from different cultures, the degree of difficulty in understanding people from different cultures, and the number of hours spent together
- *The Number of Cross-Cultural Friendships Index,* which measured the number of close and casual friends from another culture, and
- *The Cross-Cultural Attitude Index.*

Feather's direct measures

Feather (1980b) used direct measures (on the Likert scale) that were concerned with how often Australian expatriates:

- had been invited into the homes of Papua New Guinean hosts
- had been asked to parties
- had been invited to play sport
- had been invited to share recreation facilities

- mixed at school, and
- how many good friends they had among their hosts.

Feather's indirect measures

Feather (1980b) also used indirect measures (on the Likert scale) that were concerned with:

- knowledge and use of the host language, and
- perceived social distance between tourists and hosts (similarity and differences in characteristics and behaviour).

Bochner's measures

The major variables that measure cross-cultural tourist–host contact and which have been suggested by Bochner (1982) are:

- on whose territory the contact occurs
- the time span of the interaction
- its purpose
- the type of involvement
- the frequency of contact
- the degree of intimacy, status and power, and
- distinguishing characteristics of the participants.

Bochner's (1982) measurement of tourist–host contact was criticized by Levine (1979) who argued that the critical variable of contact between stranger and host is not the length of time a stranger spends in the host country or the purpose of visit but the extent of stranger-host similarities/differences and the hosts' attitudes to the stranger.

Marsh and Henshall's measures

Marsh and Henshall (1987) measured social contact by:

- the scale, frequency and intensity of interaction (number of people, length of time)
- the person who chooses to interact, and
- the style of interaction based on the needs being met (Marsh and Henshall, 1987).

Black and Mendenhall's measures

Black and Mendenhall (1989) measured the intensity of social contact by:

- frequency
- importance
- nature (how familiar/novel the interaction is)
- the direction of interaction (one-way versus two-ways)
- the type of interaction (routine versus unique)
- the form of interaction (face-to-face versus mail)
- the duration (one year versus five years), and
- the format (formal versus informal) (Black and Mendenhall, 1989).

Kamal and Maruyama's direct measures

Kamal and Maruyama's (1990) measured the amount of direct contact by the:

- time spent with hosts
- number of host friends
- interaction preferences, and
- number of parties attended.

Kamal and Maruyama's indirect measures

Kamal and Maruyama's (1990) measured the amount of indirect contact by the:

- free time spent on discretion
- length of stay
- amount of previous contact with other cultures
- difficulties of establishing friendships, and
- opinion about treating tourists as equals.

The degree of social interaction was assessed by multiplying the frequency of interaction, importance and nature of interaction (Black and Mendenhall, 1989).

Degree of social interaction = f (frequency, importance and nature of interaction)

The ability to speak a foreign language

Social contact was also measured by the ability to speak a foreign language and, in particular, whether or not the English language was spoken in the home country. It was found that Asian groups, composed of Vietnamese, Chinese and Japanese, and a Middle Eastern group composed of Lebanese and Turks, have no knowledge of the English language, therefore they were least popular among Australian born people (McAllister and Moore, 1991).

Problems in measuring tourist–host contact

Presently, there is not enough information on how to precisely and successfully measure cross-cultural tourist–host contact. The techniques used in past studies to measure tourist–host contact have been limited. They have been criticized for not measuring data on the number of hosts the tourists meet, time they spent together, or the amount of contact. They provide only a general idea of the distributions of frequency and contact time (Hoivik and Heiberg, 1980). Past studies have been criticized for not using a reliable and valid technique to measure tourist–host contact. For example, Bystrzanowski (1989) showed that the extent of contact between tourists and hosts in Hungary, Poland, Florida and the Canary Islands was high and the only differences tourists and hosts perceived between themselves was the way of spending their leisure time, and attitudes toward nature. Bystrzanowski's (1989) study was criticized by Haywood (1990) for lack of appropriate measurement scale. The problems of developing useful techniques for measuring social interaction between tourists and hosts of different cultural backgrounds still exist.

Importance of the cultural background analysis

The analysis of the cultural backgrounds of different nations and groups within each nation is necessary (Feather, 1980b; Sutton, 1967) in order to determine where differences in value priorities between these groups occur and what their influence is on individuals and the social contact within these various groups (Feather, 1980b). Such analysis can provide important information about the reasons for potential misunderstanding between different cultural groups. Since the development of international tourism has significantly increased the contact between people from different cultures, research is needed to examine cultural influences on social interaction in different tourism settings (Murphy, 2000).

Tourist–host contact studies

The literature review reveals that there have been several attempts to analyse tourist–host contact. Doxey (1975) analysed the effects of host attitudes toward tourists. DeKadt (1979) examined the nature of contact with tourists and its influence on attitudes, behaviour and values toward tourism. Mathieson and Wall (1982) analysed tourist–host contact in terms of the social and cultural impacts of tourism development. Pearce (1982b) analysed the effects of social contact between tourists and hosts and the way in which tourists and hosts view one another. Pearce and Bochner (1982) examined the effects of intercultural tourist–host contact on tourists and the visited people. Pizam (1982) examined tourist–host contact as a potential source of crime. Pearce (1984) analysed tourist-guide interaction, as well as interactions between the host and guest populations in the New Zealand farm context (Pearce, 1990). Krippendorf (1987) examined tourist–host contact in terms of understanding and communication. Mittelberg (1988) and Uriely and Reichel (2000) analysed the tourist–host encounter between working tourists and their hosts. Pi-Sunyer and Smith (1989) examined the social processes at work in tourist–host encounters. Ryan (1991) analysed the disappearance of the local language and dialect as an outcome of tourist–host contact. Srisang (1991) highlighted the unequal nature of tourist–host relations by discussing its most extreme form of child prostitution. McKercher (1993) identified the tourist–host contact as a potential source of conflict because of the differences in tourists' and hosts' demand. Sharpley (1994) examined the host adoption of foreign languages and development of stereotypical attitudes towards hosts. Burns and Holden (1995) analysed hosts' coping behaviour and efforts to avoid contact. McIntosh et al. (1995) analysed host resentment towards tourists as the outcome of the economic gaps between tourists and hosts. Pizam analysed the perceptions of British, Israeli, Korean and Dutch tour guides of tourists of different nationalities (Pizam and Sussmann, 1995; Pizam and Jeong, 1996; Pizam and Reichel, 1996; Pizam et al., 1997). Black et al. (1996) looked at the communicative messages behind the tourist–host encounter and examined whether host perceptions of their guests and of themselves change over time. Boniface (1999) addressed the issue of cultural conflict in the tourist–host encounter. Past studies have implied that cultural factors affect tourist–host contact. Thus there is a need to examine the cultural background of tourists and hosts and determine how the cultural differences in their backgrounds affect their social interaction.

Summary

The concept of social contact can be used to explain tourist–host contact. There are different forms of tourist–host contact. The contact between tourists and hosts from different cultural groups is the focus of this book. The contact hypothesis suggests that contact between tourists and hosts of different cultural backgrounds may result in positive and negative outcomes. The impact of cultural differences on tourist–host contact in less developed countries is greater. Several factors determine tourist–host contact: (a) the nature of the contact itself and the social character of the situation in which the contact occurs; (b) the opportunity for contact; (c) the place in which this contact takes place; (d) interpersonal attraction of the contact participants; (e) personal attributes; (f) social motivations; (g) rules of social behaviour; (h) attitudes; (i) social skills; (j) perceptions of costs and benefits derived from interaction; (k) resources that are exchanged; (l) status, interests, goals and activities. These factors are culturally influenced. There are also other factors that influence tourist–host contact such as stage of tourism development or type of tourism. However, these factors are not discussed, as they do not directly influence the tourist–host contact in a cross-cultural setting.

The influence of cultural factors is vital for the explanation of tourist–host contact in the cross-cultural setting. Similarity in cultural background facilitates interaction between tourists and hosts; dissimilarity reduces it. Tourists and hosts from different cultural backgrounds can experience difficulties in their social interaction. Most difficulties occur due to cultural differences in communication and rules of social interaction. Culture shock is one of the most recognized difficulties encountered by travellers in a foreign culture. Tourists experience culture shock when they travel to a foreign culture. Many symptoms of culture shock have been identified. There are several stages of culture shock. The theorized stages of culture shock have not always been supported by empirical research. There have been several attempts to measure tourist–host contact. However, this measurement has proved to be difficult because of a very large number of variables that may be used. The measurement of cross-cultural tourist–host contact is very difficult because of the differences in the meanings of the measurement variables across cultures. The existing measuring techniques can be criticized for being invalid and unreliable. Currently, there is no standardized, reliable and valid technique that allows for the successful measurement of cross-cultural tourist–host contact and there is a need to develop such a technique.

Discussion points and questions

1. Explain the concept of social interaction and how it can be applied in a tourism context.
2. Cite two studies that suggest that the social contact between tourists and hosts from different cultures results in positive outcomes, and two others that show that the same tourist–host contact results in negative outcomes.
3. Describe what characterizes tourist–host contact.
4. Describe the common stages and assumptions of culture shock. Do you think that every traveller must experience culture shock? Give an answer illustrating the various arguments.
5. Give some reasons why researchers experience difficulties in measuring social contact between tourists and hosts of different cultural backgrounds.

Since cultural differences and the difficulties that tourists and hosts face in their social contact arise from differences in their values (Wei *et al.*, 1989), the next chapter will discuss the concept of cultural values.

Further reading

Furnham, A. and Bochner, S. (1986) *Culture Shock*. London: Methuen.
Oberg, K. (1960) Culture shock: adjustment to neo-cultural environment, *Practical Anthropology* 17: 177–182.

Pearce, P. (1982) *The Social Psychology of Tourist Behaviour*. Oxford: Pergamon Press.

Pearce, P., Kim, E. and Lussa, S. (1998) Facilitating tourist–host social interaction: an overview and assessment of the culture assimilator. In Laws, E., Faulkner, B. and Moscardo, G. (eds) *Embracing and Managing Change in Tourism: International Case Studies*. London: Routledge.

Smith, V. (1978) *Hosts and Guests*. Oxford: Blackwell.

Values

Objectives

After completing this chapter the reader should be able to:

- define values, value system and values orientation

- understand the relationship between culture, values and other related concepts

- identify different types of values

- describe major value dimensions along which cultures differ

- identify techniques of value measurement

- identify major value patterns and cultural differences between Asian, European, US and Australian societies.

Introduction

The previous chapter showed that social interaction is influenced by differences in cultural background. Since most of these differences arise from cross-cultural differences in values (Triandis, 1972), it is important to introduce the concept of values.

Concept and definitions

There have been many attempts to characterize values, their functions, and the ways in which they differ from other related concepts. According to Adler (1956), the concept of value is broad, vague and lacking in real meaning. Every person has a unique set of values. Some values tend to permeate a culture. These are called cultural values and derive from the larger philosophical issues that are part of a culture's milieu.

The major problem with defining value is a lack of consensus about what constitutes value and recognizing value priorities. For instance, values have been defined as the core of culture (Kroeber and Kluckhohn, 1952); world views (Redfield, 1953); system and core of meaning (Kluckhohn, 1956; Sapir, 1949); specific preferences and beliefs about these preferences (Baier, 1969; Catton, 1959); standards and criteria (Rokeach, 1973); attributes of individuals (Barton, 1969) and collectives (Kluckhohn, 1951b). Therefore, attention has to be drawn to definitions that show an agreement in describing the concept of value (Feather, 1975; Rokeach, 1973, 1979).

Firstly, it is agreed that values possess a normative dimension. They inform a member of a culture about what is good and bad, right and wrong, true or false, positive or negative, and the like. They define what ought to be or ought not to be, what is useful and useless, appropriate and inappropriate, what is proper conduct, and what types of events lead to social acceptance and satisfaction.

Kluckhohn

Kluckhohn (1951b) reported that values are general principles that define life situations, selection, and decision-making. Without values it would be impossible to measure order in social life as social values predict social life. Kluckhohn (1951b) saw values as attributes of people; as having affective, cognitive and conative elements. Kluckhohn (1951b, p. 395) defined value as 'a conception, explicit or implicit, distinctive of an individual or characteristic of a group, of the desirable which influences the selection from available modes, means and ends of actions'. Although Kluckhohn's (1951b) definition was criticized for being ambiguous and confusing (Albert, 1968), his definition of value was supported by Rokeach (1973).

Rokeach

Rokeach (1973) defined value as 'an enduring belief that a specific mode of conduct or end-state of existence is personally preferable to an opposite mode of conduct or end-state of existence' (p. 5). He referred to values as 'beliefs about desirable goals and modes of conduct' (Rokeach, 1979, p. 41) such as to seek truth and beauty, to behave with sincerity, justice, compassion, humility, respect, honour, and loyalty. Rokeach (1973) also stressed that these desirable modes of conduct are abstract ideals, which represent ideal existence such as security, happiness, freedom, equality, state of grace, and salvation. In a similar way to Kluckhohn (1951b), Rokeach (1973) viewed values as 'means and ends'. Rokeach (1973) agreed with Kluckhohn (1951b) that values are socially shared, and are conceptions of the desirable, and with Williams (1970, 1979) that they are standards or criteria. According to Rokeach (1979, p. 48), values are criteria that we 'learn to employ to guide action ... to guide self-presentations ... to evaluate and judge ourselves and others by; to compare ourselves with others, not only with respect to competence ... but also with respect to morality. We employ values as standards ... to decide what is worth and not worth arguing about, worth and not worth persuading and influencing others to believe in and to do. We employ values to guide ... justification and rationalization of action, thought, and judgment. Thus, the ultimate function of human values is to provide us with a set of standards to guide us in all our efforts to satisfy our needs and at the same time to maintain and enhance self-esteem, ... to make it possible to regard ourselves and to be regarded by others as having satisfied socially and institutionally ... morality and competence.' Therefore, values are determinants of social behaviour (Rokeach, 1973).

Smith, Triandis, Williams and Bailey

A similar explanation of values is provided by Smith (1969), who stated that values play an important role in the evaluation process such as judging, praising or condemning. Triandis (1972) and Williams (1979) agreed with Kluckhohn (1951b) that values are preferences for actions and have strong affective components. Triandis (1972) reported that values are abstract categories. Also Bailey (1991) agreed with Kluckhohn (1951b) that 'values are individual attributes that can affect such things as the attitudes, perceptions, needs and motivations of people' (p. 78).

Value system

Rokeach (1979, p. 49) believed that the main values could be ordered in a priority of relative importance with respect to other values to create a value system (Rokeach, 1973), which is an enduring organization of beliefs concerning preferable modes of conduct or end-states of existence along a continuum of relative importance. According to Rokeach (1973), a value system is the *system* of criteria by which behaviour is evaluated and sanctions applied, a system of social guidelines that show the cultural norms of a society and specify the ways in which people should behave, a system of standards that permit individuals to make decisions about relationships with self, others, society, nature and God.

Values over time

A value system is relatively stable over time. However, as a result of changes in culture the value priorities may be rearranged in the long term (Rokeach, 1973). Changes in values affect thoughts, actions, attitudes, beliefs, and social behaviour. However, these changes depend on the intensity with which individuals within a culture hold these values.

Value conflicts

Value systems may conflict, and cultural differences in value orientations may create disagreements. On an individual level, a person may feel a conflict about being polite versus being dishonest; on a societal level, members may feel a disagreement on the importance of values. When two people are from different cultures, value differences may jeopardize the achievement of successful interaction. Violations of expectations based upon a value system can produce hurt, insult, and general dissatisfaction (Samovar and Porter, 1988).

Values and culture

Many writers suggest a relationship between values and culture. Culture is a system of shared values of its members (Bailey, 1991); culture and values held by its members are related (Hofstede, 1980); values are the core of culture (Kroeber and Kluckhohn, 1952); values depend on culture (Fridgen, 1991); culture is rooted in values (Hofstede, 1980). Values are psychological variables that characterize people within the same culture with regard to similarities in people's psychological make-up. Rokeach (1973) argued that '... differences between cultures ... are concerning differences in underlying values and value systems' (p. 26). Rokeach (1973) provided many examples of value differences between various cultural groups and concluded that values differentiate significantly among cultural groups. Differences in values indicate cultural differences in thinking, acting, perceiving; understanding of attitudes, motivations, and human needs (Rokeach, 1973). Similarly, Segall (1986) reported that people from different cultures possess different cultural values. Also, Chamberlain (1985) noted that differences in values are found between differing cultural groups and, therefore, they differentiate cultural groups. Williams (1979) argued that while there are some values that appear to be universal, societies differ in their patterns of cultural values. However, these differences involve not only differences in the relative importance of particular values but also differences in the extent to which members of each society adhere to particular values, differences in the degree to which the values are universally accepted within a society, and differences in the emphasis which each society places on particular values.

Value orientation

There is a distinction between value and value orientation. Value orientations are 'complex but ... patterned-rank ordered principles ... which give ... direction to the ... human acts ... the solution of common human problems' (Kluckhohn and Strodtbeck, 1961, p. 4). Variations in value orientations are the most important type of cultural variations and, therefore, the central feature of the structure of culture (Kluckhohn and Strodtbeck, 1961). Since different cultures find different solutions to human problems, the value orientation is a critical variable in the comparison of cultures (Zavalloni, 1980). Major cultural orientations along which cultures differ have been identified (Parson, 1951; Kluckhohn and Strodtbeck, 1961; Stewart, 1971; Hall, 1976; Hofstede, 1980; Argyle, 1986; Schein, 1992; Trompenaars, 1984, 1993; Hampden-Turner and Trompenaars, 1993; Maznevski, 1994). These will be described later.

Values as used in this book

In this book it is proposed to treat values as one of the elements of culture, and to examine whether differences in values differentiate cultural groups. The concept of cultural values as used in this book is similar to the Rokeach (1973) concept of values. Like Rokeach (1973, 1979), the authors of this book argue that values influence means and ends, guide interaction patterns, represent criteria for evaluation of self and others and standards for these evaluations, can be put in a priority of importance, and can differentiate various cultures. The concept of cultural values as used in this book is also similar to Kluckhohn's (1956, 1959) and Kluckhohn and Strodtbeck's (1961) value orientation. Since values may be applied to individuals (personal values) and groups (cultural values) (Kluckhohn, 1951b) that mutually influence each other (Barth, 1966; Meissner, 1971), cultural values can be seen as yardsticks around which personal values develop. Therefore, by examining personal values it is possible to analyse cultural values of a particular society. However, it has to be noted that dominant cultural values kept by society do not need to be identical or even similar to individual personal values.

The relationship between values and other related concepts

Many writers suggest relationships between values and other concepts such as behaviour, attitudes, perceptions, beliefs, rules, norms, interests, motivations, or needs (e.g., Allport, 1961; Campbell, 1963; Kluckhohn, 1951b; Maslow, 1943, 1959; Moutinho, 1987; Rokeach, 1973; Stewart, 1972; Williams, 1968; Zavalloni, 1980). Values seem to be superior to other concepts. For the purpose of this book, the relationships between values and the concepts of behaviour, rules, and perceptions are outlined. The aim is not only to show the superiority of the value concept to these concepts but also to justify choosing the value concept as a dominant cultural variable in differentiating cultures.

Values and behaviour

Values are related to behaviour (Kluckhohn, 1951b; Rokeach, 1973) because they are cultural determinants of behaviour (Zavalloni, 1980). Values prescribe behaviour that members of the culture are expected to perform (Samovar and Porter, 1988). They specify which behaviours are important and which should be avoided within a culture. They guide and rank behaviour (Fridgen, 1991; Peterson, 1979). Values are superior to behaviour. Most people follow normative values that indicate how to behave and failure to do so may be met with sanctions. The differences in values reflect differences in behaviour (Rokeach, 1973). The similarity between values predispose a similar way of behaviour.

Values and rules and norms

Values are also related to rules and norms. Values provide a set of rules for behaviour (Samovar and Porter, 1988) that guide behaviour (Stewart, 1972). Since values refer to desirable modes of behaviour unlike norms that refer to *just* modes of behaviour (Stewart, 1972), values decide about the acceptance or rejection of particular norms (Williams, 1968). Values are more personal and internal than rules and norms. They can better explain behaviour than rules and norms; therefore, they are superior to rules and norms.

Values, attitudes and perceptions

Values are also related to attitudes because they contribute to the development and content of attitudes (Samovar and Porter, 1988); they determine attitudes (Rokeach, 1973). Attitudes are learned within a cultural context and tend to respond in a consistent manner with respect to value orientations. For instance, valuing harmony indicates an attitude toward people and the nature of the relationship between people. Similarity in terminal values determines harmonious interpersonal interaction (Sikula, 1970). Values are standards, as opposed to attitudes. Values refer to single beliefs that focus on general situations and objects, as opposed to attitudes that refer to a number of beliefs and focus on specific objects and situations. There are fewer values than attitudes because people have

only several values concerning a desirable behaviour, and as many attitudes as encounters. Values determine attitudes (Allport, 1961). Values
are more stable over time than attitudes (Rokeach, 1973). Values provide
more information about persons, groups and cultures than attitudes
(Rokeach, 1968a, 1968b). Therefore, values are more useful than attitudes in understanding and predicting behaviour. In fact, values determine attitudes and behaviour (Homer and Kahle, 1988). Although
Campbell (1963) argued that value and attitude concepts are similar,
and Newcomb *et al.* (1965) recognized values as special cases of attitudes,
the literature agrees that values are superior to attitudes. Since attitudes
influence perceptions (Bochner, 1982), values also determine perceptions
(Samovar and Porter, 1988). Therefore, the concept of value is also
superior to the concept of perception. Since values vary from one culture
to another, behaviour, rules and attitudes also differ across various
cultures. In addition, differences between values and attitudes allow for
a clustering of societies (Ronen and Shenkar, 1985) and market segmentation (Madrigal and Kahle, 1994).

Types of values and their classification

Many researchers have attempted to classify and distinguish various
types of values (Albert, 1956; Allport *et al.*, 1960; Levitin, 1973;
Parsons, 1951, 1953; Parsons and Shils, 1951; White, 1951). One of the
descriptions of value and value differences has been provided by Rokeach
(1968b, 1971, 1973, 1979). Rokeach as well as others (Kluckhohn, 1951b;
Kluckhohn and Strodtbeck, 1961; Lovejoy, 1950; Rokeach, 1973) agreed
that there are two types of values: *instrumental* (about broad modes of
conduct) and *terminal* (about end-states of existence), or in other words,
means and ends.

Instrumental values

Instrumental values are concerned with preferable modes of conduct or
means of conduct (to be honest, obedient, ambitious, independent, to
love). These values may be moral (to behave honestly, to be helpful,
loving) and be of a social form; or not be concerned with morality (to
be ambitious, self-controlled, logical, imaginative) but with competency
or self-actualization and be of a personal form (Rokeach, 1973).

Terminal values

Terminal values are concerned with goals or the end-state of existence (salvation, world peace, freedom, comfortable life, true friendship). They may be personal (individual security, freedom, happiness, salvation) and social (national security, social recognition, true friendship), and they are worth striving for. People's attitudes and behaviour depend on whether their personal or social values have priority (Rokeach, 1973).

Number of values

The number of values is limited by a man's biological and social make-up and his needs. The total number of terminal values that a person possesses is about 18, instrumental values between 60–72 (Rokeach, 1973).

Primary, secondary and tertiary values

Values can also be classified according to their importance within a society. Samovar and Porter (1988) distinguished *primary*, *secondary*, and *tertiary* values. Primary values are at the top of the value hierarchy because they are the most important. They specify what is worth the sacrifice of human life, or worth dying for. Secondary values are very important, but they are not strong enough for the sacrifice of human life. Tertiary values are at the bottom of the value hierarchy (e.g., hospitality to guests may be a tertiary value). Whether a value is primary, secondary or tertiary depends upon the culture in which the person resides.

Measurement of values

There are two types of value measurement: (a) direct, and (b) indirect.

Direct measures

One of the direct measurements is survey research when the respondents are asked to rank values according to the importance of values (Rokeach, 1973), or rate them on a Likert scale (Millbraith, 1980; Moum, 1980).

81

Indirect measures

Values can also be measured indirectly by asking the respondents about their desired values (self-description) and desirable values (ideological statements), or by describing third people. As Hofstede (1980) pointed out, the respondents' perceptions of third people are influenced by the respondents' values. Values can also be assessed through open-ended questions, essays, by observing peoples' choices (Williams, 1978), their interests, type of rewards and punishments for particular actions, by analysing historical and literary documents, art, myths, and legends.

Value measures in cross-cultural studies

Values were measured in various cross-cultural studies. Different techniques of measurement have been used. Among well-known techniques are the following:

- The Allport-Vernon Values Scale (Allport *et al.*, 1951)
- The Allport-Vernon-Lindzey Values Scale (Allport *et al.*, 1960)
- The Ways to Live Test (Morris, 1956)
- The Survey of Interpersonal Values (Gordon, 1960)
- The description of value orientations (Kluckhohn and Strodtbeck, 1961)
- Personal Value Scales (Scott, 1965)
- Ranking procedures (Kohn, 1969; Rokeach, 1973)
- The antecedent-consequent procedure (Triandis *et al.*, 1972a)
- Osgood's semantic differential technique (Osgood *et al.*, 1957)
- The Value Survey of Rokeach (Rokeach, 1973)
- Ideographic procedures (Zavalloni, 1980), and
- A variety of questionnaire measures and procedures developed for specific purposes (Mirels and Garrett, 1971; Scott, 1965).

Shortcomings of the value measures

Not all of these techniques gained universal acceptance. For instance, Morris' (1956) ways of living test was criticized for being suited to only highly educated respondents. Kluckhohn and Strodtbeck's (1961) value orientation survey is appropriate only for peasant populations. Scott's (1965) Personal Value Scale is a normative rather than an ipsative test (forced-choice format). Although the Allport-Vernon-Lindzey (AVL) test is regarded as one of the best available tests for the assessment of values (the test-retest and split-half reliabilities ranged from 0.84 to 0.95, and the validity has also been assessed successfully) (Graham and Lilly, 1984), this test was also criticized for using an ipsative scoring method. According to Hicks (1970), the ipsative measure is a very serious limitation of the instrument and should not be used. High scores on one scale can be obtained only if scores on the other scale are low, forcing negative intercorrelations among the scales. Since the scores are dependent, it is also not appropriate to use ipsative scores for prediction and examination of group differences (Graham and Lilly, 1984). Therefore, the only way to avoid this shortcoming is to normalize the scores from the ipsative scale.

Value surveys

Feather (1975) and Rokeach (1973) reported that value surveys are very useful in studying adult values. The value surveys were praised for not only measuring a person's value but also perceived values of others (Feather, 1970b, 1971, 1972a, 1972c).

Rokeach Value Survey

The Rokeach Value Survey (RVS) (Rokeach, 1973) is considered to be the best available instrument for measuring human values. In his value survey Rokeach (1973) introduced two lists of 18 alphabetically arranged instrumental and terminal values. These two sets of values are accompanied by short descriptors that were added after tests showed they improved the reliability of the instrument. The terminal values that include such concepts as salvation, equality, world of peace, lasting contributions, comfortable life, exciting life, and social recognition refer to preferred end-states of existence. The instrumental values that include such concepts as being courageous, responsible, honest, polite, and clean describe preferred modes of conduct. Rokeach (1973) asked the respondents to arrange values in order of importance to them from 1–18. Rokeach (1973) found that the highest valued terminal values were: world peace, family security, and freedom. The highest valued instrumental values were: honesty, ambition, and responsibility.

The RVS is 'based on a well-articulated conceptualization of value' and its success in 'finding specific values that differentiate various political, religious, economic, generation and cultural groups' (Braithwaite and Law, 1985, p. 250). The RV is relatively economical because respondents have to deal with only thirty-six concepts in all, each being represented by two or three short phrases. Rokeach (1968b, 1973, 1979) used his value survey in wide-ranging research to investigate topics such as a relationship between values, attitudes and behaviour; the distribution of value priorities at different times; political ideologies; the effect of inconsistencies among the individual values; value educations, and institutional values.

Several researchers have used the RVS to measure human values (e.g., Feather, 1970a, 1970b, 1971, 1972a, 1972b, 1972c, 1980a, 1980b, 1980c, 1986a, 1986b; Ng et al., 1982). The results of the studies indicated numerous cultural differences in values between various Western and Asian countries. The RVS was also used to construct the 'List of Values' (Kahle and Timmer, 1983) that included values such as a sense of belonging; fun and enjoyment; warm relationships with others; self-fulfilment; being well respected; sense of accomplishments; security; self-respect; and excitement. The 'List of Values' was used several times for marketing research purposes.

Criticism of value surveys

The value surveys were criticized for their content being removed and being to far from what is meant by 'the desirable'. According to Rokeach (1973), a person's belief does not imply that the belief is to be desirable. Therefore, it was argued that the value surveys do not have high priori validity. Cantril (1965) noted that cross-cultural value surveys attempting to determine cultural differences in values do not allow for explanations of these differences either. The RVS was also criticized for its shortcomings. Kahle (1986) believed that use of the RVS would be inappropriate in less developed societies and for groups with low verbal comprehension. Some of the values might be misunderstood or irrelevant to some cultures. Rokeach (1973) argued that the ranking procedure yields a hierarchy of values understandable to groups with little education. However, many researchers have questioned the meaningfulness of the ranking procedure (Gorsuch, 1970; Keats and Keats, 1974; Lynn, 1974). Consequently, the most recent value studies applied a rating rather than a ranking system (e.g., Braithwaite and Law, 1985).

Value analysis

Various analytical procedures have been used to analyse values. In the earlier studies Jones and Bock (1960) applied multiple discriminant analysis. Bales and Couch (1969) applied factor analysis and reduced 900 different statements of values to four basic values such as authority, self-restraint, equality, and individuality. In more recent studies researchers have used multidimensional scaling techniques such as factor analysis, cluster analysis, discriminatory and smallest space analysis (e.g., Feather and Peay, 1975; Hofstede and Bond, 1984; Ng et al., 1982; Schwartz and Bilsky, 1986).

Difficulties in measuring and analysing values

In general, it is difficult to measure and analyse values in cross-cultural research. Values are abstract constructs, not easily observed, difficult to translate into different languages and their interpretations depend on the cultural backgrounds of respondents and researchers. 'Often values ... and evaluations of the behaviours of strangers are based on the values and belief system of the observers' (Damen, 1987, p. 192). Therefore, there is a problem of matching researchers' value interpretations and respondents' behaviour. There is also a problem of confusing values with other related concepts. A number of studies that claimed to measure values assessed specific attitudes and interests (Feather, 1980c). Problems in choosing which particular values should be assessed (Rokeach, 1973) add to the difficulties in measuring values. Past study findings also suggested that values that are central to the individual receive high rankings. Atkinson and Murray (1979) found that social values such as love, family, or friendship were given a higher priority than economic values. Leisure values have been ranked low (Bharadway and Wilkening, 1977). Chamberlain (1985) recommended focusing on values that are less central to the individual.

The choice of technique used to measure values in cross-cultural research also creates problems. Only techniques that are appropriate to the cultures that are being compared and that are equivalent across cultures (Feather, 1975), should be chosen. Problems also concern the *emic* versus *etic* approach, the appropriate equivalence of measures and meanings, ways of maximizing reliable and valid measurements, and the logic of comparative analysis. Studies that use multiple methods of measurement of values give the best understanding of cultural values (Feather, 1986b).

Value studies in tourism

Not many value studies have been done in tourism. Shih (1986) used a Values, Attitudes, and Lifestyles (VALS) technique to assess whether personal values affect the selection of Pennsylvania as a holiday destination. Four groups of nine lifestyle segments emerged including experientials who focus on interpersonal relationship experiences. Pitts and Woodside (1986) found values to be useful in describing visitors to tourist attractions versus non-visitors, and identifying 'a value profile' of each group. They found values to be indicative of the motives and needs a particular attraction satisfies. Differences in cultural values could predict visitation to tourist attractions. Pizam and Calantone (1987) developed a value scale related to tourist vacation behaviour. They used numerous scales from previous studies measuring values: the RVS; Scott's Personal Values Scales (Scott, 1965); Webster, Sanford and Freeman's New 'F' Scale (Webster *et al.*, 1955); Rosenberg's Self Esteem Scale (Rosenberg, 1965); Bales and Couch's Value Profile (Bales and Couch, 1969) and Rehfisch's Rigidity Scale (Rehfisch, 1958). The original scale consisted of twenty-three bipolar statements on a 1–9 scale that were related to various aspects of vacation travel behaviour. Pizam and Calantone (1987) found that travel behaviour was significantly associated with a person's general and vacation-specific values. They concluded that values predict travel behaviour. Muller (1991) found that different segments of American tourists to Toronto attached different importance to destination attributes and, thus, possessed different values. Madrigal and Kahle (1994) segmented English-speaking tourists to Scandinavia on a basis of their values and found the differences in vacation activity preferences among tourists to be based on the relative importance they placed on four value domains. It appeared that values are important variables in predicting tourist visitation to a destination and behaviour.

Differences in cutural value patterns between Asian, US, European and Australian societies: empirical and non-empirical evidence

An attempt is made to summarize the available empirical and non-empirical evidence of differences in cultural values between Asian, US, European and Australian societies. The focus is mostly on the United

States, Western Europe and Australia as representative of Western culture and Southeast Asian countries as representative of Eastern cultures.

Early studies

Several multinational studies have been conducted (Eckhardt, 1971; Rusett, 1968; Stewart, 1971; Vincent, 1971). There were some attempts to cluster countries (Cattell, 1950; Hofstede, 1980; Rummel, 1972; Russett, 1968; Sicinski, 1976; Sirota and Greenswood, 1971):

- Gordon (1967) clustered Chinese, Japanese, Philippino and Indian together
- Ando (1965) clustered together Indian and Philippino; Japanese and Norwegian, and as distinct, Chinese and American
- Hofstede (1980) clustered forty countries into eight cultural areas including Asian, Near-Eastern and Anglo groups
- Russett (1968) and Tung (1989) made a distinction between Eastern and Western clusters.

The cross-cultural differences in values between the countries belonging to these clusters were analysed (Ando, 1965). The Eastern clusters were characterized as more conservative, pessimistic, conformist, compulsive, socially oriented, nationally dissatisfied, and unstable as opposed to Western clusters (Eckhardt, 1971).

Religious philosophies

The cultural differences in values between Eastern and Western societies could be explained by distinct religious philosophies adapted in various regions of the world. Smart (1968) described Eastern values in terms of major Eastern religions like Buddhism and Hinduism. Ryan (1985) assessed how religious philosophies influenced the Chinese way of life, thinking and behaviour. For instance, Confucius dictated the correct naming, use of precise words, speaking with a proper degree of hierarchy, respect and the ability to foresee how their own behaviour affects others. It restricted the expression of emotions. Taoism stressed emotional calm, being in harmony with nature, discouraged assertiveness and self-expression. Buddhism emphasized common coexistence. Buddhists (Chinese, Koreans, Japanese) were described as people, who do nothing to hurt others, respect life, morality, control one's own feelings and thoughts, and practise proper conversation. Taoism dictated leading a simple, close to nature life, and avoiding social obligations. Shintoism dictated the worship of ancestors. The Eastern cultures stressed belongingness and ego that protects from creating conflict. The Japanese were presented as people- and society-oriented, receptive to nature, achievement-oriented, less materialistic (Kikuchi and Gordon, 1966, 1970; Stoetzel, 1955), independent and open to experience (Jones and Bock, 1960). The Chinese were presented as self-sufficient and progress-oriented. Differences between Eastern and Western approaches to the concept of self were noted (Chung, 1969; Hsu, 1971a). Western values could be explained by the Christian religious philosophy, which teaches love, respect and worship of God and others, and dictates non-violence and caring for one another, and is based on the Ten Commandments. Unfortunately, many of the Christian laws have been violated in modern times.

Comparison of cultural orientations

The Western and Eastern cultures exhibit distinct 'orientations' towards the world and other people. According to Kluckhohn and Strodtbeck (1961), these orientations represent human problems for which people in all cultures must find solutions: how to relate to (1) human nature; (2) nature; (3) human activities; (4) other people; and (5) time. Different cultures may be compared on the basis of how their members solve these problems. Different leading authors in the field developed different sets of cultural orientations, however, they all appear to relate to Kluckhohn and Strodtbeck's cultural dimensions. Table 3.1 shows a comparison of the major cultural orientations. The explanation of these orientations, which follows Table 3.1, indicates the interdependence among various aspects of culture.

Parson's pattern variables

Parson (1951) identified six pattern variables, which represent the choices individuals have to make before engaging in any behaviour: universalism-particularism, ascription-achievement, diffuseness-specificity, affectivity-affective neutrality, instrumental-expressive orientation, and self-orientation–collective orientation.

1. *Universalism-Particularism*. This dimension differentiates between cultures depending on the manner by which people describe each other and objects and the rules they use for this purpose. In cultures

Table 3.1 Comparison of cultural dimensions

	Human Nature	Relation to Nature	Activity Orientation	Human Relationships	Relation to Time	Context	Space Orientation	Information Flow	Language
Parson (1951)	Universalism Particularism		Achievement Ascription Diffuseness Specificity	Affectivity Affective neutrality Instrumental Expressive Self-oriented Collective-oriented					
Kluckhohn and Strodtbeck (1961)	Good Evil Neutral Mixed Changeable Unchangeable	Subjugation Harmony Mastery	Doing Being Being-in-becoming	Individualistic Collateral (collectivistic) Linear (hierarchical)	Past Present Future		Public Private Mixed		
Stewart (1971)	Changeable Unchangeable	Subjugation Harmony Control	Doing Being Becoming	Formal Informal Egalitarian Hierarchical Direct Indirect Self-oriented Group-oriented	Present Future				

Table 3.1 (*continued*)

	Human Nature	Relation to Nature	Activity Orientation	Human Relationships	Relation to Time	Context	Space Orientation	Information Flow	Language
Hall (1960, 1966, 1973, 1976) **Hall and Hall** (1987)	Agreements		Monochronic Polychronic	Amount of space Possessions In- and out-groups Friendship Authority	Past Future Monochronic Polychronic	Low/high context	Public Private Intimate Personal Social	Covert/overt messages	Low/high context
Hofstede (1980)	Low/high Uncertainty Avoidance	Low/high Uncertainty Avoidance	Masculinity Femininity	Low/high Power Distance Individualism Collectivism					
Bond (1987)/ **Chinese Culture Connection** (1987)					Long/short-term Orientation				
Argyle (1986)				Formal Informal Contact Non-contact					
Triandis (1994)				Tight/loose cultures					

90

Schein (1992)	Evil Good Mixed	Subjugation Harmony Control	Doing Being Being-in-becoming Work Family Personal	Individualism Groupism Participation Involvement Role relationships	Planning Development Discretionary time horizons (function/occupation/rank) Temporary symmetry Pacing Past Present Near/Far Future Monochronic Polychronic	Physical Social Individual Moralism Pragmatism High/low context	Intimacy Personal Social Public High/low status
Trompenaars (1984, 1993) Hampden-Turner Trompenaars (1993)	Universalism Particularism	Inner/outer directed	Achievement Ascription Analysing Integrating	Individualism Communitarianism Equality Hierarchy Affective Neutral	Sequential Synchronic Past Present Future		
Maznevski (1994)	Good Evil Changeable	Subjugation Harmony Mastery	Doing Being Containing Controlling	Individual Collective Hierarchical			

with a *universalistic* orientation, people describe themselves and objects according to universal and general rules by following a standardized pattern. In cultures with a *particularistic* orientation people use particular rules and describe others in specific categories that are unique to the situation. In universalistic cultures people interact and communicate with strangers in the same way regardless of social situations and circumstances, while in particularistic cultures the interaction and communication patterns with strangers differ depending upon situations. Bellah (1985) found the US and Canada the more universalistic cultures on earth, and Japan, Singapore, Hong Kong, China, Thailand and South Korea more particularistic (Hampden-Turner and Trompenaars, 1996).

2. *Ascription-Achievement*. This dimension differentiates between cultures depending on how people assess each other. In *ascription* orientation people assess others on the basis of the inherent qualities (e.g., gender, family heritage, race, ethnic group) and predict others' behaviour on the basis of qualities ascribed to them (India, China, Japan, Indonesia, France). In the *achievement* orientation people and objects are judged on the basis of the performance and measurable results, and predict others' behaviour on the basis of their efforts and occupational status and achievements (US, Britain).

3. *Diffuseness-Specificity*. This dimension differentiates between cultures depending on whether people categorize others and objects in a holistic manner by integrating the details, looking for patterns, structures and theories (collectivistic cultures, *diffuseness* orientation), or categorize others according to specific details such as facts, tasks and numbers and respond to a particular aspect of a person or an object only, e.g., role or responsibility assigned (individualistic cultures, *specificity* cultures). Hampden-Turner and Trompenaars (1996) reported that Japan, Thailand, Malaysia, China, Hong Kong and Singapore tend to be holistic oriented. Canada, Australia, France, Germany, US, Netherlands and UK are more specifics oriented.

4. *Affectivity-Affective Neutrality*. This dimension differentiates between cultures depending upon the nature of the gratification people seek (Parsons, 1951), their association with emotional and non-emotional responses and the way their decisions are based. In *affective* orientation people look for immediate gratification; their behaviour and decisions are guided by emotions (Latin American cultures such as Spain, Italy, or Mexico). In *affective neutrality* orientation people express self-restraint; their behaviour and decisions are guided by cognitive information and facts (US, Australia, Great Britain).

5. *Instrumental-Expressive Orientation*. This dimension differentiates between cultures depending on the nature of the goals people seek to achieve in their social interactions. In *instrumental* orientation social interactions are important because they help to achieve certain goals (US), while in the *expressive* orientation social interactions are valued for their own sake (Latin America, Arab cultures). In the expressive orientation people value friendships more than in instrumental orientation (Gudykunst and Kim, 1997).

6. *Self-Orientation–Collective Orientation*. This dimension differentiates between cultures by identifying those cultures that focus on the enhancement of individuals, their needs and rights and those that care about the welfare of others and the community. In the *self-oriented* cultures the individual goals are emphasized; people are supposed to look after themselves and take initiatives (US, Great Britain). In the *collective* cultures people are concerned about the interests and well being of others (Asia). Americans and Canadians are the most self-oriented and individualist nations on earth (Bellah, 1985); the Chinese, Singaporeans, Hong Kong, Malaysians and Koreans are more concerned with a group of people with whom they work or interact socially (Hampden-Turner and Trompenaars, 1996).

Kluckhohn and Strodtbeck's value orientation

Kluckhohn and Strodtbeck (1961) compared cultures on a basis of five value orientations toward human nature, nature, human activities, time, and other people.

1. *Orientation toward human nature*. The human nature orientation deals with the innate character of human nature. Humans can be viewed as good, evil or a mixture of good and evil. Western societies perceive man as good, while Eastern societies perceive man as good or bad. For instance, the Chinese assume that a man is either born good or bad. The orientation toward man's nature has a significant impact on people's attitudes to each other and consequently on their interpersonal contact. However, no studies have been done on the cultural differences between Eastern and Western value orientation towards human kind.

2. *Orientation toward nature*. There are three potential types that exist between humans and nature: mastery over nature, harmony with nature, and subjugation to nature. Gudykunst and Kim (1997) reported that the distinction is not quite that simple. Humans can

also be viewed as able to change (mutable) or not able to change (immutable). There are numerous combinations of these various aspects: (a) humans are evil but mutable; (b) humans are evil and immutable; (c) humans are neutral with respect to good and evil; (d) humans are a mixture of good and evil; (e) humans are good but mutable; and (f) humans are good and immutable. Western societies believe they can control nature and all natural forces can and should be overcome (e.g., floods, storms). However, it is not always easy to decide which of the six combinations predominates. For example, in the United States people see human nature as evil but mutable; they use discipline and self-control to change their nature. Many believe that human nature is a mixture of good and evil (Gudykunst and Kim, 1997). Eastern societies believe people should live in harmony with nature and worship it (e.g., China, Japan, North American groups). The Eastern societies see nature as a creation of God and life as God's will. They regard members of Western societies, who imply the alternatives for God and spiritual dimensions as untrustworthy, unintelligent, and biased. In cultures such as Spanish Americans, people are subjugated to nature and believe that nothing can be done to control nature if it threatens. The orientation towards nature affects people's attitudes to religion, aesthetics, material possession, life quality and, consequently, interpersonal relations.

3. *Orientation toward human activities.* Human activity can be handled in three ways: doing, being and being-becoming. Western cultures such as the United States or Germany are 'doing' and 'action' oriented. They emphasize activity, task completion, goals achievements, getting things done, and competition. Activities are tangible and can be externally measured. A common question in the United States is 'What do you do for a living?' Eastern cultures are either 'being' or 'being-in-becoming' oriented. The being orientation is opposite to the doing orientation. People engage in spontaneous activities, indulge in pleasures and reveal their spontaneity as an expression of their human personality. The examples of this orientation are most Latin cultures, e.g., Mexico. The being-in-becoming orientation is concerned with spiritual life more than a material one, who people are, not what they have. The focus is on self-development, contemplation, meditation, and self-improvement (e.g., Hinduism, Zen Buddhist monks). In both being and being-in-becoming cultures people emphasize passivity, defensiveness and strive for social harmony in interpersonal relations at the expense of efficiency. They are people oriented and harmony oriented. Members of

Eastern cultures try to be humble and tolerant and refrain from open confrontations. They emphasize individual obligations to society and group harmony. As Beatty *et al.* (1991) reported, people who value highly other people and warm relationships with others also give more gifts and put more effort into gift selection, than people who exhibit more self-centered and self-concerned values. An understanding of the activity orientation can give insight into the people approach to work and leisure. In the 'being' oriented societies decisions are most likely to be emotional and people oriented. In the 'doing' oriented societies decisions are most likely to be economically driven and task oriented. The activity orientation dimension has a significant influence on interpersonal relations.

4. *Orientation toward time*. The focus of human life can be directed on the past, present and future. Western societies are future time-oriented. They perceive time as a scarce resource and try to use it effectively. They value change and see the future as 'bigger and brighter' (e.g., United States). Eastern societies are past and tradition oriented. They worship ancestors and have strong family traditions (e.g., China, Japan). They attach relatively small importance to time schedules and punctuality. They perceive time as circular rather than linear (e.g., Indonesian). However, in Western influenced Hong Kong the majority of Chinese act according to precise time schedules. Present-oriented societies believe that the moment has the most significance. The future is vague and unknown and what really matters is 'now'. People pay relatively little attention to what has happened in the past and history. People believe they must 'enjoy their moments'. People of the Philippines, Mexico and Latin America usually have these beliefs. Also, in societies such as Navajo Indians of northern Arizona the present orientation predominates. Time orientation has a significant impact on people's attitudes to tradition, ceremony, etiquette and, consequently, on interpersonal relations.

5. *Orientation towards other people*. This dimension appears to be the most crucial in governing human interactions and the most differentiating between Eastern and Western cultures. Kluckhohn and Strodtbeck (1961) distinguished three types of orientations towards other people: (a) *individualistic* (individual goals take primacy over group goals); (b) *collateral* (the individual is part of 'social order which results from laterally extended relationships' (p. 18), e.g., preference for group consensus, agreement with group norms); and (c) *linear* (stresses the 'continuity of the group through time in

ordered positional succession' (p. 19), for example, stresses submission to the elders or superior position).

(a) *Individualistic relationships*. According to Hofstede (1980), Western cultures such as the United States emphasize individualism in interpersonal relations. People primarily perceive themselves as individuals rather than as members of a group. They maximize efforts to achieve personal benefits and enhance personal status. Social relations are competitive and self-image is important. People relate to each other informally.

(b) *Collateral relationships*. Eastern cultures emphasize both collaterality and linearity (hierarchical). Collateral (collectivistic) relationships are characterized by the strong relationship between an individual and a group. There are studies that support Hofstede's (1980) findings and give evidence that collaterality in interpersonal relations in Eastern cultures is characterized by smooth interpersonal relations, group harmony, and concern for the welfare of others. DeMente (1991c) observed traditional Chinese values, such as politeness, thrift, and saving face, and reported that causing someone else embarrassment is regarded as inappropriate behaviour. Lynch (1964), Bulatao (1962), Jocano (1966) and Hollnsteiner (1963) emphasized the Philippino pattern of 'smooth interpersonal relations', the importance of 'being together', emotional closeness with the family, and friendly relations outside the family. Komin (1990) emphasized the Thais patterns of 'smooth interpersonal relations': being polite, kind, pleasant, conflict-free and superficial. Gardiner (1972) found that Thai people value smiling as an important element in interpersonal relations. Forrest (1971) indicated that the Vietnamese frequently display affection and they are ready for social contact with strangers.

(c) *Linear relationships*. There is also evidence that Eastern cultures employ linearity in interpersonal relations which are characterized by hierarchy of society, obedience and loyalty to authority, feelings of duty, responsibility, submission to the group and elders, desire to comply, and respectful conduct. Leung (1991) reported that the prevalent Confucian value teaches modest behaviour and that the superiority of higher status cannot be challenged. Earle (1969) indicated that the Chinese scored highly on the authoritarianism and dogmatism scales. According to Meade (1970), the Chinese operate with greater cohesiveness of judgment under authoritarian leadership. Hare and Peabody

(1971) noted that Philippinos agreed with both the anti-authoritarian and authoritarian scales. According to Ettenson and Wagner (1991), in Chinese culture politeness and deference to authority are considered to be virtues. Huyton (1991) noted that one of the aspects of a Confucian value characteristic for the Chinese people is that of filial piety – giving of unquestioning respect to parents and the elderly through understanding and expectations of authority. Forrest (1971) reported the importance of filial piety, desire to comply and submissiveness to authority in the Vietnamese culture. Lynch (1970) stressed the importance of conformity, endurance and deference with regard to the Philippino 'smooth interpersonal relations'. Noesjirwan (1970) found that Asian students in Australia were significantly more dependent on authority than Australian students. Doi (1981) emphasized that Eastern countries are more conforming and that people depend more on each other. According to Yau (1988), values, which are important for the Chinese are group orientation, face saving, deference to age and authority, and connections. Huyton (1991) noted that the needs to maintain harmony, saving own and others' face, the needs for prestige and social respect manifest themselves by a Chinese student being both unwilling and unhappy to answer questions in public. According to the Chinese, it is better to perform acts of self-effacement rather than break the group harmony. Several studies have noted the importance of external control in Hong Kong (Hsieh et al., 1969) and in Thailand (Reitz and Graff, 1972).

Importance of harmony

Harmony in interpersonal relations appears to be an extremely important value in Eastern cultures. The Eastern cultures emphasize self-restrain, avoidance of negative emotions, criticism, negative opinions, complaints, and conflict in interpersonal relations. Members of Eastern cultures try to 'save face', avoid embarrassment, and maintain harmony in interpersonal relations (Dodd, 1987). Openly disagreeing or saying 'no' is considered rude and damaging to social harmony (Elashmawi, 1991). Criticizing in public makes people lose face and damages their relationships with those who criticize. For instance, in China one confirms a negative statement with a 'yes' (Leung, 1991). The Thai response to criticism, where criticism is rare and face saving common, was rigidity and withdrawal as opposed to the American response, which was an increased cognitive flexibility (Foa *et al.*, 1969). The Easterners' (Hong Kong, Japan, Thailand, Vietnam) admission to failure and criticism were limited to protect the individuals from loss of face; the Westerners' reaction to failure was an attempt to improve performance. Gardiner (1968) found that Thai students regarded 'keeping calm' and 'facial expressions' as the most acceptable expressions of anger. Forrest (1971) noted that the Vietnamese talked around the subject. Ellis and Ellis (1989, p. 24) reported that the 'Japanese place more emphasis on good human relationships than on money'. Social relations are seen in Japan as mutual responsibilities and the smallest favours put the receiver in debt. Huyton (1991) noted that for the people of Hong Kong harmony in social relations is paramount. In Western societies interpersonal relationships are seen as creating frictions and these societies are less concerned with apologies; they value self-esteem. Lynch (1970) indicated that Philippinos avoided social disruption, embarrassment or disagreement, which could bring shame. The Philippine and Indonesian concept of shame is very similar, as well as the Chinese and Japanese concept of 'saving face'. However, these concepts appear to be in contrast with the Western emphasis on truthfulness or forthrightness.

Importance of apology

In order to maintain social harmony, people in many Asian cultures frequently apologize. The apologetic and humble attitude is regarded as a sign of good behaviour in Asian cultures. Wagatsuma and Rosett (1986) noted that the Japanese apologized by acknowledging their fault even when the other party was at fault, in order to indicate their will to maintain or restore relations. On the other hand, Americans blamed others even when they knew they were at fault. Coulmas (1981) reported that the Japanese tend to apologize if repayment is not possible. The Japanese are sensitive to fulfilling their social obligations and are concerned with apologies for not meeting their obligations. Barnlund and Yoshioka (1990) noted that the Japanese offered compensation for the other person in order to maintain harmony in relations. Americans, on the other hand, gave explanations and justified their acts.

Stewart's cultural patterns

According to Stewart (1971), a culture's underlying patterns consists of orientations to activity, social relations, the self, and world.

Activity orientation

This orientation is similar to Kluckhohn and Strodtbeck's (1961) activity orientation and differentiates between cultures on a basis of how people view human activities and how they express themselves through activities (doing/being/becoming). *Doing* cultures value action and 'getting things done'; people seek change and want to control their lives (Euroamericans). *Being* cultures focus on non-action (African-American, Greek); people believe that all events are determined by fate (Hindus from India). *Becoming* cultures see human beings as evolving and changing (Native Americans, South Americans).

According to Lustig and Koester (1993), the activity orientation determines the pace of people's life. 'Doing cultures' are governed by time schedules and appointments, and are characterized by a fast pace of life. 'Being' and 'becoming' cultures are characterized by a slower and more relaxed pace of life. The activity orientation also determines how people measure their own success. In 'doing' cultures people set the goals for their activities and evaluate the results of their activities by measurable criteria. In 'being' and 'becoming' cultures the process rather than final result is more important. Further, the activity orientation influences the relationship between work and play. In 'doing' cultures work is separated from play. Employees are supervised and controlled. In 'being' and 'becoming' cultures work is a means to an end and there is no clear distinction between work and play. Employees mix together and socialize. Moreover, 'doing' cultures challenge and solve a problem when a difficulty occurs. 'Being' and 'becoming' cultures accept the difficulty rather than challenge and eliminate it. Further, in 'doing' cultures interpersonal interaction and communication are characterized by accomplishing specific tasks and solving problems. In 'being' and 'becoming' cultures social interactions are characterized by being together.

Social relations orientation

This orientation shows similarity to Parson's (1951) self-and-group orientation and Kluckhohn and Strodtbeck's (1961) individualistic-collateral and linear relationships. It differentiates cultures on a basis of how people relate to one another (formal/informal; egalitarian/hierarchical; direct/indirect). In *formal* cultures people follow rules of social etiquette and address others in an official way by using appropriate titles (Japan, Germany). In *informal* cultures social relations are based on equality and informal ways of interacting and communicating (US, Australia).

In *egalitarian* cultures (European and US American) emphasis is on equality and evenness in interpersonal relationships. In *hierarchical* cultures such as South Korea, Japan or Mexico emphasis is on status differences between individuals. Also, in egalitarian cultures focus is on independence and a minimum number of obligations and responsibilities (US, Australia, Britain); in hierarchical cultures focus is on obligations and dependence (Japan, China). The degree of dependency in hierarchical cultures depends on the social status and formality that exist between individuals. In *direct* cultures members emphasize directness and openness in interpersonal interactions and communication (Europe, US). In *indirect* cultures an emphasis is on indirectness, ambiquity and the use of third parties and intermediaries (Japan, Korea, Thailand, China, Africa) (Lustig and Koester, 1993).

Self-orientation

This orientation, similar to Parson's (1951) self-orientation and Kluckhohn and Strodtbeck's (1961) individualism-collectivism orientation, differentiates between cultures depending on how people view themselves, form their identities, whether their nature is changeable, what motivates their actions and who is valued and respected (self/group orientation). In *self-oriented* US and Europe the emphasis is on individual self, children are encouraged to make their own decisions and be independent from an yearly age. People seek innovation and change. Alternatively, in group-oriented Asian cultures people define themselves through their relationships with others. An individual cannot exist without the group. People depend on each other at work, school and at home. Members of the group are motivated by loyalty to a group, duties and responsibilities (e.g., family, company). They also seek advice from elders who have valuable life experience and are a source of knowledge.

World orientation

This orientation differentiates between cultures on the basis of how people relate to the spiritual world and nature (subjugation/harmony/control). Europeans, US Americans and Canadians believe in the power of an individual to control, manipulate and change nature. They also believe in separate physical and spiritual worlds. Reality is what can be tested and proved, as opposed to spirituality. On the other hand, Latino cultures believe that humans have very little power to control the forces of nature and, thus, are subjugated to nature. They also place a great value on spirituality. According to Stewart (1971), the world orientation determines the way people view time. For example, US Americans and Europeans are future oriented, Native Americans and Latinos are present-oriented.

Hall's cultural differentiation

Hall differentiated cultures on the basis of different styles of communication (Hall, 1976) and orientation toward the world and people (Hall, 1960, 1966, 1973; Hall and Hall, 1987). In terms of communication style he distinguished between cultures on the basis of the context the communication takes place (low/high context), handling personal space (public/private), information flow (covert/overt messages), and language (low/high context). In terms of the orientation toward the world and people, Hall distinguished between cultures on the basis of orientation toward human nature (agreements), activity (monochronic/polychronic), human relationships (amount of space, possessions, friendships, communication) and time (past/future, monochronic/polychronic).

Communication

Context

Hall (1976) distinguished between the low-context cultures (LCC) and high-context cultures (HCC) depending on the level of information included in a communication message. In the *low-context cultures* most of the information is contained in verbal messages, very little in the contextual message (Hall, 1983; Ting-Tomey, 1985). Messages have clear meanings. There is a tendency to emphasize line logic, explicit direct verbal communication and clear intentions. Hofstede (1980) indicated that Western cultures (Germany, Sweden, Switzerland, Australia, USA, France) belong to LCC where there is a need for explicit instructions, signs, and procedures that explain how to behave. In the *high-context cultures* (China, Japan, Korea, Taiwan, Vietnam, Latin America, Mexico) very little information is coded in the verbal message as most information is coded in the non-verbal, contextual message. All events can be understood only in context, meanings can vary depending upon circumstances, situations can change. There is a tendency to emphasize spiral logic, implicit, imprecise indirect non-verbal communication, non-clear intentions, discretion in expressing own opinions (Ting-Toomey, 1991), and use of an indirect communications system (Hall, 1976; Gudykunst *et al.*, 1988b). Since the HCC value face saving, honour shame and obligations that reflect status, position and power, they avoid confrontations in groups, and use smoothing strategies to manage conflicts in interpersonal relations (Kim and Gudykunst, 1988). Members of HCC are also more cautious in initial interactions and have a greater tendency to make assumptions based upon a stranger's cultural background. They also ask more questions (Gudykunst, 1983b). However, direct questions are considered by Asians to be rude (Elashmawi, 1991). The Japanese, Chinese, Southeast Asians, Indonesians, Micronesians, and Indians belong to HCC that expect others to sense the rules of behaviour (Dodd, 1987).

Information flow

Cultures have been distinguished on a basis of the structure and speed of messages between individuals. Members of high-context cultures use *covert messages* that are high in context. The focus is on non-verbal codes and implied meanings. People know the meanings of particular messages in specific situations and they do not need to be explicit. Little is left for interpretation. In low-context culture, members use *overt messages* that are low in context. People need explicit messages, which include clear instructions to convey exact meanings. Precise verbal codes and words are used to transmit the meanings.

Language

Language determines what is said and how it is said. This can be observed in appropriate subjects of discussion (family, politics, religion) and the degree of expressiveness. In high-context cultures being direct and open, using many verbal codes, expressing emotions or showing feelings may be considered as a sign of immaturity. Silence and reserved reactions are necessary to maintain social harmony and not to threaten the face or self-esteem of others. In low-context cultures it is acceptable to express anger, show excitement, and be noisy and confident.

Space

Hall distinguished cultures depending on the ways people communicate through handling of personal space. In *public* space cultures people are suspicious of activities conducted in secret, social closeness is encouraged and public meetings are valued. In *private* space cultures members respect personal ownership, value privacy, and keep social distance.

Orientation toward the world and people

Human nature
In high-context cultures agreements between members tend to be *spoken* rather than written. Written contracts are not binding and can be changed depending on the situation. In low-context cultures agreements tend to be *written* rather than spoken. Written agreements are final and legally binding.

Human relationships
Amount of space. According to Hall (1966), people differ in their use of space and interact within four spatial zones or distance ranges: *intimate* (for loving, comforting, protecting or fighting), *personal* (for conversations with intimates, friends), *social* (for impersonal and social gatherings) and *public* (for lectures, speeches, concerts, ceremonies, plays). By following the rules of space people know how far to remain from others in different social situations without interrupting conversations and jeopardizing privacy. Space distances are culture-specific. People from colder climates (Germany, Scandinavia, England) use larger physical distance when they communicate. They expect others to keep their distances. People from warm weather climates (Italy, Greece, Spain, Africa) prefer close distances.

Possessions. In various cultures people differ in their motivations. Achieving an external success in the form of possessions, positions and power motivates individualists. Collectivists are motivated by a responsibility and duty to a group, loyalty, and social harmony.

In-groups and out-groups. In high context cultures there is a strong emphasis on *in-groups* and a clear distinction between those who belong to a group (in-groups, insiders), e.g., families, friends, neighbours, work groups and those who don't (out-groups, outsiders), e.g., non-members, clan, organizations, and foreigners. Individuals identify themselves with only a few groups, with which they have strong bonds (Japan, Korea, China). In high context cultures people know how they should act according to rules and situations and what to expect from the behaviour of others. This is in contrast to the low-context cultures, where the emphasis is on *out-groups* (US, Europe); people typically belong to many groups through lifetimes. Membership in these groups is temporary; people change groups (e.g., change jobs and companies).

Friendship. In high context-cultures relationships are relatively *long lasting*, based on the individual's commitment to each other, loyalty, trust, and obligations. In low-context cultures relationships are relatively *shorter* in duration and more casual, the bonds between people are fragile, and the extent of involvement to long-term relationship is low. Deep personal involvement with others is valued less.

Authority. In high-context cultures people are personally responsible for the actions of subordinates. In low-context cultures authority is diffused and personal responsibility is difficult to determine.

Relation to time

Cultural attitudes to time differ in the relative importance attached to *past* and *future*. Americans are not concerned about the past, which is relatively unimportant when compared to the future. In contrast, in Europe and Asia people have a long history and deeply rooted traditions, thus they pay attention to the past and follow traditions. In high-context cultures time is viewed as open, less structured, more responsive to the needs of people and less to external goals. In low-context cultures time is highly organized in order to be able to live and work with others.

Assumptions about time indicate cultural differences in perceiving time. Similarly to Kluckhohn and Strodtbeck (1961), Hall (1983) also acknowledged the importance of time in differentiating cultures. According to Hall (1983), *monochronic* cultures such as Anglo-Saxon (US, Canada, Australia, Britain) and northern European cultures (Sweden, Norway, Finland, Germany) are task, time schedules and procedures oriented. Time is seen as limited, treated as money and regarded as a finite resource, which can be spent, saved, borrowed, lost or even killed. Activities are synchronized with a watch and can be stopped because 'time is up' (Gudykunst and Kim, 1997). Human relations are time dependent, and compartmentalize their time and activities. Time is used in a structured, sequential and linear fashion. There is a concern about punctuality, time, and appointments schedules. On the other hand, *polychronic* cultures such as southern Europe (Spain, Italy, Portugal), and the Middle East experience time as unlimited and expandable. People are human relations and family oriented. Human relations are not time dependent. Being late and interruptions are excusable for the sake of the relationship. Punctuality is not as important, focus is on task completion rather than adherence to time schedules. Time can be sacrificed (Latin America, Arab states). Thus, the polychronic cultures are more effective for building relationships and solving human problems (Schein, 1992). Further, Asian cultures believe in a cyclical concept of time as phases, rather than circular in form. One season follows the next; one life leads into another (Sithi-Amnuai, 1968).

Relation to activity

Time orientation also influences attitudes to activities and change. In high-context cultures people are cautious of change. In low-context cultures people desire change, they live faster and change their cultural behaviour faster. For example, US Americans tend to view change as good and desirable, they constantly search for new and better ways of doing things. Europeans may view change as risky since it can threaten traditions. In Asia change may be seen as dangerous since it brings uncertainty that needs to be avoided (Schneider and Barsoux, 1997). In monochronic cultures only 'one thing can be done at a time'. In polychronic cultures people engage in several activities at the same time because time is expandable.

Hofstede's dimensions of cultural variability

Hofstede (1980, 2001) distinguished between cultures by analysing work-related value orientations in different countries. There is empirical evidence of cultural differences between societies as related to Hofstede's (1980, 2001) dimensions of cultural variability. These dimensions reflect value differences that influence interpersonal interactions.

Power Distance. The Power Distance (PD) dimension refers to the extent to which a society accepts the unequal distribution of power in institutions and organizations. Hofstede (2001) reported that in the *high PD cultures* (Malaysia, Guatemala, Panama, Philippines, Mexico, Venezuela, Arab countries, Ecuador, Indonesia, India) societies hold that people are not equal but that everyone has a rightful place. Societies value obedience, conformity, authority, supervision, and co-operation; there is a social hierarchy and inequality. In *low PD cultures* (Austria, Israel, Denmark, New Zealand, Ireland, Sweden, Norway, Finland, Switzerland, Great Britain) societies hold that inequality should be minimized. They value independence, personality, and consultancy instead of autocratic decision-making; there is a strong ethic of competition. It was found that members of low PD cultures respect equality as antecedents to freedom, while members of high PD cultures view servitude and money as antecedents to freedom (Triandis, 1972). Australia, United States and Canada scored relatively low on the PD scale.

Uncertainty Avoidance. The Uncertainty Avoidance (UA) dimension refers to the extent to which a society feels threatened by uncertain and ambiguous situations and tries to avoid them. In the *high UA cultures* (Greece, Portugal, Guatemala, Uruguay, Belgium, Salvador, Japan, Yugoslavia, Peru, Spain) societies feel that uncertainty in life is a threat that must be fought. Therefore, they try to avoid uncertainty and ambiguity by avoiding conflict, disapproving competition, not tolerating deviant behaviours and ideas that are considered dangerous, providing greater stability with little risk. A high level of anxiety, aggressiveness, emotional restraint, loyalty, consensus, and group decisions characterizes societies. People believe in absolute truths, knowledge and the attainment of expertise. They emphasize a need for hard work; they are achievement motivated, and desire law and order. They have a strong need for written rules, are nationalistic, suspicious toward foreigners, conservatist, and concerned with security in life. They are pessimistic about the future. Japan scored the highest among all Asian countries on the UA dimension. This indicates that the Japanese avoid ambiguous and uncertain situations (Gudykunst *et al.*, 1988a). In the *low UA cultures* (Singapore, Jamaica, Denmark, Sweden, Hong Kong, Ireland, Great Britain, Malaysia, India, Philippines) societies tolerate ambiguity and uncertainty, take more risk, accept deviant behaviours, and do not find new ideas threatening. People are less stressed. Societies focus on advancement, individualism, and competition. There are as few rules as possible. Societies believe not so much in expertise as in common sense. Conflict is natural. People are optimistic about the future and accept foreigners with different ideas. However, the degree of uncertainty avoidance varies in collectivistic cultures (Kim and Gudykunst, 1988). Australia, United States and Canada scored relatively low on the UA dimension.

Individualism/Collectivism. The Individualism/Collectivism (I/C) dimension refers to the extent to which people emphasize their own needs. In the *highly individualistic cultures* (United States, Australia, Great Britain, Canada, Netherlands, New Zealand, Italy, Belgium, Denmark, Sweden) societies emphasize individual goals, concerns, rights, needs, self-actualization and development. Importance is attached to freedom, challenge, autonomy, initiative, individual decisions, activity, achievement, own opinion, pleasure, and financial security. People are self-oriented and emphasize the right to private life and opinion. The social ties are loose. In *highly collectivistic cultures* (Guatemala, Ecuador, Panama, Venezuela, Colombia, Indonesia, Pakistan, Costa Rica, Peru, Taiwan) societies emphasize group goals, rights, needs, decisions, consensus, and cooperation. Individual initiative is discouraged and people are 'we' oriented. The social and family ties are tight. There is a distinction between in-groups and out-groups. The in-group members are expected to look after the other members, in exchange for absolute loyalty. Friendships are predetermined by long, stable relationships. Hofstede (1980) found that East Asian countries are particularly high on collectivism and English-speaking countries are particularly high on individualism.

Triandis (1995) argued that individualistic and collectivistic cultures could differ according to whether relations among people in the culture are horizontal or vertical. In horizontal cultures people are treated equally, and there is an emphasis on valuing equality. In vertical cultures people see themselves as different from others, and equality is not valued highly. Also, in horizontal collectivistic cultures little value is placed on freedom and members of those cultures are not expected to stand out (e.g., Japan). In vertical collectivistic cultures (e.g., India) individuals are expected to fit into the group and at the same time they are allowed and expected to stand out in the group. In vertical, individualistic cultures (e.g., the United States, Britain, France, Germany) people are expected to act as individuals and stand out from others. In horizontal, individualistic cultures (e.g., Sweden, Norway) people are expected to act as individuals, and at the same time, not stand out from others.

Masculinity/Femininity. The Masculinity/Femininity (M/F) dimension refers to the extent to which a culture values masculine behaviours such as assertiveness, acquisition of money and material possessions, and lack of care for others and the quality of life. In the *highly masculine cultures* (Japan, Austria, Venezuela, Italy, Switzerland, Mexico, Ireland, Jamaica, Great Britain, Germany) societies are money and possessions oriented. Emphasis is on performance, growth, ambition, independence, living to work, successful achievement, excellence, dominance, and assertiveness. People accept the company's interference in their private lives. There is high job stress; sex roles are differentiated and unequal. Japan scored the highest on the masculinity index, 95/100 among all Asian countries. In the *high feminine cultures* (Sweden, Norway, Netherlands, Denmark, Costa Rica, Yugoslavia, Finland, Chile, Portugal, Thailand) societies are people oriented. The emphasis is on quality of life, welfare of others, and sympathy for the unsuccessful. Sex roles are equal. Australia and United States scored relatively high on the masculinity index, Canada scored between high and low.

Table 3.2 presents a ranking of fifty-three countries on Hofstede's (2001) four value dimensions.

Table 3.2   Ranking of fifty-three countries on Hofstede's (2001) four value dimensions

Country	Power distance	Uncertainty avoidance	Individualism	Masculinity
Arab countries	7	27	26/27	23
Argentina	35/36	10/15	22/23	20/21
Australia	41	37	2	16
Austria	53	24/25	18	2
Belgium	20	5/6	8	22
Brazil	14	21/22	26/27	27
Canada	39	41/42	4/5	24
Chile	24/25	10/15	38	46
Colombia	17	20	49	11/12
Costa Rica	42/44	10/15	46	48/49
Denmark	51	51	9	50
East Africa	21/23	36	33/35	39
Ecuador	8/9	28	52	13/14
Finland	46	31/32	17	47
France	15/16	10/15	10/11	35/36
Germany	42/44	29	15	9/10
Great Britain	42/44	47/48	3	9/10
Greece	27/28	1	30	18/19
Guatemala	2/3	3	53	43
Hong Kong	15/16	49/50	37	18/19
India	10/11	45	21	20/21
Indonesia	8/9	41/42	47/48	30/31
Iran	29/30	31/32	24	35/36
Ireland	49	47/48	12	7/8
Israel	52	19	19	29
Italy	34	23	7	4/5
Jamaica	37	52	25	7/8
Japan	33	7	22/23	1
Malaysia	1	46	36	25/26

Mexico	5/6	18	32	6
Netherlands	40	35	4/5	51
New Zealand	50	39/40	6	17
Norway	47/48	38	13	52
Pakistan	32	24/25	47/48	25/26
Panama	2/3	10/15	51	34
Peru	21/23	9	45	37/38
Philippines	4	44	31	11/12
Portugal	24/25	2	33/35	45
Salvador	18/19	5/6	42	40
Singapore	13	53	39/41	28
South Africa	35/36	39/40	16	13/14
South Korea	27/28	16/17	43	41
Spain	31	10/15	20	37/38
Sweden	47/48	49/50	10/11	53
Switzerland	45	33	14	4/5
Taiwan	29/30	26	44	32/33
Thailand	21/23	30	39/41	44
Turkey	18/19	16/17	28	32/33
Uruguay	26	4	29	42
USA	38	43	1	15
Venezuela	5/6	21/22	50	3
West Africa	10/11	34	39/41	30/31
Yugoslavia	12	8	33/35	48/49

Source: Hofstede, G. (2001) *Culture's Consequences: Comparing Values, Behaviors, Institutions and Organisations Across Nations.* 2nd ed. London: Sage Publications.
Note: A low ranking (e.g. 3) indicates a high rating on that dimension.

Weaknesses of Hofstede's theory

The Hofstede's (1980) theory of cultural differentiation has been often criticized for: (a) assuming that a national territory corresponds with a cultural group (many countries include a range of culture groups); (b) data being collected in a single industry (computer industry) and a single multinational corporation; (c) data not being representative of other members of the cultures; (d) the questionable validity of the items used to construct the indices; (e) the western bias because of the methodology used in collecting the data; and (f) not being exhaustive.

Strengths of Hofstede's theory

Although the Hofstede's (1980) study has been criticized, his four cultural dimensions embraced major cultural values and made comparisons between national cultures possible (Mead, 1998). Hofstede's cultural dimensions gained acceptance as distinguishing cultural groups according to differences in cultural values. Hofstede's (1980) cultural dimensions were related to various concepts, e.g., the power distance dimension was related to the concepts of freedom, power, respect, and wealth in Triandis' (1972) study. Evidence suggests that Hofstede's (1980) cultural dimensions are applicable not only to work-related values but to cultural values generally (Forgas and Bond, 1985; Hofstede and Bond, 1984) and are cross-culturally universal. Most importantly, Hofstede's (1980) study has been replicated more than 60 times (Sondergaard (1994) and the results confirmed on different samples. Thus, Hofstede's (1980) method has proved to have considerable life (Mead, 1998).

Studies based on Hofstede's cultural dimensions

Many studies have been done on cross-cultural differences based on Hofstede's (1980) cultural dimensions. Hofstede's (1980) dimensions are very useful in explaining the cross-cultural differences in interpersonal interactions. The differences between British, Hong Kong, Malaysian, and Indonesian cultures have been researched (Wright et al., 1978; Wright and Phillips, 1980). The four cultures scored similarly on Hofstede's (1980) UA and M/F; and differently on the PD and I/C dimensions. The Asian cultures differed on power distance. These findings were supported by Hofstede (1980) who also indicated differences in the PD and I/C dimensions in Hong Kong Chinese and other Asian cultures. Some studies indicated differences in PD and I/C in the Chinese and Australian cultures (Hofstede, 1980; Kroger et al., 1979). Chinese culture was characterized by high power distance and authority differences with strong collectivist social structure, accepting inequality, solidarity, and group orientation. The Australian culture was characterized by small power distance and strong individualism, low tolerance of inequality and authority, loose social networks, and weak sense of social obligations. The Chinese also seemed to emphasize social values in human interactions, while Australians favoured competitiveness and individualism. Hsu (1971a) showed that in the Chinese culture individualistic behaviour is regarded to be at the expense of others, therefore, the concept of personality does not exist at all. Hsu (1953, 1971b, 1972, 1981) also noted that the Chinese are very socially and psychologically dependent on others. They give support for parents, tradition, duty, obligations, acquiring wisdom; they are emotionally restrained, and partially socially withdrawn. They are concerned with self-control and social conformity accompanied by shyness.

Importance of I/C and M/F dimensions

According to studies that analysed the I/C dimension (Kim and Gudykunst, 1988; Schwartz, 1990; Triandis, 1988), this dimension is the major dimension that differentiates cultures. The I/C dimension explains the cross-cultural differences in interaction patterns (Hui and Triandis, 1986). Its understanding enables us to predict implications for social interactions (Triandis, 1988). For instance, individualists confront others, feel responsible for their own success and failures (Hui and Triandis, 1986), and are concerned only with self-face maintenance (Kim and Gudykunst, 1988). Therefore, they experience separation and distance from their in-groups (Hui and Triandis, 1986). Collectivists consider the implications of their own behaviour for others, share material and non-material resources with others, are controlled by shame, emphasize harmony in relations with others (Hui and Triandis, 1986), are concerned with both self- and other face maintenance, and also with reciprocal obligations (Kim and Gudykunst, 1988). Therefore, they experience closeness with their in-groups.

According to Triandis *et al.* (1988) and Schwartz (1994), the dimension of I/C and M/F can explain communication differences between cultures. Noesjirwan (1978) examined communication in in-group and out-group relationships and found that Indonesian members of the group could adapt to the group (collectivism). In Australia the group members are expected to 'do their own thing' even if they must go against the group (individualism). The literature indicates evidence of cultural differences in communication between Japanese and Americans (Barnlund, 1989; Gudykunst and Nishida, 1983; Okabe, 1983). Markus and Kitayama (1991) argued that cultural variations in individualism and collectivism are linked to the ways members of cultures see themselves and behave, e.g., whether they feel as part of social relationship or emphasize the self. Gudykunst and Ting-Toomey (1988) argued that low- and high-context communication styles are also a function of individualism-collectivism. For example, members of individualistic cultures are more emotion and pleasure oriented, members of collectivistic cultures are more concerned with avoiding hurting others and imposing on them. Members of individualistic cultures use direct requests as the most effective strategy for accomplishing their goals, while members of collectivistic cultures perceive direct requests as the least effective strategy (Kim and Wilson, 1994).

Other studies

There are other empirical studies concerning cultural differences in interpersonal interactions between Eastern and Western societies that use Hofstede's (1980) cultural dimensions. It was shown that since interpersonal relationships are culture bound (Ting-Toomey, 1991), different values are placed on *interpersonal styles* in different cultures (Argyle, 1972). Individualistic cultures are concerned with individualized relationships; collectivistic cultures with group relationships (Hui and Triandis, 1986; Triandis, 1988). A further example, interpersonal relationships in Japan differ depending on the role of the individual and group interaction (Damen, 1987). In Japan there is a distinction between the *omote* (public, formal) and *ura* (private, informal) style of interaction (Okabe, 1983). Argyle (1986) and Argyle *et al.* (1986) found that in the collectivistic Japan and Hong Kong cultures maintaining harmonious relations is highly endorsed. These cultures perceive in-group relationships as more intimate than individualistic cultures (Gudykunst and Nishida, 1986). In Japan and Korea human relations are treated as more personal than in individualistic cultures (Gudykunst *et al.*, 1987). The importance of time invested in building trustful relationships is crucial to the Japanese (Elashmawi, 1991).

Cultural differences were found in *network patterns* (Yum, 1985). Asians develop close networks and Confucianism provides them with basic rules for social relationships (Yum, 1985, 1987). Successful relationships begin with the establishment of a personal bond between participants, and thereafter are based on the careful maintenance of these personal ties. Personal face-to-face contact is a vital aspect of all relationships in China (DeMente, 1991c).

There are cultural differences in *self-presentation* (Tu, 1985). In individualistic cultures (e.g., Australia) self-presentation is of importance. In collectivistic cultures (e.g., China, Korea and Japan) self-presentation depends on the situation.

Cultural differences also exist in *self-disclosure*. Members of individualistic cultures tend to self-disclose more in intimate topics than members

112

of collectivistic cultures (Ting-Toomey, 1991) and they use open communication systems in relationships. For instance, the Japanese are more subtle and discrete in managing relationships than Americans or French, as they put emphasis on group harmony and cohesion (Ting-Toomey, 1991).

Several studies suggest that there are cultural differences in *interacting with strangers and with in-group members* (Leung and Bond, 1984; Triandis, 1972).

There is evidence that cultural differences exist in *experiencing emotions* (Schrerer *et al.*, 1986) and anxiety. For instance, Asians experience greater anxiety in interaction with strangers and guilt compared to Caucasians, regardless of whether they are less assertive or not, because they emphasize preserving harmony in relationships, particularly in those that involve conflict and are threats to interpersonal harmony (Zane *et al.*, 1991).

There is also evidence of cultural differences in the *feelings of responsibility for the other people* (Argyle, 1972). In individualistic cultures people help those who depend on them; in collectivistic cultures helpfulness is a function of reciprocity (Berkowitz and Friedman, 1967).

The *understanding of morality* is different. The Koreans emphasize personal welfare and Americans puritanical morality (Retting and Pasamanick, 1962). The Chinese show a great moral ethic value and a strong group orientation (Hsu, 1953).

Cultural groups also differ in *accepting compliments*. The Japanese are less likely to accept compliments and complain less often in interactions than Americans (Barnlund and Araki, 1985).

Perceptions of social interactions are also different in different cultures. Social interactions in China are perceived in terms of collectivism and social usefulness as opposed to Western societies that perceive social interactions in light of competitiveness, self-confidence, and freedom (Kim and Gudykunst, 1988). Similar interaction episodes also have different meanings for people from different cultures (Kim and Gudykunst, 1988).

Bond's Confucian cultural patterns

Michael Bond, a Canadian who lived in Asia for twenty-five years, organized a group of researchers from Hong Kong and Taiwan called the Chinese Culture Connection (CCC) (1987). The CCC developed a Chinese Value Survey to overcome a Western bias of the previous studies developed by scholars from Europe and the United States that measured cultural values. The instrument was developed on a basis of forty important Chinese values and was administered to university students in twenty-three countries around the world. The aim was to test Hofstede's (1980) findings and see whether there is any association between the Hofstede's and CCC instruments. The CCC found four dimensions of cultural variability: integration (social stability, tolerance, harmony with others, non-competitiveness, interpersonal harmony, group solidarity, intimate friendships), human heartedness (patience, courtesy, compassion, sense of righteousness, kindness toward others), moral discipline (restraint, moderation, keeping oneself disinterested and pure, having few desires, prudence), and *Confucian Work Dynamism* (persistence, thriftiness, a sense of shame, status differences, ordering relationships, reciprocation and protecting face, importance of tradition).

According to Bond (1987), the values of the Confucian work dynamism describe patterns that are consistent with the teachings of Confucius (social order, unequal relationships between people ordered by status, importance of family, proper social behaviour, education, hard work, modesty, patience, persistence and perseverance). Four of the Confucian work dynamism values that are associated positively with the dimension are: ordering relationships, thrift, persistence, and having a sense of shame. The CCC argued that these values reflect a hierarchical dynamism present in Chinese society. Hofstede (2001) argued these and other values such as adaptability to new circumstances, reciprocation, education, hard work, importance of the future, and savings characterize people who have a *long-term orientation* toward life. The other four values such as protecting the face of self and others, personal steadiness, respect for tradition, and reciprocation are negatively associated with the dimension and reflect distractions to the Confucian work dynamism (Hofstede, 1991). According to Hofstede (2001), these and other values such as tolerance, leisure, importance of the past and present, and spending characterize people who have a *short-term orientation* toward life. The six major countries that scored highly on the Confucian values dimension were China, Hong Kong, Taiwan, Japan, South Korea, and Brazil. The six major countries that scored low on the Confucian values dimension were Pakistan, Nigeria, Philippines, Canada, Zimbabwe, and Great Britain (Hofstede, 2001). Australia, the US and Great Britain scored relatively low on the Confucian values dimension (Hofstede, 2001).

The first three dimensions of CCC corresponded to dimensions of cultural patterns described by Hofstede (1980). The integration dimension was closely related to Hofstede's (1980) individualism-collectivism and masculinity-femininity dimensions, the human heartedness dimension was similar to Hofstede's (1980) masculinity-femininity dimension, and moral discipline was correlated with Hofstede's power distance dimension. Only the Confucian Work Dynamism did not relate to any of Hofstede's (1980) four dimensions.

Argyle's and Triandis' cultural differentiation

Argyle (1986) differentiated cultures according to the degree of formality in interpersonal interactions and an acceptable level of physical contact between people.

Formality

Argyle (1986) and Samovar and Porter (1988) reported that cultures tend to range from very formal to very informal (e.g., US). The degree of formality associated with a culture may be recognized by the way in which people are able to interact with one another. In *formal* cultures (Japan, Korea, China, Egypt, Turkey, Iran, Germany) all human behaviour, greeting, addressing, dressing, talking, sitting and even eating reflects their adherence to the strict social rules of behaviour and status differences. For example, people use formal titles in face-to-face encounters to identify people and their positions in society. In *informal* cultures (US, Australia) little attention is paid to formal rules of behaviour. People treat each other informally, address directly by first names, dress casually and do not focus much on hierarchical positions in social structures.

Touch

In *contact cultures* people touch more, face each other more directly and stand closer. Western societies belong to contact cultures. In *non-contact cultures* people touch less, face each other less directly, and stand further apart (Argyle and Cook, 1976). Asian cultures are non-contact cultures. For instance, in Japan people do not look each other in the eye much

(Morsbach, 1973). Too much gaze is regarded as disrespectful, threatening, or insulting by Asians (Argyle and Cook, 1976). However, too little gaze is interpreted as not paying attention, impolite, insincere, dishonest or shy.

Structural tightness

Triandis (1994) reported that in *tight cultures* there are many rules and constraints imposed on social behaviour. In tight cultures the rules and norms are clear and people are expected to follow them (Pelto, 1968). Sanctions are imposed on people if they violate the norms and rules of culture. Japan is an example of a tight culture where one must carry out 'all the rules of good behavior' (Benedict (1946), p. 225). In *loose cultures* there are few rules and constraints. Rules and norms are vague and flexible and people are allowed to deviate from them. The sanctions for violating rules in loose cultures are not as severe as they are in tight cultures (Pelto, 1968). Thailand is an example of a loose culture where the behaviour of people lacks discipline and regularity (Phillips, 1965).

Schein's, Trompenaars' and Maznevski's cultural differentiation

Schein's cultural dimensions

Schein (1992) distinguished cultures on the basis of the following dimensions: Human Nature (evil, good, mixed), Relationship with Nature (subjugation, harmony, control), Human Activity (doing, being, being-in-becoming; work, family, personal), Human Relationships (individualism, groupism; participation and involvement; role relationships), Time (planning, development; discretionary time horizons (function, occupation, rank); temporary symmetry, pacing; past, present, near or far-future; monochronic, polychronic), Reality and Truth (physical, social, individual; high/low context; moralism, pragmatism), and Space (intimacy, personal, social, public; high/low status).

The Nature of Human Nature   This dimension defines what it means to be human and the attributes of human beings, and is similar to the one of Kluckhohn and Strodtbeck (1961). Western and Asian societies have very different concepts about self. Asians are less focused on separating the individual from the group and pay less attention to self-actualization, whereas Eastern societies have a strong sense of the individual and the self (Redding and Martyn-Johns, 1979).

The Nature of Relations with Environment   This dimension defines what is the right thing for human beings to do in relation to the natural environment and is similar to one of Kluckhohn and Strodtbeck's (1961) and Stewart's (1971) dimensions. The environment can be subjugated and controlled (the Western tradition), harmonized with (the assumption of Oriental religions and societies), or subjugated to nature (the assumption of South-east Asian societies).

The Nature of Human Activity This defines the appropriate level of human activity, and also the relationship between work, play, family and personal concerns, and is similar to one of Kluckhohn and Strodtbeck's (1961) and Stewart's (1971) dimensions.

The Nature of Human Relationships This dimension distinguishes various assumptions about the right way for people to relate to each other and distribute power and love. It resembles Parson's (1951) and Stewart's (1971) self- and group-orientation. Kluckhohn and Strodtbeck (1961) distinguished between individualistic and competitive (US), collateral and group cooperative (Japan), and linear, hierarchical and authoritarian (Latin countries) cultures. Hofstede's (1980) dimensions of 'power distance' identified a related variable. Stewart also referred to hierarchical relationships. Schein (1992) referred to a number of ways authority can be used and what level of participation is expected: autocrative, paternalistic, consultative or democratic, participative and power sharing, delegative and abdicative.

The Nature of Time This dimension defines the basic concept of time, kinds of time and its importance and measurement. According to Schein (1992), monochronic cultures are characterized by time *planning;* people believe that time can be treated as an object and manipulated; the length of activities can be measured in terms of the time they take to complete. Polychronic cultures are characterized by *development* time; people believe that time cannot be slowed-down or speeded up, and 'things will take as long as they will take'. Time is open-ended and can be extended into the future.

According to Schein (1992), people in different cultures work with totally different time horizons. They use different measurements of time in relation to given tasks (annual, monthly, hourly). 'On time' or 'soon' may mean completely different things depending upon situations. Time horizons differ by function, occupation and rank. The period of time is dependent upon the time needed for doing one's basic job. Time is also determined by the way activities are paced and the degree to which the pacing of the activities are similar or symmetric at different occupations, ranks and levels.

The Nature of Reality and Truth This dimension distinguishes cultures on a basis of their assumptions about what constitutes reality and truth. Reality can exist at physical, social and individual levels, and the assessment of what is real depends on scientific tests, social consensus or individual experience. The Anglo-Saxon cultures believe that *physical reality* or truth is in facts and figures, and can be established only if logically proven and assessed by scientific tests. Other cultures rely more on feelings, intuition, and spirituality (Brazil, Asia). They regard a spiritual world as external reality. *Social reality* refers to the things that members of a cultural group agree upon, i.e., group identity, its values, nature of relationships, the distribution of power, meaning of life, ideology, religion, and culture itself. *Individual reality* refers to what an individual has learned from one's own experience and believes to be true. Individual reality may not be shared with anyone else. Members of *moralistic* cultures seek truth and validation in a general philosophy, moral system, religion and tradition; *pragmatic* cultures seek truth and validation in own experience, wisdom based on authority, and legal system. Europeans were found to be more moralistic while Americans tended to be more pragmatic.

The Nature of Space This dimension introduces assumptions about space, how it is allocated and owned, its meaning and role in relationships, and influence on intimacy and privacy. It resembles Hall's (1966) space dimension.

Trompenaars' cultural dimensions

Trompenaars (1984, 1993) and Hampden-Turner and Trompenaars (1993) provided a set of parameters to differentiate cultures according to the relationship to human nature (universalism/particularism), nature (inner-directed/outer-directed), activity (achievement status/ascription, analysing specifics/integrating wholes), human relationships (individualism/communitarianism, equality/hierarchy, affective/neutral), and time (sequence/synchronization, past/present/future). The *universalism versus particularism orientation to human nature* is similar to Parson's (1951) universalism/particularism dimension. The *achieved status versus ascribed orientation towards activity* is similar to Parson's (1951) achievement versus ascription dimension. The *analysed specifics versus integrated wholes* resembles Parson's (1951) diffuseness versus specificity dimension.

Individualism and communitarianism orientation towards human relationships This dimension is similar to Parson's (1951) self- and group-orientation, Kluckhohn and Strodtbeck's (1961) individualistic versus collateral and linear dimensions, Stewart's (1971) egalitarian versus hierarchical relations and self- and group-orientation, Hofstede's (1980) individualism and collectivism, and Schein's (1992) individualism and groupism dimensions.

Inner-directed versus outer-directed orientation to nature This dimension differentiates between those who are inner-directed, use internal motives to guide their behaviour and believe they can and should control nature (US, Britain, Canada), and those who are outer-directed, use external motives to direct their behaviour and go along with nature (Hong Kong, Japan, Korea, China).

Equality versus hierarchy orientation towards human relationships This dimension differentiates between those who focus on equality (US, Canada, Netherlands, Sweden, UK) and those who base their decisions on the basis of authority to judge and elicit from others the best they have to give (Pakistan, Hong Kong, Indonesia, Thailand, Turkey).

Time as sequence versus time as synchronization This dimension shows the differences between those for whom it is important to plan, do things fast in a sequential manner, and in-time (US, English-speaking countries) and those who synchronize all efforts to get things done, do many things simultaneously, treat time as elastic and use the past to advance the future (China).

Maznevski's cultural dimensions

Maznevski (1994) used a modified version of Kluckhohn and Strodtbeck's (1961) Value Orientations Instrument to distinguish cultures on a basis of orientation toward: Human nature (good/evil, changeable), Nature (subjugation/mastery/harmony), Activity (doing/being, containing and controlling), and Human relationships (individual/collective, hierarchical).

Schneider and Barsoux's cultural assumptions

Schneider and Barsoux (1997) organized cultural assumptions according to 'relationships with the environment', which include assumptions regarding control and uncertainty, the nature of human activity, and the nature of truth and reality (*external adaptation*), and 'relationships among people'. These include assumptions regarding the importance of relationships over task achievement, relationships with superiors and subordinates (hierarchy), and relationships with peers (individualism and collectivism) (*internal adaptation*). The assumptions, which relate to both relationships with nature as well as relationships with people, are those regarding time, space, and language (see Table 3.3).

Table 3.3   Schneider and Barsoux's (1997) cultural assumptions

External adaptation	Internal adaptation	Linking assumptions
Relationship with nature Control Uncertainty avoidance	**Human nature** Good versus evil	**Space** Personal and physical
Nature of human activity Doing versus being Achievement versus ascription	**Nature of human relationships** Social versus task orientation Particularism/ universalism Hierarchical Individualism/ collectivism	**Language** High-low context
Nature of reality and truth		**Time** Monochronic/ polychronic Past, present, future

Asian cultures and values

Japanese cultural characteristics

The review of popular literature revealed that much has been written on Japanese culture and values (Argyle, 1975; Agrusa, 1998; Befu, 1980; Benedict, 1946, 1974; Doi, 1971, 1973a, 1973b; Fontaine and Severance, 1990; Graburn, 1983; Hendry, 1987; Izard, 1969; Lebra, 1976; Lundberg, 1990; Moeran, 1983, 1984; Morsbach, 1981; Nakane, 1973; Neustupny, 1987; Ramsey, 1984; Vogel, 1965; Zimmerman, 1985). It is agreed that there are cultural differences between Japanese and Western societies in:

- cultural motivations
- morality
- displaying emotions
- courtesy
- shame
- humility
- non-verbal communication
- gift giving
- correct protocol of presentation

- meanings of concepts such as duty (*giri*) and face (*kao*)
- sense of obligation
- loyalty to others (*gimur*)
- situational interaction
- rituals
- attitudes to strangers
- importance of status

It was reported that the Japanese value peacefulness, passivity, collectivism, reciprocal obligation, and hierarchical structure (Isomura *et al.*, 1987). They are expected to conform and cooperate with one another, to avoid conflict and competition. They emphasize harmony and their behaviour is formal to reduce conflict and embarrassment. Japanese subordinate individual interests to group goals and remain loyal to the group (Moeran, 1984). *Seishin* spirit teaches them order, individual sacrifice, self-discipline, dedication, hierarchy, loyalty, devotion, discipline, responsibility, goodwill, group activity, be 'beautiful' for themselves and others, disregard for material disadvantages (Moeran, 1984). It stresses the importance of duty (*giri*), indebtedness (*on*) and obligation (Lebra, 1976). Buddhism teaches the Japanese to be integrated with nature, that a stranger is not an enemy but a friend, and the aim is to reach consensus and compromise (Schinzinger, 1983).

Confucianism and Buddhism prescribe collectivism, a hierarchical structure of authority, status, and obedience of superiors (Chinese, Japanese, Korean and Indo-Chinese). Differences in status influence the differences in non-verbal behaviour (Matsumoto and Kudoh, 1987). The importance of status was explained in terms of high scores on power distance and masculinity, and low scores on individualism. Benedict (1946), Lebra (1976) and Nakane (1973) described Japanese culture as collectivistic emphasizing conformity, belongingness, empathy and dependence, however, with the tendency to more individualistic attitudes, and achieving individual goals and profits. Triandis (1972) reported that the Japanese value courage, sense of justice, love, companionship, trust, friendship, and are concerned with war and peace. Laughter is not only associated with funny events but also satisfaction and happiness. Responsibility, achievement, aesthetic and general satisfaction are emphasized, and to lie is criminal. Rules are desired and success depends upon thinking, learning, research, cooperation, high motivation, and will power. Comfort is not valued, as opposed to self-adjustment, advancement, and serenity.

However, Frager (1970) reported a high degree of anticonformity among the Japanese (inability to adapt) that correlated with a measure of alienation. Mouer and Sugimoto (1979) indicated that the Japanese are group oriented, emphasize harmony in interpersonal relations, solidarity, loyalty, belongingness to society, an informal level of socialization, and that society is closed to outsiders. Kracht and Morsbach (1981) reported reciprocal dependency, passivity in being loved, cooperation and conformity, suppression of open conflict and competition, formal behaviour, harmonious relationships, support for group welfare, perceptions of Westerners as 'odd' people due to their focus on individualism, differentiation between what people say and actually do, between *tatemae* (outside behaviour) and *honne* (real intentions), between formal and informal behaviour, dependence of attitudes and behaviour in situations.

Japanese tourists

Much has been written on Japanese tourists (Kennedy, 1988; Leiper, 1985, 1987; Lethlean, 1988; Maurer, 1988; McArthur, 1988; McGee, 1988a, 1988b; McGown *et al.*, 1988; Moeran, 1983; Morris, 1988; Polunin, 1989; Reisinger, 1992a; Reisinger and Turner, 1999a, 2000, 2002c; Reisinger and Waryszak, 1994a,b,c, 1996; Warner, 1986; Watson, 1986). For instance, Ziff-Levine (1990) noted that the Japanese evaluate new ideas (e.g., product/service) by giving consideration to the effect on others and relations with them. He emphasized that Japanese tourists are not leisure oriented but activity-oriented unlike the Western tourists who travel to do nothing on their holidays. He reported the importance of shopping to the Japanese tourists while on a vacation, obligatory gift giving, polite inexplicitness motivated by not wanting to humiliate, offend or disturb the harmony of the group. He stressed the importance of trust and relationship building. Reisinger (1990) noted the importance of the service providers' attributes to the Japanese tourists in Australia. Unfortunately, no empirical evidence about the Japanese tourist values system was found.

Other Asian cultures and values

Past studies also indicate that there is some work done on Korean values (Kim, Q. Y., 1988). For instance, Koreans believe in inequality among people based on virtue, loyalty to authority, filial piety to parents, and sincerity to friends. The fundamental value is secular personalism – a commitment to personal relations (Kim, Q. Y., 1988). There is little evidence for individualism (Bellah, 1970). Thai values were also described and the nine major Thai values are: the ego, grateful relationships, smooth interpersonal relationships, flexibility and adjustment, religion-psychical orientation, education and competence, interdependence, fun and pleasure, achievement-task orientation (Komin, 1990). There is work done on the expression of anger among Thais (Gardiner, 1968). There is research on Vietnamese values (Iwao, 1986; Redick and Wood, 1982; Truny, 1988); Chinese values (Bond and Wang, 1983; Craig, 1979; Eberhard, 1971; Hsu, 1981; Redick and Wood, 1982; Shenkar and

Ronen, 1987); and Singapore Malay and Indian values (Craig, 1979). A number of values have been found that are common to all Asian cultures: respect for elders, parents, ancestors, importance of the family as a source of personal self-worth, a sense of obligation and shame, harmony, face-saving, consensus, cooperation, ambiguity and silence, indirectness and respect for tradition, differentiation between in-groups and out-groups, loyalty to a group, hierarchy contrasts, emotional restraint (Dodd, 1995), patience, avoiding strong emotions, having connections, self-respect, and reputation (Tung, 1996).

US and European cultures and values

The United States
Seven major values that guide behaviour of a majority of people in the United States were identified by Vander Zanden (1965).

1. *Materialism*: people are consumption oriented and evaluate things in material and monetary terms. They often judge people by their material possessions (Samovar *et al.*, 1998).
2. *Success*: people believe in another chance, achievement and goals attainment. They believe that all people have a right to succeed in life and be materially well off. They are very competitive and assertive and they always rank, grade, classify and evaluate to know if they are the best (Samovar *et al.*, 1998). McClelland (1976) noted that Americans have a high need for achievement and want to excel.
3. *Work and activity*: people are motivated by work values and believe in 'doing' things; people are valued as long as they work. In conversation among Americans one has to know what the other does for a living. Work is a means for recognition, money, and power. Activities and performance determine self-identity and self-worth (Samovar *et al.*, 1998).
4. *Progress:* people place great importance on progress and change representing the major tool for improving and understanding life. They desire 'the new' and 'the best'. Americans are optimistic and focus on the future rather than present and the past because the future is 'bigger and brighter'. Americans are confident, take new chances, and explore new possibilities (Samovar *et al.*, 1998).
5. *Rationality*: people believe in the rational approach to life and that humans should act on the basis of reasons; they search for reasons, and more efficient and effective ways of doing things. Everything is possible to accomplish when scientists, researchers and inventors get

together. Scientific methods allow people to predict and control life (Samovar *et al.*, 1998).

6. *Democracy*: there is a belief that all people are equal and all have a right to freedom of expression, success, material well-being, and the power of their government (Samovar *et al.*, 1998).

7. *Humanitarianism:* people pay a lot of attention to social welfare, charity, and voluntary work.

According to Samovar *et al.* (1998), for Americans each individual is unique, special and completely different from all other individuals, thus the interests of the individual are paramount. People in the United States believe that individual satisfaction comes from personal achievement. They are successful in controlling the natural environment; they attempt to dominate space as well. According to Jandt (1998), people in the United States place a high value on time, efficiency, good planning, organization, and practicality. They believe in the scientific method of solving problems. They think that human nature can be changed and education is an important element in improving human nature. Importance is placed on learning to be an individual, independent, self-motivated and achievement oriented. The US Americans view time as a commodity and believe that the future can be planned and controlled (Mead, 1998). The majority of US Americans are optimistic and believe that everything is possible if worked for. However, 'the dependence upon legal remedies to forestall conflict indicates pessimism' (Mead, 1998, p. 24). Lipset (1963) indicated that the United States are achievement, egalitarian, universal, and specificity oriented. Dodd (1995) noted that US Americans value equality of people, personal freedom, humanitarianism, directness, work, time, success, individualism, and material well-being.

Europe

Lessem and Neubauer (1994) attempted to characterize the European values and philosophies that dominate European culture. They determined the four most significant European values as pragmatism, rationalism, holism, and humanism. However, they also noted that European countries are quite different from each other in terms of their value orientations. According to Hofstede (1996), Europeans are different in their mental programming and the differences are quite large. Table 3.2 shows the ranking scores, which represent the relative positions of the selected European countries on Hofstede's (2001) cultural dimensions. According to Hofstede (2001), the most individualistic European countries are Great Britain, Netherlands, Italy, Belgium and Denmark; the most collectivistic are Portugal, former Yugoslavia, Greece and Turkey. Most of the Western European countries are low on power distance. High power distance values are characteristic of former Yugoslavia and France only. The highest on uncertainty avoidance and the most threatened are Greece, Portugal, Belgium, Yugoslavia and Spain; the lowest on uncertainty avoidance are Denmark, Sweden, Ireland and Great Britain. The most masculine are Austria, Italy, Switzerland, Ireland, Great Britain and Germany; the most feminine are Sweden, Norway, Netherlands, Denmark, former Yugoslavia, Finland and Portugal.

Hofstede (2001) reported that on individualism the extreme countries are Britain and Greece; Greece scored very highly on collectivism. Greece also scored extremely highly on uncertainty avoidance. Sweden is the most feminine country; Austria the most masculine. The Germanic countries (Britain, Denmark, Germany, Ireland, Luxembourg and the Netherlands, all speaking a German language) are characterized by smaller power distance and weak to medium uncertainty avoidance. In the Germanic group the extreme country is Denmark, characterized by very small power distance and very weak uncertainty avoidance. Belgium, on the other hand, is characterized by a quite high uncertainty avoidance. Britain and Ireland are low on both power distance and uncertainty avoidance dimensions. Germany occupies a middle position on the scale and is characterized by small power distance and medium uncertainty avoidance. Germany is seen as more collectivistic than Britain. It was noted that Germans value cooperation, mutual support, team spirit, avoidance of conflict, and punctuality. However, the degree of formality in Germany is extreme. Germans address others and conduct themselves in a very formal manner; they use titles and identify people by their positions in social structures (Samovar et al., 1998). Further, the Latin countries (Belgium, France, Italy, Portugal, Spain, all speaking a Roman language, plus Greece) are characterized by medium to large power distance and medium to strong uncertainty avoidance.

In terms of the Confucian Work Dynamism dimension Netherlands, Sweden, Poland and Germany are in the middle rank on the Confucius Long-Term Orientation (Hofstede, 2001). Their value orientations are in between the long-term orientation (persistence, ordering relationships by status, thrift, having a sense of shame) and short-term orientation (personal stability, protecting 'face', respect for traditions, reciprocation, adaptation).

According to Hampden-Turner and Trompenaars (1993), in Europe the most universalistic cultures can be found in Britain, Germany and Sweden, and the most particularistic in France. The most individualistic are Britain, Netherlands and Sweden; the most collectivistic France and Germany. The most equitable are Germany, Britain and Netherlands, the most hierarchical is France. Countries in which people are inner directed are Britain and Germany, countries with outer-orientation are Sweden, Netherlands and France. The most analytical are Britain, Netherlands and Sweden; the most integrative are France and Germany. Countries in which status is gained by achievement are Britain, Sweden, Germany and Netherlands; the country in which status is ascribed is France. Countries which view time as sequential are Sweden, Netherlands, Britain and Germany; the country which views time as synchronized is France.

According to Hofstede (1996), the Eastern European countries are extremely diverse and very heterogeneous in terms of their populations, traditions, history, and cultural values. Although they all experienced communism, which failed nearly a decade ago after forty-five years of domination, communism was a native development in Russia only. In all other Eastern European countries it was forcefully imposed by the military. Today many elders in the Eastern European bloc believe that living under communism was better and easier than in the free market economy that encourages an individualistic mentality and demands looking after one's own existence. In these countries a national materialism, based on group collectivism, is highly developed. People do not want to accept the responsibility for making their own living and being responsible for their own existence, and demand financial and social support from government. Since many members of the Eastern European countries experienced wars and lived for many decades in insecurity, they don't want risk in their lives, and seek security and order. National materialism is less developed in the Czech Republic, Poland and Hungary. These countries have the best chances to develop capitalism, free market economies, and individualist entrepreneurship. These countries are more individualistic, risk-takers, and masculine.

Russia

According to Jandt (1998), in Russia individualism, personal gains, and self-orientation have been discouraged. People had to subjugate to a state that totally controlled their lives. In schools and at universities Russians were taught discipline, subordination and sacrifice of their well being for the welfare of the state. The society was very hierarchical; power distance between the communist leadership and the people was great. There were different rules and rights for those who were in government and those who weren't. Russian values reflect more feminine than masculine cultural values. Importance is attached to friends, family life, social relations and cultural life rather than money and material possessions. Love, ethics, morality, feelings and friendships are taught as being important values in human life. Currently, Russia is at a transition stage after the collapse of the Soviet Union where people are attempting to rebuild their rich Russian tradition and culture. However, the distance between the working class and those in government is now even greater than under communism. A distribution of wealth is inequitable. The Russian economy is chaotic, generating a fear of the unexpected, particularly for those who are at the bottom level of social class.

According to Jandt (1998), Russian values reflect both Asian and European values. For example, Russian people attach importance to family, relationships with others and social harmony, and seek Western values of personal rights and freedom. They are passive in nature and autocratic, and believe in the governing class. They need some authority to establish social and economic order. They distrust outsiders, particularly foreigners. They respect the past; they worship history and traditions, and respect elders. They attach importance to the present. They are pessimistic about the future due to experiencing hardship and insecurity for long decades. They believe that people are bad or a mixture of good and evil, and they believe they cannot control the environment (Jandt, 1998).

Australian cultural pattern

There have been some studies done on Australian values and Australian identity (Bennett *et al.*, 1977; Carroll, 1984; England, 1975; Feather, 1975; Hofstede, 1980; Spillane, 1984; White, 1981). Australian contemporary values have been described as those of: achievement, success, activity, work, humanitarianism, democracy, equality, aggressiveness and independence, all deriving from a value of self-reliance (Elashmawi, 1991). Many commentators have referred to egalitarianism in Australian society and the Australian concern for mateship (Encel, 1970; Hancock, 1930; Lipset, 1963; Taft and Walker, 1958; Ward, 1958). Mateship was related to true friendship, loneliness, hardship of outback life, need for companionship, joint activities, support, equality, reciprocal favours, and conformity to group norms. According to some theorists, mateship is related to collectivistic and egalitarian values and contradicts a successful achievement value. However, Lipset (1963) found no evidence for this. He found that Australians are more egalitarian but less achievement oriented, universalistic and specific than Americans. Other theorists have noted the tendency for Australians to appraise those successful in sport, to be critical and less respectful of successful intellectuals 'tall poppies', and to play down and devalue their accomplishments (Encel, 1970; Sharp, 1992). Others found a tendency for admiration for the 'Aussie battler' and those who stand out against authority (Feather, 1986b). Feather (1985) noted that in Australia there is a conflict between collectivistic ideology that favours mateship, group solidarity and equality, and a system that rewards personal accomplishments and individual enterprise. There is also a conflict between masculine, assertive values and feminine, communal values (Feather, 1986a). Australia's affluence and stability promotes less concern for safety and security at the personal and national levels and more concern with love, affiliation, self-definition, and self-fulfilment (Feather, 1975, 1980a, 1986a; Feather and Hutton, 1973).

Australian value studies

Several studies on Australian values have been conducted by Feather (1970a, 1972a, 1972b, 1972c, 1980a, 1986a, 1986b) and Rim (1970). The results of these studies showed that Australians place importance on friendships and equality more than Americans and Israelis. Australians are less achievement oriented than Americans but more than Canadians and Israelis. Australians ranked family, security, happiness and intellectual values lower than do the other groups. Australians ranked exciting life, world of beauty, inner harmony, mature love, friendship, and being cheerful higher than Americans; and a comfortable life, salvation, and ambition lower than Americans (Feather, 1975).

The value differences between Australians, Papua New Guineans and Chinese have been compared. Australians are concerned with love, accomplishments, self-respect, friendships, happiness, pleasure, and being cheerful when compared with Papua New Guineans. The Chinese assigned more importance to scholarship (wisdom, being capable, imagination, intellect, and logic), respect, hard work and self-restraint (e.g., social recognition, being ambitious, self-controlled), and national security than Australians (Feather, 1986a). These differences were consistent with the study by Hsu (1972) who reported that the Chinese are more situation-oriented, more concerned with appropriate behaviour in relation to others, and more emotionally restrained. They are more socially and psychologically dependent on others and they form a big network of relationships. They support respect for parents, tradition, duty, obligations, and the getting of wisdom. Scholarship is the most important criterion for membership in the highest social class. Therefore, it brings power, prestige, and wealth. The Chinese are also more concerned with freedom. Australians, as compared with the Chinese, are more individually centred, less concerned with scholarship and ranked self-related values and excitement (happiness, inner harmony, exciting life) as more important, and they emphasized affiliate and altruistic values (being cheerful, forgiving, helpful and loving).

The most and least important values

It was found that the four most important terminal values for the Australian sample were happiness, inner harmony, freedom, and true friendship. For instance, friendship emerged as a strong value, reflecting the cultural emphasis on mateships. The four least important terminal values for the Australian sample were pleasure, social recognition, national security, and salvation. For the Chinese sample, the four most important terminal values were true friendship, wisdom, freedom, and mature love. The four least important terminal values were family security, a comfortable life, an exciting life, and salvation. The four most important instrumental values for the Australian sample were being honest, loving, broadminded, and cheerful. The four least important instrumental values were being logical, polite, clean, and obedient. The four most important instrumental values for the Chinese were being ambitious, broadminded, intellectual, and courageous. The four least important instrumental values were being forgiving, helpful, clean, and obedient. Some of these differences overlap with findings for the Australian and Papua New Guineans students (Feather, 1976, 1980a) and are consistent with those that one would expect on the basis of the analysis of cultural differences between Western and Eastern cultures presented previously.

Further, Feather and Hutton (1973) applied the RVS to compare Australians and Papua New Guineans students' values. The Australian students showed concern with self-definition and self-fulfilment and gave much lower priorities to equality, national security, salvation, social recognition, and comfortable life. Noesjirwan (1977) studied differences between Indonesian and Australian values. Maxwell (1979) and Nurmi (1986) analysed the similarities and differences between the Australian and Finish values. Hofstede (1980) found that there are value differences between South Asians and Australians.

Summary

Values are culturally determined standards of socially desirable behaviour. They determine rules of social behaviour. They characterize people within the same culture and distinguish those from other cultures. They are superior in differentiating cultures and explaining cultural differences. There are two types of values: instrumental and terminal. There are direct and indirect methods and techniques for measuring values. The Rokeach Value Survey (1973) is accepted to be the best method for measuring values. According to Kluckhohn and Strodtbeck (1961), different cultures can be compared on a basis of how their members relate to human nature, nature, human activities, other people, and time. Different researchers in the field have developed different sets of cultural orientations, however, they all appear to be related and interdependent. Cultural value patterns in Asia, Europe, the United States and Australia are identified based on the value orientations that differentiate cultures.

Discussion points and questions

1. Why do we use cultural dimensions to explain similarities and differences in behaviour across cultures?
2. What are the major cultural differences between collectivistic and individualistic cultures?
3. Why is status a major issue in high power distance cultures, but not in low power distance cultures?
4. What are the major differences in communication in individualistic and collectivistic cultures?
5. How do you explain the influence of cultural differences on interpersonal relations?

6. How does uncertainty influence the way people communicate?
7. Which cultural orientation is the most influential on the development of social relations in all cultures?
8. Are there any similarities in cultural value patterns between Asia, Europe, US and Australia?
9. Find two examples that demonstrate how Hofstede's (1980) dimensions can cause clashes in tourist–host interaction.

Since cultural values determine the rules of social interaction (e.g., Argyle *et al.*, 1986), which indicate what is permitted or not between those in contact (e.g., Argyle and Henderson, 1984), the next chapter examines the concept of rules, and their influence on social interaction.

Further reading

Hofstede, G. (1980) *Culture's Consequences*. Beverly Hills, CA: Sage Publications.

Kluckhohn, F. and Strodtbeck, F. (1961) *Variations in Value Orientations*. New York: Row, Petersen.

Lustig, M and Koester, J. (1993) *Intercultural Competence: Interpersonal Communication Across Cultures*. New York: Harper College Publishers.

Schein, E. (1992) *Organizational Culture and Leadership*. San Francisco, CA: Jossey-Bass Publishers.

Triandis, H. (1995) *Individualism-Collectivism*. Boulder, Co.: Westview.

4

Rules of social interaction

Objectives

After completing this chapter the reader should be able to:

- define rules of social interaction, their role and types

- understand the difference between rules, commands, laws and norms

- understand the relationship between rules and culture

- understand differences between universal and specific rules

- describe the reasons and consequences of rules violations

- identify techniques of rules measurement

- identify cultural differences in rules of social interaction as based on Hofstede's (1980) cultural dimensions.

Introduction

The aim of this chapter will be to introduce the concept of rules of social interaction and to present the cultural differences in rules of social interaction between culturally different societies.

Concept and definitions

The literature review indicates that the concept of rule is widely used and has been discussed by many writers: Berne (1966), Garfinkel (1967), Goffman (1961, 1969), Harre (1972, 1974), Harre and Secord (1972), Segal and Stacey (1975), Toulmin (1974). Since cultural systems can be analysed in terms of the rules (Kim and Gudykunst, 1988), this concept is presented below.

Definitions

Rules were defined as directives for people's behaviour and guidelines for their actions (Harre and Secord, 1972). Rules apply to most social relationships; they indicate to participating persons what actions are appropriate or inappropriate in social interaction and how people ought or ought not to behave (Argyle and Henderson, 1985b). They define the responsibilities and obligations within a given social relationship (Kim and Gudykunst, 1988). Rules allow coordination and exclusion of certain behaviours (Argyle *et al.*, 1986). Kim Y. Y. (1988, see p. 34) defined rule as a system of expected patterns of behaviour that serves to organize interaction between individuals in the host country. 'Knowing the rule ... provides some ground for expectations one may have of the behavior of other people who accept the rule' (Harre and Secord, 1972, p. 182). Since rules determine expectations (Harre and Secord, 1972) and 'frame the expectational levels of the interactants in terms of what constitute appropriate or inappropriate behaviors in a situation' (Gudykunst *et al.*, 1988b, p. 68), the rules are future oriented and can predict behaviour.

In this book, rules are conceptualized as guidelines that direct behaviour of the individuals in relationships and make actions consistent with the expectations of the other members of the relationship (Moghaddam *et al.*, 1993); prescriptions for obligated, preferred, or prohibited behaviour (Shimanoff, 1980); and regulations in the sense that they are prescriptions that are used to regulate, evaluate, and predict social conduct (Searle, 1969).

Role of rules

Rules are developed to understand events, actions and behaviour; to define the meaning of a situation and behaviour within that situation. Rules provide recipes of how to achieve an end-state (Kim, Y. Y., 1988) of existence. Thus, rules are developed to achieve certain goals in situations and relationships such as harmony of interaction (Moghaddam *et al.*, 1993), satisfaction with interaction, or as Goffman (1971) puts it, to achieve 'public order'. Rules solve problems of social behaviour and make interaction easier, more predictable (Cohen, J. B., 1972), and more understandable to others (Kim, Y. Y., 1988). They set up expectations and provide meanings and standards of evaluation. 'Without a knowledge of the rules, we cannot understand the intention and meaning of an act' (Noesjirwan and Freestone, 1979, p. 20) and cannot evaluate the behaviour of others.

Rules creation

Rules are created by mutual consent of society and, therefore, they are socially accepted. Behaviour that conforms to socially accepted and shared rules is more predictable (Shimanoff, 1980). However, rules are conditional. They can be followed, or can be broken (McLaughlin, 1984). They may be modified, changed, or ignored.

Types of rules

There are many types of rules: interpersonal (should be nice to each other) and task rules (should help). There are rules that require reward (should support) and rules that prevent conflict (should cooperate). There are rules for actions and rules for conduct (Martin, 1971). There are enabling rules (for actions that create episodes) and restricting rules (that limit the appropriate behaviour). There are explicit (e.g., school and work rules) and implicit rules (e.g., rules of etiquette). Rules can explain formal episodes and enigmatic episodes that are social acts not governed by explicit and formal rules (Harre and Secord, 1972). There are specific and general rules (Collier *et al.*, 1986).

Situation rules

Situation rules indicate how people should or should not behave in certain situations e.g., how to greet each other, exchange gifts, how to initiate conversation, what to talk about during conversations, or the mood that is appropriate. Rules may relate to general or specific social situations. Rules also indicate how people should or should not behave in relation to others such as guests, strangers, or friends. Rules govern verbal and non-verbal behaviour.

Relationship rules

Rules are important components of relationships (Argyle and Henderson, 1985a,b). Relationship rules can be explicit, formally coded within the written or spoken language and directly stated, and are usually well known, as in the case of public or institutional regulations. They can also be implicit, informal, not visible, coded in non-verbal behaviour or indirectly stated, and are usually learned through the process of socialization, observing the actions of others, as in the case of rules related to intimacy levels, status, and dominance (Kim, Y. Y., 1988; Moghaddam *et al.*, 1993). In voluntary relationships, there is less need for the behaviours to be regulated by explicit rules, as opposed to involuntary or permanent behaviours where there is greater need for explicit rules to guide interactions. Therefore, it is common that in cultures where the relationships are involuntary (collectivistic), there is a need for more explicit relationship rules, as opposed to individualistic cultures. Since the tourist–host contact is a form of voluntary relationship, there is less need to regulate it by explicit rules; the implicit rules play a more important role in this contact (Kim, Y. Y., 1988; Moghaddam *et al.*, 1993).

Universal and specific rules

Some of the social interaction rules are universal and apply to nearly all situations and cultures, while others apply to specific situations and cultures only. Argyle *et al.* (1979) studied the rules of twenty-five social situations and found that rules 'should be friendly', 'should keep to pleasant topics of conversation', apply to all social situations. Pearce (1988) reported that the universal social rules tourists and hosts agreed to follow are: to be polite, honest, open, friendly, and genuine. Hosts reported that visitors should treat them with respect. These will be discussed later.

Three orders of rules

There are three orders of rules (Harre, 1974):

- First order rules 'constitute the etiquette for social situations' (p. 162). Rules of etiquette differ across cultures.
- The second order rules 'construct social relations ... by maintaining hierarchy' (p. 163). These rules specify 'how rights and privileges ... are to be socially distributed' (Goodenough, 1971). The first and second order rules define what is appropriate.
- The third order rules apply to self-presentation or self-performance and create a self-image (Goffman, 1969).

In this book reference is made to only the first and second order rules because these rules provide guidelines for socially accepted behaviour and indicate how people should or should not behave in relations with others.

Rules variations

Rules vary in respect to clarity and range (Gudykunst *et al.*, 1988b). For instance, the high context cultures have a more specific and greater range of rules because these cultures need more rules to coordinate activity and accuracy with implicit understanding than the low-context cultures (Hall, 1976). Rules also vary with respect to the degree of consensus. For instance, in high context cultures there is a need for more accurate understanding of rules in a communication system (Cushman and Whiting, 1972).

Rules versus commands, laws and norms

There is a distinction between rules, commands, laws, and norms. Rules are general and can be followed; commands are specific and must be followed (Harre and Secord, 1972). Rules are not enforceable; law is enforceable (Harre and Secord, 1972). Rules show reasons for behaviour and can be changed whereas laws show causes of behaviour and cannot be changed. Norms are special rules and refer to regularities in behaviour. They are 'generalizations which guide behavior' (Moutinho, 1987, p. 7). The violation of a norm brings sanctions. The violation of a rule has only consequences because rules may be subjected to different interpretations. Like rules, norms describe how a person is expected to act in various situations in interactional contact (Brislin, 1981). Norms contain a statement of the ideal behaviour. They involve beliefs related to values

(Triandis, 1972). They are 'specifications of values relating to behavior in interaction' (Peterson, 1979, p. 137).

Fundamental norms

There are two fundamental norms that influence cultural interaction:

1. *Norm of justice*
2. *Norm of reciprocity*.

Norms of justice

There are two norms of justice: norm of equity (indicates the concept of deservingness) accepted in individualistic cultures and norm of equality (indicates even distribution regardless of the contribution) accepted in collectivistic cultures. These two types of norms explain the cultural differences in the meaning of fairness. The individualistic cultures reward people on a basis of their contribution. The collectivistic cultures reward people regardless of their contributions (Gudykunst *et al.*, 1988b).

Norm of reciprocity

The norm of reciprocity means that people should help and not injure those who have helped them (Gouldner, 1960). Members of individualistic cultures stress a voluntary reciprocity norm (Ting-Toomey, 1986b). Members of collectivistic cultures emphasize an obligatory reciprocity norm (the debtors should repay the debt and engage in face-saving activities). They practise long-term reciprocity unlike those in individualistic cultures who practise short-term reciprocity (based on monochronic values of time) (Hall, 1983). Also, the individualistic cultures with low power distance follow symmetrical reciprocity that does not reflect status, unlike the collectivistic cultures with high power distance that follow the complementary reciprocity that reflects role, status, and power (Gouldner, 1960).

Rules are culturally determined

Rules that govern social situations and interactions are culturally determined. Culture provides the 'rules of the game' (Kim, Y. Y., 1988). Rules vary along cultural dimensions, or as Harre (1972) puts it, rules have cultural dimensions. Rules are ordered and patterned by underlying principles of cultural values (Barth, 1966; Noesjirwan and Freestone, 1979). Therefore, rules vary according to the dominant values and culture (Mann, 1986) and together with values they define the dominant culture (Goodenough, 1971). Consequently, members of the same culture generally understand the social interaction rules of their culture (Gudykunst et al., 1988b). However, the members of different cultures that have different rules may not understand them. For instance, in different cultures there are different rules for defining interpersonal relations and attributing importance to social interactions (Wagatsuma and Rosett, 1986), establishing and maintaining relations, greetings, self-presentations (Argyle, 1967), beginning of conversation, degree of expressiveness, frankness, intensity, persistency, intimacy, volume of interaction (Jensen, 1970), understanding of what constitutes friendship (Wei et al., 1989), expressing dissatisfaction and criticism (Nomura and Barnlund, 1983), describing reasons and opinions, exaggerations and telling the truth (Argyle, 1978). There are differences in the use of space, physical proximity, and privacy (Argyle, 1972; Hall, 1966), gestures, facial expressions, expressions of intimacy, status, and politeness (Argyle, 1972), eye and body movements (Goffman, 1963), expressing negative opinions, joking, showing warmth, apologizing, farewelling, use of time, perceiving sense of shame, feelings of obligations, responsibility, avoiding embarrassment, confrontation, taking initiatives, responses, and external appearance (Argyle, 1972, 1978; Dodd, 1987; Gudykunst and Kim, 1984a; Hall, 1983). There are cultural differences in rules regarding social distance, bodily contact, and self-presentation (Argyle, 1972). There are cultural differences in gift giving, tipping, eating, and drinking. Certain cultures have developed specific rules related to entertaining guests (Argyle, 1972).

Cultural differences in travel behaviour

Cultural differences were found in the travelling behaviour of the Asian markets (March, 1997). The differences included: (1) the ability and the desire to speak English (Indonesians speak better English than Koreans); (2) eating patterns dependent upon religious factors (Koreans have strong preference for their own cuisine, Indonesians require halal food); (3) level of adventurous spirit (Koreans are more adventurous than Japanese); (4) degree of overseas travel experience; (5) consumer expectations from overseas travel; (6) different travelling patterns and demands in terms of desired accommodation (luxury versus budget), purpose of travel, seasonality due to different school holiday calendars, and shopping behaviour (big versus moderate spenders). It was found that when deciding about their vacation destinations, the Japanese relied more heavily on the print medium as an information source, while the Germans relied more on word-of-mouth advice from family and friends (Mihalik *et al.*, 1995). In response to unsatisfactory service in a hotel Americans were more likely to stop patronizing the hotel, complain to hotel management and warn family and friends. Japanese, on the other hand, were more likely to take no action (Huang *et al.*, 1996). Pizam and Sussmann (1995) noted that behavioural differences between tourists from Japan, France, Italy and the US were attributable to cultural influences. Ibrahim (1991) reported that these differences were caused by the differences in value systems.

Impact of the cultural differences in rules on social behaviour

Since different cultures have different rules of interaction, the expectations and meanings of rules also differ across cultures. The rules that are socially accepted in one culture may have quite different meanings in another. Thus, members of different cultures may misunderstand and misinterpret the rules of other cultures that can cause difficulty interacting with those from different cultures, lead to confusion, generate tension, and even conflict. This is specifically relevant to tourist–host contact. Many tourists and hosts reported interaction difficulties due to cultural differences in rules of social interaction (Pearce, 1982b). Stringer (1981) noted that in bed-and-breakfast establishments even different customs of handling cutlery and eating habits caused irritation. Difficulties also occur because rules are not written but held unconsciously (Noesjirwan, 1978). Consequently, an analysis of the rules governing contact with foreigners is important (Argyle *et al.*, 1986) and can facilitate the improvement of social relationships (Argyle, 1981) in tourism.

Breaking rules

People often break the rules, either because they ignore them or because they are unaware of the cultural differences in the meanings of rules, and breaking rules disrupts interaction (Goffman, 1963). Tourists often break social rules on the streets, in shops, banks, at meal times, at religious services by inappropriate clothes or gestures. Pearce (1988) reported that American tourists often seriously breach social rules by excessive drinking, which was embarrassing to hosts in New Zealand farms. Tourists break the social rules because they do not know what rules apply to social encounters in the receiving countries, and they are socially unskilled in culturally different countries. Unfortunately, due to the special character of the tourist–host contact, tourists have little opportunity to learn about the rules and proper interaction with culturally different hosts. The lack of cultural awareness in social rules develops stereotypes of tourists as ignorant and abusing and with little respect for the host community. Such stereotypes add to a negative tourist evaluation by hosts and development of negative hosts' attitudes toward tourists. Unfortunately, cultural awareness of the differences in rules develops when they are already broken (Argyle, 1972).

Consequences of rules violations

Cultural differences exist not only in rules but also in the expected consequences for action due to different rules (Applegate and Sypher, 1988; Cronen et al., 1988). In every culture the rules have specific consequences, and these consequences are visible and measurable (Kim, Y. Y., 1988). For instance, there are sanctions for violations of the rules. These sanctions are clearly defined for the violations of the explicit rules. They are not clearly defined for violations of implicit rules. However, since compliance with implicit rules is also necessary for developing and maintaining smooth relationships, violations of both explicit and implicit rules lead to disruption and deterioration of the relationships.

Learning rules

Learning rules of the host culture requires a deep cultural understanding, not only of the verbal and non-verbal patterns, but also how and why the natives interact the way they do. Cultural understanding can make a stranger able to share and understand the experiences of the natives (Kim, Y. Y., 1988). Such deep understanding of the foreign interaction rules requires a broad knowledge of historical, political, economic, religious, and educational practices as well as the natives' values, beliefs, attitudes, and thought patterns. Without such knowledge it is impossible to make sense of the rules and behaviours of those who are culturally different, and understand and deal successfully with them (Kim, Y. Y., 1988). Knowledge of the cultural rules of social interaction can facilitate an understanding of tourists' and hosts' behaviour in tourism social situations (Levine, 1979). However, such knowledge can never be complete, and the knowledge of others' rules can be understood only in relative terms (Kim, Y. Y., 1988). Since tourism development creates increasing opportunities for cross-cultural contact between tourists and hosts who will be interacting on a regular face-to-face basis (Machlis and Burch, 1983), there is a need to develop cultural awareness and learn the rules of social interaction within cultures in order to facilitate this contact.

Measuring rules

There are several ways of investigating and measuring the rules of social interaction. For instance, one can ask to rate the appropriateness of the social rules in a specific situation. If there is an agreement between respondents one can conclude that a rule exists (Argyle *et al.*, 1981). In order to ascertain the existence of interaction rules in communication between tourists and hosts, one can also ask them to rate the social rules. One can also refer to the rules applied in social interactions with strangers (Pitt-Rivers, 1968) since the concept of a tourist is similar to the concept of a stranger. However, since people from different cultures hold different beliefs about the appropriateness of rules in interaction, tourists and hosts may also apply different interaction rules, each according to their own standards.

Cross-cultural differences in rules of social interaction

There are many studies done on rules of social relationships. These studies indicate that there are cultural differences in the rules of social relationship between Eastern and Western societies (e.g., Hofstede, 1980; Foa *et al.*, 1969; Nakamura, 1964).

Rules of social relationships in Japan

Many empirical and non-empirical writers have discussed the rules of social relationships in Japan (Argyle *et al.*, 1978; Befu, 1971; Benedict, 1967; Lebra, 1976; Morsbach, 1977; Nakane, 1973; Shimoda *et al.*, 1978), and in Hong Kong (Bond and Wang, 1983; Dawson *et al.*, 1972; Meade and Barnard, 1973; Whitney, 1971). They reported that there are a number of rules specific to each culture. For instance, the Japanese have more rules of endorsement than other cultures (Argyle *et al.*, 1986). They have

141

many rules in respect of public criticism, about the exchange of obligations, repaying debt, and rewards (Befu, 1971), gift-giving and receiving, etiquette (Benedict, 1967; Morsbach, 1977), restraining emotions and suppressing natural feelings (Argyle *et al.*, 1986). However, rules concerning emotions are difficult to decode because of the so-called Japanese 'display rules' (Shimoda *et al.*, 1978). The Japanese also have more specific rules related to human interaction and situation rather than to person (Argyle *et al.*, 1978). According to Doi (1973a), the Japanese have more formal rules regulating public interactions than rules guiding private interactions because they control themselves more in public and more things are prohibited in public. The Japanese also have more work and group relational rules. Lebra (1976) stated that the Japanese have more rules regulating relations with supervisors and subordinates that concern roles and specific behaviour in particular situations. The reason for this is the Japanese concern with order and hierarchy in society. The Japanese have more rules about restraints and obedience since they endorse obedience significantly more than other cultures. They also have more rules concerned with loyalty and group harmony since they emphasize loyalty to group and concern for harmonious relations. According to Lebra (1976), the Japanese have more rules of conflict avoidance and they value 'face saving' to maintain harmony in interpersonal relations. In Hong Kong there are more rules respecting privacy, parents, ancestors, and obligations.

Rules of social relationships in Hong Kong

In general, Eastern cultures such as Hong Kong have many rules dealing with public and human interaction, regulating conflict, avoiding public disagreement and criticism, maintaining group harmony, restraining emotional expressions, saving face, hierarchy and power differences, obeying people in authority, prohibiting jokes, teasing, and teaching positive regard (Argyle *et al.*, 1986).

Rules of social relationships and Hofstede's (1980) cultural dimensions

The findings of the past studies are related to Hofstede's (1980) cultural dimensions. They indicate that Eastern cultures endorse rules underlying collectivistic values. Members of collectivistic cultures high on uncertainty avoidance (who desire less ambiguity in relationships, are more cautious about strangers, draw sharper distinctions between in-groups and out-groups, and perceive in-group relationships to be more intimate) need more rules concerning the out-groups than members of individualistic cultures. In collectivistic high power distant cultures (where the relationships between superiors and subordinates differ) there is a need for more formal rules for hierarchical work relations. In high-context cultures (where members are more cautious in initial interactions with strangers, make more assumptions about strangers based on their backgrounds, and ask more questions about strangers than do members of low-context cultures) (Gudykunst, 1983a), there is a need for more rules concerned with strangers. Members of collectivistic cultures (who tend to not commit themselves in relationships with individuals from out-groups) use indirect forms of communication and tend to have less self-disclosure in the relationships. In masculine cultures there are more rules of performance, than rules maintaining harmonious relations. Members of collectivistic cultures who emphasize multiple relationships need more rules regulating social relations. In collectivistic cultures with high power distance (where members are willing to spend more time to cultivate social relationships and reciprocate social information) there are more rules governing these relationships, unlike in individualistic cultures with low power distance (where most of the time is spent on developing personalized relationships, self-disclosure, and risk-taking in exchanging information on one's private life (Gudykunst et al., 1988b). In collectivistic cultures (Hong Kong, Japan) rules of public criticism are endorsed by avoiding public confrontations and negative criticism, unlike in individualistic cultures where people are less concerned with public criticism. In collectivistic cultures that emphasize group harmony more rules are related to harmonious relations, unlike in individualistic cultures that emphasize self-assertion and self-reliance (DeRiviera, 1977). Members of high uncertainty avoidance cultures (Japan) also support rules of conforming behaviour and they need more formal rules to maintain social order, unlike the members of low uncertainty avoidance cultures who tolerate violation of rules of behaviour and deviation from the formal rules of interaction.

Importance of universal relationship rules

The important role of rules in the relationships of people within various cultures was demonstrated by British researchers (Argyle and Henderson, 1984, 1985a, 1985b; Argyle et al., 1985b; Argyle et al., 1986). Several years later Argyle and his colleagues examined the presence and nature of relationship rules in England, Italy, Hong Kong and Japan (Argyle *et al.*, 1986). Subjects were asked to rate the importance of common and relationship specific rules on a 9-point bipolar scale. The results showed that all cultures had rules for social relationships. These rules were seen as important elements of interpersonal relationships in all four cultures, and there were numerous similarities among the cultures in relation to certain rule endorsement. For instance, there were consistent rules for professional formal relationships such as watching one's personal appearance, showing courtesy and respect, and avoiding social intimacy.

It was found that the universal rules that are highly endorsed across most of the social relationships and common to all situations are as follows:

1. one should respect others' privacy
2. one should look the other person in the eye during conversation
3. one should not discuss what is said in confidence
4. one should or should not indulge in sexual activity
5. one should not criticize the other in public
6. one should repay debts, favours, or compliments no matter how small (Argyle and Henderson, 1984; Argyle *et al.*, 1985b).

The only rule endorsed in all four cultures for all social relationships was respect for privacy (Argyle *et al.*, 1985b). However, this rule might have different meanings in different cultures.

Specific rules

Argyle *et al.* (1986) found that there are also specific rules for social relationships in the four cultures: England, Italy, Hong Kong and Japan. For instance, the rules for close friendships endorsed in Japan were quite different from those endorsed in Italy. The Japanese placed less emphasis on the expression of emotion, opinions, showing affection, and requesting help and advice than did Italians. There was a noticeable difference in rules relating to intimacy. Further, there were differences in rules between Eastern and Western clusters. In the Eastern clusters there were more rules about obedience, avoidance of conflict and saving face, maintaining harmonious relations in groups, and restraining emotional expressions. For instance, in Eastern cultures there are more rules regarding 'losing face' than in Western cultures because self-presentation is of great importance. However, the cultural differences were less noticed in

Hong Kong due to the influence of Western cultural values. In Hong Kong rules about showing respect for parents were important. In Japan there were more rules for hierarchical work relations, fewer for family and more rules concerned with avoidance of conflict and out-groups. Although reward and control rules were found in each culture, the Japanese did not have many rules about exchange of rewards (Argyle *et al.*, 1986). This finding is not supported by the well-known custom of gift exchange in Japan (Morsbach, 1977), and may result from a bias due to not including all Japanese culture-specific rules in the measuring instrument.

The findings for Hofstede's (1980) masculinity, power distance, and uncertainty avoidance dimensions were not supported in Argyle's *et al.* (1986) study, probably, due to the wider range of relationships examined by Argyle and the fact that Hofstede's (1980) study was limited to work relationships only. The Argyle *et al.* (1986) study had a British origin and it did not include many Japanese specific rules such as: should express humility, should use indirect form of refusal, can ask strangers personal questions, and should not express personal opinions (Naotsuka and Sakamoto, 1981).

Summary

Rules of social relationship play a central role in human interactions. Their role is to maintain harmonious interactions. They create the framework for stable relationships by coordinating behaviour and avoiding conflict (Argyle *et al.*, 1986). There are universal and culture specific rules of social relationships. There are differences in rules of social relationships between various cultures. Argyle *et al.* (1986) suggested an analysis of the rules governing contact with strangers such as foreigners, including international tourists. Such an analysis would be useful for understanding and interpreting social interaction between culturally different tourists and hosts. Knowledge of the rules of social relationship governing cross-cultural tourist–host interaction would be an important element for improving tourists' and hosts' relationships with each other (Argyle, 1981; Brislin and Pedersen, 1976). It would also positively influence the tourists' and hosts' mutual perceptions.

Discussion points and questions

1. What is the role of rules of social interaction?
2. Why are the rules of social interaction determined by culture?
3. Identify five rules of social interaction, which are universal in all cultures, and five that are different.
4. Identify universal rules of behaviour that should be followed by tourists and hosts in their social interaction.
5. Why do people break rules of social behaviour? Why do tourists break social rules when on a vacation in different countries?
6. Identify cultural differences in rules of social behaviour that are related to Hofstede's (1980) four cultural dimensions, i.e., individualism and collectivism, power distance, uncertainty avoidance, and masculinity and femininity.

Because the concept of perception is inherent within tourist–host contact, this concept will be reviewed in the following chapter.

Further reading

Argyle, M. (1986). Rules for social relationships in four cultures. *Australian Journal of Psychology* 38(3): 309–318.

Argyle, M. and Henderson, M. (1984). The rules of friendship. *Journal of Personal and Social Relationships* 1: 211–237.

Argyle, M. and Henderson, M. (1985). *The Anatomy of Relationships: and the Rules and Skills Needed to Manage Them Successfully.* London: Heinemann.

Argyle, M., Graham, J. and White, P. (1979). The rules of different situations. *New Zealand Psychologist* 8: 13–22.

Argyle, M., Henderson, M. and Furnham, A. (1985) The rules of social relationships. *British Journal of Social Psychology* 24: 125–139.

Argyle, M., Henderson, M., Bond, M., Iizuka, Y. and Contarello, A. (1986). Cross-cultural variations in relationship rules. *International Journal of Psychology* 21: 287–315.

Harre, R. and Secord, P. (1972). *The Explanation of Social Behavior.* Oxford: Basil Blackwell.

5

Perception

Objectives

After completing this chapter the reader should be able to:

- understand the concept of perception and its key characteristics

- understand the influence of culture on perception

- understand the influence of perception on tourist–host social interaction

- identify major techniques for measuring perceptions

- identify major studies of tourists' and hosts' perceptions

- understand the relationships between perceptions, attitudes, image, attribution, stereotyping and ethnocentrism.

Introduction

This chapter concentrates on the concept of perception and will present studies on its various aspects. The aim is to explain the concept of perception with specific reference to tourist–host contact. The relationship between culture, social interaction and perception will be discussed. A brief review of the concepts related to perception such as attitude, image, attribution, stereotyping and ethnocentrism, that can also determine tourist–host contact, will also be presented in this chapter. However, for a full and more comprehensive review of these concepts references will be made to various authors. Techniques for measuring perception along with numerous studies analysing tourists' and hosts' perceptions will be outlined.

Reasons for choosing perceptions instead of attitudes

The concept of perception was chosen for the analysis as its use is most appropriate and can be used more effectively in the analysis of tourist–host contact than the concept of attitude (Ap, 1992). There are several reasons why this is so.

- Firstly, there is a clear distinction between the terms perception and attitude. By definition, perception represents the process by which meaning is attributed to an object, event or person encountered in the environment, whereas attitude represents a predisposition to think and act in a certain way towards an object, event or person (Kurtz and Boone, 1984). An attitude, as opposed to perception, is created on the basis of experience during the process of learning, and acquiring knowledge (Moutinho, 1987). Perception can be created without experience and knowledge of the object/person. This is often the case when tourists develop perceptions of a destination prior to its visitation.
- Secondly, tourists and hosts may attribute meanings to each other (perceive each other) without having previous experience and knowledge of each other. Consequently, they develop perceptions rather than attitudes to each other.
- Thirdly, not all tourists and hosts meet and experience each other. Those who do may have only very limited experience, which does not allow for the acquiring of a complete and accurate knowledge of each other and, consequently, attitude development.
- Fourthly, the decision to travel comes from a perception in the first instance, and attitudes develop later after travel has commenced.

Concept and definitions

In general terms, perception is the process through which people see the world around themselves (Schiffman and Kanuk, 1987). In academic terms, perception is a 'process by which an individual selects, organizes, and interprets stimuli into a meaningful and coherent picture of the world' (Schiffman and Kanuk, 1987, p. 174). Samovar and Porter (1991) defined perception as the process by which stimuli are selected from the external environment and interpreted into meaningful internal experiences. Mitchell (1978) referred to perceptions as the processes that shape and produce what we actually experience. Similar definitions have been introduced by Moutinho (1987) and Markin (1974). Cole and Scribner (1974) reported that '... perceptions, memory, and thinking all develop as part of the general socialization ... and are inseparably bound up with ... social relations ...' (p.11). Perceptions were also defined as 'the impressions people form of one another and how interpretations are made concerning the behaviour of others' (Hargie, 1986, p. 47). Particularly important are first impressions because they decide whether one associates with others (Huston and Levinger, 1978). For instance, first impressions of taxi drivers, security officers, airline hostesses, baggage assistants, registration staff and so on, decide whether or not tourists will be willing to interact with hosts in the future.

Subjectivity of perceptions

Perceptions and their meanings are subjective. The meaning of the object or event differs depending on the perceiver. People differ in their perceptions because they have different views of the world (Krech and Crutchfield, 1948; Robertson, 1970). These views reflect the environment in which people live. For instance, the perceptions of tourists and hosts may vary depending on the external and internal environment in which they live. The environment and culture determine which stimuli will be chosen, and how they will be interpreted and judged. According to Schiffman and Kanuk (1987) and Cohen, J. B. (1972), perceptions depend on people's value orientations, expectations, experiences, and interests that are culturally determined. The stronger the cultural value orientation, the higher awareness of stimuli relevant to the value. For instance, those who value the most interpersonal interaction with other people are very highly aware of the stimuli relevant to their interpersonal values. Therefore, it is vital to understand the individual value orientation that affects perceptions.

Subjective versus objective perceptions

Subjective perceptions also differ from objective reality. For instance, the perceptions of tourists who had never experienced the product before (or had very limited experience of it), and whose perceptions are mostly created on the basis of the knowledge gained from promotion instead of first-hand experience, may differ from the perceptions of tourists who had experienced the product. In the absence of experience (for example, first-time visitors), the product is assessed on the basis of subjective perceptions, not reality. The same applies to the perceptions of people. In the absence of experience with hosts, tourists evaluate their hosts on the basis of their subjective perceptions. The construction of perceptual mapping allows for finding out individual subjective perceptions and deciding what can be done to maintain, change, or use the perceptions as criteria for evaluation.

Importance of perceptions for social interaction

The concept of perception is very important for social interaction (Cook, 1979), its initiation, maintenance and termination (Forgas, 1985) because the way people perceive each other determines the way they interact with each other. As Singer (1982, p. 54) pointed out, 'individuals ... can only act or react on the basis of their perceptions ...'. This means that perceptions influence social interaction and, thus, are vital for the analysis of tourist–host interaction.

Key aspects of perceptions that influence social interaction

According to Gudykunst and Kim (1997), there are three key aspects of perceptions that may influence social interaction and communication. Firstly, perceptions are highly selective and limited to one person or one situation only in the specific context in which social interaction takes place. Secondly, perceptions involve categorization, that is, grouping people or objects according to their common characteristics, which allows drawing distinctions among them. Thirdly, there are sharp distinctions between categories, which inhibit the development of accurate perceptions. The individual variations within the categories cannot be easily recognized and thus create perceptual bias. In order to increase the accuracy of the predictions and interpretation of others' behaviour Gudykunst and Kim (1997) suggested perception checking, which consists of three processes: describing others' behaviour, telling others one's own interpretation of others' behaviour, and asking others if one's own perceptions are accurate. Perception checking should be used when one thinks that one's perceptions may not be accurate and one needs to base one's own behaviour on accurate perceptions (Gudykunst and Kim, 1997).

Types of perceptions

There are three types of perceptions that play an important role in social interaction.

1. *Perceptions of other people* (for example, tourist perceptions of hosts and host perceptions of tourists)
2. *Perceptions of one's own* (tourists' perceptions of themselves and hosts' perceptions of themselves)
3. *Perceptions of the perceptions*, called metaperceptions, indicate how others perceive they are perceived (tourist perceptions of how they are perceived by hosts).

According to Hargie's (1986) theory of metaperceptions, if the tourists like their hosts, tourists will perceive that their hosts like tourists, and vice versa. Similarly, if tourists perceive hosts positively, tourists will also perceive that hosts perceive tourists positively, and vice versa. This theory has vital consequences for the assessment of tourist and host perceptions. Similarity in perceptions may determine tourist and host mutual acceptance, affiliation, treatment (Huston and Levinger, 1978; Rokeach *et al.*, 1960) and, consequently, satisfaction with interaction. In this book the perceptions of other people (tourist and host perceptions of each other) are analysed.

Importance of positive perceptions

Perceptions may be negative or positive, and vary in intensity depending on the environmental influences on judgment. It is critical to develop positive perceptions in the minds of potential tourists. For instance, the tourists' positive perceptions determine the selection of the tourist destination (McLellan and Foushee, 1983). The more favourable perceptions, the greater the likelihood of choosing a product from similar alternatives (Goodrich, 1978). Similarly, tourists' positive perceptions of hosts determine the decision to interact with hosts. The more favourable the perception of the host, the greater the probability of choosing particular hosts from others for social interaction.

Perceptions versus satisfaction

Perception affects satisfaction. As Mayo (1975) reported, tourists usually do not have knowledge about the destinations they have not previously visited. However, they hold perceptions of alternative and ideal destinations. The differences between their perceptions and reality affect tourist holiday satisfaction (Phelps, 1986). The smaller the differences between actual and ideal perceptions, the higher the tourist satisfaction. The perceptions of a destination, which promise to be similar to an ideal, provide tourists with the greatest satisfaction (Mayo, 1975). On the other hand, the greater the gap between actual and ideal perceptions, the less likely the destination provides tourists with satisfaction and the less likely tourists will choose the destination for visitation (Crompton, 1979b).

The same rule applies to tourist–host contact. The perceptions of hosts may determine the degree of tourist holiday satisfaction and the actual selection of a holiday destination. The smaller the gap between the actual and ideal perceptions of hosts, the greater the satisfaction tourists can achieve from interacting with hosts, and the more likely tourists opt for repeat visitation, and vice versa. The destination that promises interaction with ideal hosts and provides tourists with the greatest satisfaction has the greatest chance for repeat visitation. Consequently, it is vital to analyse the tourists' perceptions of their hosts.

Relationship between culture, social interaction and perception

Perceptions are shaped by a number of external (e.g., economic, social, cultural, geographical) and internal (e.g., demographic, psychographic, behaviouristic) environmental factors. These factors are often related to each other. Many researchers have noted the relationship between culture, social interaction and perception.

The influence of culture on perception

One of the major elements that directly influences the meaning of perception is culture (Samovar and Porter, 1991). Culture strongly influences the environment in which people are raised, it exposes them to experiences and produces meanings. Culture teaches people how to perceive experiences and interpret meanings. The ways in which people learn to perceive the world indicate how they should behave. People usually behave in the way they learned to perceive the world. In the judgmental processes of own and others' behaviour, people respond to stimuli learned from their culture. Which stimuli reach awareness and influence the judgmental aspect of perceptions and the attachment of meaning to the stimuli depends upon culturally determined perceptual processes (Samovar and Porter, 1988). People respond to stimuli that are important to them. Culture determines which stimuli and criteria of the perceptions are important. In similar cultures people are exposed to similar experiences and respond to similar stimuli. Different cultures tend to expose themselves to dissimilar experiences as people respond to different stimuli and their perceptions of the external world vary.

Cultural variations in perception

There are cross-cultural variations in the perceptions of social objects and events. These cross-cultural variations in perceptions create barriers to social interaction (Samovar and Porter, 1988). Since social interaction is based on the culturally conditioned perceptions of other people, people bring their unique perceptions of the world to their social contact with others. They are affected in their interaction processes by their culture, which teaches them to perceive others from their own unique perspectives. The way they perceive others is determined by cultural values they have adopted as they grew. Therefore, cultural variations can explain differences in perceptions. Often, culturally determined perceptual differences create problems in cross-cultural social interaction. Only a knowledge and understanding of cultural factors can facilitate social interaction across cultural boundaries.

Empirical studies: the influence of culture on perception

Several empirical studies have been done on the influence of culture on perceptions (Mayo and Jarvis, 1981; Schneider and Jordan, 1981). Redding (1980) and Mayo and Jarvis (1981) pointed out that culture causes different nationalities to perceive differently. People who grow up in different environments perceive differently because they interpret causes differently (Segall *et al.*, 1990). Richardson and Crompton (1988a) suggested that differences in perception between French and

English Canadians were caused by the differences in their cultures resulting in a different response to market strategies. Keown *et al.* (1984) reported the influence of culture on differences in tourist perceptions of retail stores in twelve selected countries. Singer (1982) pointed out, that differences in cultural values created differences in people's perceptions. For instance, culturally determined aesthetic values determined the perception of physical appearance and attractiveness. Ritchie (1974) found significant differences in individual perceptions of leisure activities that were caused by differences in personal values and cultural backgrounds. People with significant differences in personal values had significantly different perceptions.

Perceived cultural similarity and social interaction

Tajfel (1969) reported that perceptions are influenced by cultural similarity and familiarity. According to Robinson and Nemetz (1988), cultural similarities bring people together and dissimilarities separate people. Perceived cultural similarity and familiarity in values decides about acceptance (Rokeach *et al.*, 1960) and the liking of others (Byrne, 1961; Byrne and Nelson, 1964; Freedman *et al.*, 1981; Robinson and Nemetz, 1988). The interaction is more likely to progress when people come from similar backgrounds (Forgas, 1985). The cultural familiarity of physical appearance generates positive affiliation between people. According to Huston and Levinger (1978), people desire to associate with those who are physically attractive to them and will give such people preferential treatment. Perceived cultural dissimilarity and lack of familiarity results in negative perceptions and inhibits affiliation (Robinson and Nemetz, 1988).

Similarity of attitudes

Perhaps the most important influence on perceptions and initial contact is the similarity of attitudes. Those with positive attitudes toward each other perceive more of the others' behaviour because more signals can be filtered (Hargie, 1986). Those with positive perceptions receive and understand more signals about others' behaviour, than those with negative perceptions. The receiving of these signals and their judgments depends on their meanings to the receiver. If the meanings are culturally similar and familiar, positive perceptions develop. If the meanings are culturally dissimilar, negative perceptions result.

Perception of verbal and non-verbal signals

The verbal signals that directly influence perceptions of others in social interaction may be perceived differently in different cultures. The more someone else's language is familiar and culturally similar, the more positive is the perception of the language and the user of that language, and the reverse (Robinson and Nemetz, 1988). However, the same verbal signals may contain different cultural messages. In one culture loudness may be perceived as strength, in another as aggressiveness.

The meanings of non-verbal signals such as use of time, space, gesture, or expressions of emotions may be perceived positively or negatively, depending on culture. For instance, the Japanese may be perceived as happy, whereas, their smiles or giggles may also be perceived as embarrassment (Robinson and Nemetz, 1988). The sequence of events and the appropriateness of the behaviour in social interaction can also be perceived differently (Robinson and Nemetz, 1988). For instance, in some cultures gifts should be opened and shown (France), in other cultures gifts should be acknowledged and put away (Japan). People who behave according to rules of appropriate social behaviour are liked more than those who violate such norms (Huston and Levinger, 1978). Those who do not comply with the rules and do not follow the expected sequence of events might be perceived as bad mannered.

Perception of interaction patterns

Interaction patterns can be perceived differently in various cultures. For instance, Australians might perceive the formality of Japanese social behaviour negatively because it is associated with a negative value, and informality with a positive value. Also, the expectations from interactions as well as experiences with interactions (Freedman et al., 1981; Zimbardo and Ruch, 1977) can differ. In addition, interaction skills and the skills necessary to avoid difficulties in social situations; as well as personalities, motivations, and many other aspects (Shibutani, 1962) can vary across cultures and create differences in perceptions. However, as Robinson and Nemetz (1988) pointed out, the perceptions of culturally different people might be inaccurate because of situation and environmental factors.

Perceptions and media

Perceptions depend also on the source of information and the way the information is interpreted in various cultures. Marketing efforts such as advertising (Gartner and Hunt, 1987), travel agents (Perry, 1978), and travel brochures (Phelps, 1986) play important roles in the development of tourist perceptions. Unfortunately, there is often a disparity between information presented in travel brochures and reality (Phelps, 1986). The culturally influenced media and the need for a certain type of information only to be sent to tourists can cause this disparity. Thus, the information presented in the media can also influence the perceptions of others.

Perception distortion

Perceptions can be distorted by biased sources of information, culturally influenced media, stereotypes, ethnocentrism, physical appearance, quick jumping to a conclusion, or 'hallo effect'. Therefore, perceptions can be inaccurate (Cook, 1979), often negative and often do not reflect reality. However, if necessary, they can be changed by culturally correct and unbiased advertising through media, personal communication or persuasion, or perception checking (Gudykunst and Kim, 1997).

Negative perceptions

The development of negative perceptions of culturally different people depends upon: (1) the degree of cultural dis/similarity in the signals and meanings; and (2) the knowledge of the others' culture and its influence on the meanings of the signals (Robinson and Nemetz, 1988). When there are great cultural dissimilarities between perceivers, the probability of negative perceptions of each other is high. Perceived cultural dissimilarity in values generates perceptual mismatching in interpretations (Robinson and Nemetz, 1988), and consequently cross-cultural misunderstanding. Negative perceptions last longer and it is very difficult to change them once they are developed (Robinson and Nemetz, 1988).

Importance of cultural understanding

In order to avoid negative perceptions of people with different cultural backgrounds it is important to understand the target culture, how and why people from other cultures perceive the way they do and the reasons for cultural dissimilarities, and consequently modify one's own cultural understanding (Robinson and Nemetz, 1988). It is particularly important to know *how* differences in cultural backgrounds determine differences in perceptions, and *which* cultural factors create positive and negative perceptions. Such understanding could facilitate the development of positive perceptions and deepen understanding between culturally different people.

Measurement of perception

Measurement of perception focuses on the measurement of a respondent's feelings or beliefs about the object, event or person. The most common measurement techniques are:

- Open-ended questions
- Interviews
- Likert Scale (requires indication of degree of agreement or disagreement with a variety of statements related to the perception of an object/person)
- Thurstone Scale (requires generation of a large number of statements or adjectives reflecting all degrees of favourableness toward an object/person and for classification of them according to their degree of favourableness or unfavourableness, usually on a bipolar scale, with 'very favourable' at one end, 'very unfavourable' at the other end, and neutral in the middle)
- Semantic Differential Scale (requires rating of perceptions on a number of five- or seven-point rating scales bounded at each end by polar adjectives or phrases (monopolar or bipolar)
- Multidimensional scaling (gives a visual comparison of the perceptions of different objects/people by plotting the mean ratings for each object/person on each scale).

Difficulties in measuring social perceptions

Social perceptions (perceptions of people) differ from the perceptions of physical objects and are more difficult to measure. The perception of objects is directed at surface characteristics, which are immediately observable such as size, or volume. The perception of people is concerned with characteristics, which are not immediately observable, but must be inferred such as intelligence and attitude. Therefore, social perception judgments are more complex and difficult to make than judgments about physical objects. Since social perception is based on inferences about hidden qualities, more mistakes are made in perceiving people than in perceiving objects (Forgas, 1985). Additionally, perceived similarities and differences between perceivers and the people perceived can be sources of bias. The personal bias and the difficulty of detecting them and then correcting mistakes present serious threats to the accuracy of judgment and the measurement of social perceptions.

Pre- and post-travel perceptions

One technique, which has been introduced to avoid bias in measuring social perceptions, is a comparison of pre- and post-travel perceptions. This technique allows for understanding how perceptions develop and change over time and has been used numerous times within the tourism context (Pearce, 1980a; Reisinger, 1990; Cottrell *et al.*, 1999). Researchers found that tourist pre-travel perceptions of the visited hosts change as a result of their holiday experience. However, Yum (1988) argued that the travel experience couldn't bring changes in post-travel perceptions. Tourists can modify their perceptions of hosts (Pearce, 1982c) regardless of whether their perceptions are negative or positive. This view suggests that pre- and post-travel perceptions are similar and the apparent change in post-travel perceptions is not significant. For example, Pizam *et al.* (1991) found that the travel experience did not change the attitudes of US students towards the USSR and the Soviet people. Similarly, Milman *et al.* (1990) found that the travel experience did not change the attitudes of Israelis towards Egypt and the Egyptian people. Consequently, tourist–host contact does not always result in positive/negative change in perceptions/attitudes.

Tourists' and hosts' perceptions of each other – Asia, Europe, US and Australia

Tourists' perceptions of hosts

There are some studies that suggest that tourists form perceptions of their hosts. Although most of these studies did not distinguish between different types of travellers they emphasize the importance of the perceptions tourists develop of hosts in the overall destination perception.

Importance of the tourists' perceptions of hosts

Hosts represent an important part of the tourism product. Thus, the perception of hosts is an important part of the overall tourist perception of their holiday. Perceptions of hosts are important (Gee *et al.*, 1989) because the perceptions may detract from, or contribute to the success of the tourist destination (Hunt, 1975). They can influence the tourists' choice of holiday destination and may motivate repeat visitation. Tourists are inclined to visit a destination where they believe the hosts are friendly and courteous (Gee *et al.*, 1989). For instance, when hotel employees are perceived as professional and welcoming, tour guides as knowledgeable about their product, shop assistants as concerned with tourists' needs and helpful, then the tourism product quality is enhanced, the tourists' needs are satisfied, and their repeat visitation is encouraged. However, when hosts are perceived negatively, tourists are discouraged from visitation. Therefore, negative perceptions of hosts influence tourist dissatisfaction (Mill and Morrison, 1985) and lead to criticism and a decrease in visitation.

Empirical studies

Several studies on international tourist perceptions of their hosts have been done. Many have emphasized the importance of tourist perceptions of the host community. According to Hoffman and Low (1978), the tourist's perception of local people was the important variable in the decision to return to the destination. The tourists to Phoenix, Arizona, who perceived residents as friendly were likely to rate the destination as excellent, whereas those who perceived the locals as neutral were less likely to rate it as excellent. Similarly, Ross (1991) reported similar findings for tourists who visited North Queensland, Australia. Pearce (1980a) pointed out that the degree of liking or disliking of people encountered on holidays influences the tourists' perceptions of the region visited. Pearce (1980a, 1982b) also suggested that the tourist pre-travel favourability toward the visited nationality influenced the tourists' more positive post-travel evaluation. 'When the pre-travel favourability is initially high, tourists will be mentally prepared ... to evaluate visited people positively' (Pearce, 1980a, p. 14). In other words, the post-travel evaluation of the host community depends on the tourists' pre-travel perceptions. If the pre-travel perceptions are favourable, the evaluation and attitudes towards the host community will also be favourable, and the probability of achieving tourist satisfaction high.

One of the largest studies was carried out by the British Tourist Authority (BTR) (1972a,b,c) in which American (1972a), Canadian

(1972b), and European tourists (1972c) were surveyed about their perceptions of the British people. Shipka (1978) surveyed European tourists about their perceptions of Americans. These studies showed that many tourists have clear perceptions of the hosts and the countries they visit.

In Australia, the most relevant research on international tourist market perceptions was conducted by the Australian Tourist Commission (ATC, 1989, 1990). During airline disruptions Australian hosts were perceived as not caring and unable to serve tourists properly. For this reason many Japanese tourists chose other destinations for their holiday. Wilson (1988, p. 49) reported that the 'Japanese perceptions of anti-Asian attitudes held by some Australians' deterred Asian tourists from visiting Australia. Kennedy (1988) reported that Japanese tourists perceived Australian hosts as rude, bad mannered, and lazy. McArthur (1988) reported that Japanese tourists were dissatisfied with the lack of professional service at restaurants and shops, language and communication difficulties, and poor organization of tours. However, the ATC study (1990) challenged many negative opinions and showed that not only do Australian hosts meet Japanese expectations but they surpass them, declaring that 90 per cent of surveyed Japanese tourists were satisfied with Australian friendliness, politeness, sincerity and helpfulness, and 82 per cent of Japanese tourists were impressed by the tour guides performance.

Furthermore, most Japanese tourists wanted to interact with Australian hosts. These findings were supported by the BTR (1995) study indicating that 95 per cent of Japanese tourists were satisfied with the service provided in hotels and restaurants, while 31 per cent were dissatisfied with the service provided in shops and 10 per cent with the availability of service providers with Japanese language skills. Similarly, Reisinger's (1990) study showed that Japanese tourists perceived Australian hosts as professional, friendly, honest, patient, polite, helpful, concerned about customers, punctual, good looking, with humour, formal, and not exploitative financially, although less able to speak the Japanese language than expected. As per other Asian tourist markets, 99 per cent were satisfied with the service provided in hotels and restaurants, while 30 per cent were dissatisfied with the service in shops and 29 per cent with the availability of service providers with Asian language skills (BTR, 1995).

Indonesians perceived Australians as more friendly and less naive, arrogant, or insular than in the past (Broinowski, 1992). However, Hong Kong tourists perceived Australian hosts as unfriendly (Lam, 1992).

Importance of Australian studies

The important element of the ATC study (1989, 1990) was the presentation of the vital role of tourist perceptions of Australian people as one of the motives for tourist visitation to Australia. Tourists' perceptions involved hosts with whom tourists came into direct contact while holidaying in Australia, and their abilities to serve the tourists and to develop positive tourist–host relationships that make tourists feel happy and welcome. Until the ATC study findings, there was little research done on tourist perceptions of hosts and detailed information on the Asian tourist market available to the Australian tourist industry. The ATC study was most innovative in its approach to Asian tourist market research. The findings showed that the 'people factor' and the issue of satisfaction with service are of great significance to the Australian tourism industry. However, there are many other aspects that could have been covered in this study such as factors influencing the perceptions of the interpersonal element of service provision. Such analysis would enable a deeper understanding of the important factors influencing the interaction between tourists and hosts, and the service provided to tourists.

Future research issues

The rapid development of tourism and its internationalization calls for more studies on tourist behaviour in a cross-cultural environment. Since the majority of international tourists are from totally different cultural backgrounds from their hosts, the influence of culture on the interpersonal contact between culturally different tourists and hosts needs to be analysed. Dimanche (1994) called for more studies that explore other cultures and test cultural differences in a tourism context. 'We have much to learn about international tourists and the differences they show in terms of behaviour, attitudes toward destinations, spending patterns, motivations, satisfaction levels, etc.' (p. 127). Dimanche (1994) noted that researchers in consumer behaviour and marketing should examine the impact of cultural differences on the quality of cross-cultural interactions between tourists and locals working in the tourism industry. What do international tourists perceive as most important in social contact with hosts? How do they relate to and perceive hosts who are culturally different? Do they want to interact with the hosts? Are there any obstacles to their interaction? What causes international tourist dissatisfaction with interpersonal contact? These are only a few of the questions that should be answered in order to respond better to culturally different tourists.

Another important issue is to recognize that the influence of culture on the tourist and host behaviour varies depending on different types of tourists and hosts, and different types of travel arrangements (Nozawa, 1991; Sutton, 1967), the role of culture broker such as tour guide (Nozawa, 1991), the stage of tourism development and the number of tourists and hosts, at the destination visited (Husbands, 1986; Nozawa, 1991), amount of information both parties have on each other (Nozawa, 1991), or types of tourism. The distinction between different types of tourists such as day-trippers, psychocentrics and allocentrics, wanderers, explorers, etc.; their motivation, length of stay, travel arrangements (individual versus group) or type of tourism (e.g., cultural, sport or visiting friends and relatives tourism) affects the way culture differences influence tourist behaviour and interaction with hosts. Unfortunately, not many researchers took these factors into account in their perception studies. More studies that examine the impact of the above factors on tourist and host behaviour in a cross-cultural context are needed. Also, the tourism industry officials, marketers and managers must learn about the differences in the international tourist behaviour caused by different demographic and psychographic characteristics of tourists and hosts, and explore whether the differences, if any, are observed or are attributable to cultural background or perhaps to socio-economic or demographic variables. Are all international tourists influenced by cultural differences in the same way regardless of their age, occupation or socio-economic status? Are all international tourists influenced by cultural differences to the same degree regardless of their personality, interests, and preferences for activities or life style? Are there any cultural obstacles to their satisfaction and repeat visitation? What does stop international tourists from repeat visitation of the same destination? These are again only a few of the questions that should be answered, to be able to respond better to culturally different tourist needs.

Hosts' perceptions of tourists

The hosts' perception of tourists refers to how tourists are seen by their hosts. Host perceptions of tourists have been studied more frequently than the tourists' perceptions of hosts (Pearce, 1982b). However, the examination of the literature reveals major drawbacks in past studies.

- Firstly, there is a problem in defining the concept of hosts. Some studies refer to hosts as host communities or local residents, others to service providers and people in the tourism trade. Therefore, there is a major conceptual problem in the previous studies analysing host perceptions.

■ Secondly, many studies used tourists' nationality to differentiate among tourists. The nationality variable was criticized for not adequately reflecting the cultural differences between tourists.

■ Thirdly, many studies are concerned with perceptions in developed economies only (Doxey, 1974, 1975; Perrin et al., 1975; Pizam, 1978) and little is known about perceptions in the developing countries.

Importance of tourists' nationality

The literature review indicates that many host communities perceive tourists of different nationalities to be different and behave in different ways from themselves. It was found that in the destinations where the majority of the tourists were of different nationality, tourists were perceived to be different on a variety of characteristics such as behaviour, attitudes, ways of spending leisure time and morality (Pizam and Telisman-Kosuta, 1989). For example, Wagner (1977) noted that locals saw Scandinavian tourists as a completely different group of people, with different life style, behaviour, and dress. However, in destinations that were visited mostly by domestic tourists, the residents perceived only small differences between themselves and the tourists (Pizam and Telisman-Kosuta, 1989).

Several studies have been conducted to analyse the influence of nationality on tourist behaviour (Pizam and Sussmann, 1995; Pizam and Jeong, 1996; Pizam and Reichel, 1996; Pizam et al., 1997; Pizam, 1999). These studies investigated the perception that British, Israeli, Korean and Dutch tour guides had of tourists of different nationalities on escorted motor-coach tours. These studies showed that nationality influences the tourist culture and that there was a significant perceived difference between the nationalities. For example, in the study of the Dutch tour-guides' perceptions of French, Italian, Japanese and American tourists in the Netherlands the results showed that in eighteen out of the twenty behavioural characteristics there was a significant perceived difference between the four nationalities. The Americans were perceived to be the most distinct from and the Italians the most similar to other nationalities. The Italians-Americans were perceived by the tour guides as being the most similar to each other in their behaviour, followed by French-Italians, Japanese-French, Japanese-Italians, Japanese-Americans and French-Americans, who were perceived to be the most dissimilar (Pizam et al., 1997).

In the study of the Israeli tour guides' perceptions of American, British, German and French tourists the results also showed that in eighteen out of twenty behavioural characteristics there was a significant difference between the four nationalities. The Americans, again, were perceived to be the most different and the French the most similar to other nationalities. The tour guide perceived the French-British to be the most similar to each other in their behaviour, followed by French-Germans, French-Americans and British-Americans, who were perceived to be the most dissimilar (Pizam and Reichel, 1996).

Similarly, the study of the Korean tour guides' perceptions of Japanese and American tourists showed that in eighteen out of twenty behavioural characteristics there was a significant perceived difference between the three nationalities. Korean tour guides perceived the Americans to be the most distinct among the three. The Japanese were perceived to be the most similar to other nationalities. The Koreans and Japanese were perceived to be the most similar to each other, followed by Japanese-Americans. The least similar were perceived to be the Koreans and Americans (Pizam and Jeong, 1996).

Dann (1993) criticized the studies that used nationality as a basis for explaining cultural differences in tourist behaviour. He argued that it is difficult to define nationality. Nationality of tourists is not always an indication of their culture. Many tourists may belong to several cultural groups and/or may have more than one nationality regardless of their country of birth, ethnic background, and country of origin. Also, the rapid globalization of the world and increasing growth in multiculturalism of generating and receiving countries diminishes the validity of nationality as a differentiating variable; the nationality concept slowly disappears.

Positive perceptions in developed countries

The perceptions of tourists vary from negative to positive (Belisle and Hoy, 1980; Cohen, 1971; Pearce, 1982b; Pi-Sunyer, 1978; Pizam, 1978; Sethna and Richmond, 1978; Smith, 1989; Thomason et al., 1979). Many positive perceptions of tourists have been noted in technologically developed countries. For instance, despite negative social effects of tourism development, Londoners were happy about the tourist presence (English Tourist Board, 1978). Although Americans complained about the increase in the number of tourists, they developed friendships with tourists (Rothman, 1978). Arab males developed friendships with Western tourist girls visiting Israel (Cohen, 1971). Perceptions were found to be significantly more positive if the traveller had a strong affiliation with a country visited (Langlois *et al.*, 1999). Positive perceptions of tourists and the development of friendships between tourists and hosts have also been noted in technologically unsophisticated countries (Boissevain, 1979). According to Sutton (1967), these positive perceptions have been developed because the opportunity for exploitation and mistrust did not exist, and a sense of a welcoming and pleasant atmosphere was created.

Negative perceptions in developed countries

Negative perceptions of tourists have also been noted in technologically developed countries. Catalans perceived English hosts as stiff and dependable. French tourists were perceived as pushy, Germans as stingy, and Italians as untrustworthy (Pi-Sunyer, 1978). Tourists did not seem to be welcome in Bali. The Balinese hosts' friendly attitude to tourists was superficial (Francillon, 1975). The Basques found tourists unpleasant and conflictful (Greenwood, 1972).

Destinations with a great number of tourists

A number of studies indicated that hosts developed negative perceptions of tourists in the destinations receiving a great number of tourists such as Spain, Greece, Hawaii, and the Caribbean (Bryden, 1973; Kent, 1977; Matthews, 1977) and that due to tourism development the hosts' perceptions of tourists became complex (Schild, 1962; Yum and Wang, 1983). According to Butler (1980), as tourism expands 'the large numbers of visitors and the facilities provided for them can be expected to arouse some opposition and discontent among permanent residents' (p. 8). Feelings of anxiety, jealousy, xenophobia, disinterest, rudeness, and even physical hostility develop among host communities (Pearce, 1982b; Smith, 1977, 1989). Smith (1977) reported that as the tourist numbers increased, Eskimo hosts began to resent tourists due to lost privacy. Hosts felt social stress when tourists invaded their day-to-day life (Smith, 1977). There was a perception that tourists were responsible for the deterioration in the hosts' standard of living. Negative perceptions of tourists were also emphasized (Taft, 1977). Many studies indicated that with the development of mass tourism, tourists are no longer seen as individuals but as an exploitative out-group. Mass tourism results in a growing lack of concern, loss of empathy, and even intolerance toward outsiders (Pi-Sunyer, 1978). The positive perceptions of tourists disappear and turn into negative stereotypes (Pi-Sunyer, 1978). The Catalan community locals showed dislike towards tourists (Pi-Sunyer, 1978). Negative perceptions justified discrimination of tourists in the area of services and prices (Pi-Sunyer, 1978). Similarly, as the number of Japanese tourists increased in Australia, the public became hysteric, intolerant, and biased against the Japanese, who were being abused and insulted (White, 1988). People in the service sector displayed negative attitudes toward Japanese tourists on the Gold Coast in 1988 and 1989. Many Japanese tourists were going home complaining (McArthur, 1988), dissatisfied, with negative perceptions of Australian hosts.

Perception versus attitude, image and attribution

The concept of perception is related to the concept of attitude, image and attribution that can also influence tourist–host contact.

Attitude
Attitude is formed on a basis of perception (Chon, 1989) and consists of similar components to perception (Krech and Crutchfield, 1948; McGuire, 1969; Moutinho, 1987; Newcomb et al., 1965). It is possible to predict attitude from perception. Attitude as perception may be positive or negative, and may vary in intensity.

Attitude measurement
A well-known technique for attitude measurement is Bogardu's (1925) Social Distance Scale, in which subjects are asked to indicate whether they would be willing to be in close relationships with members of a particular group. The Semantic Differential technique is also a well-known, accepted and reliable method of measuring attitudes (Snider and Osgood, 1969). In addition, several multi-attribute models have been developed in an attempt to relate attitudes to behaviour (Fishbein and Ajzen, 1975).

Attitude studies
The literature reveals that there are many studies done on attitudes and they can give some insights into the analysis of tourist–host contact. Much of the research has been done on the hosts' attitude toward tourists (Pi-Sunyer, 1978; Rothman, 1978), tourists' post-travel attitude change (Anastasopoulos, 1992; British Tourist Authority, 1972a, 1972b, 1972c; Chon, 1991; Cort and King, 1979; Milman et al., 1990; Pearce, 1980a, 1982b, 1988; Pizam et al., 1991; Shipka, 1978; Smith, 1955, 1957; Steinkalk and Taft, 1979; Stringer and Pearce, 1984), local residents'

attitudes to the impact of tourism and tourists (Bystrzanowski, 1989; Milman and Pizam, 1988; Pizam, 1978; Sheldon and Var, 1984; Thomason et al., 1979; Akis et al., 1996), students-tourists attitudes to hosts (Pizam et al., 1991; Steinkalk and Taft, 1979; Smith, 1955, 1957), influence of social interaction on tourists' attitudes (Sheldon and Var, 1984), influence of seasonality on attitudes (Sheldon and Var, 1984), influence of tourist–host ratio on attitudes (Long et al., 1990), tourists' attitudes to foodservice styles (Cai and Ninemeier, 1993), and the tourists' attitudes to tourist destinations (Weber and Mikacic, 1995). Some studies demonstrated the existence of anti-tourists attitudes (Jacobsen, 2000). The interesting finding was that those employed directly in the tourism industry have more positive attitudes towards tourists than those not so employed (King et al., 1993; Milman and Pizam, 1988), probably due to greater experience with dealing with tourists and easier access to information about tourists. However, Liu and Var (1986) did not agree that dependence on tourism is a significant factor in developing positive attitudes toward tourists. Some researchers tried to explain the positive and negative attitudes to tourists as a function of the stage of tourism development (Belisle and Hoy, 1980). Several researchers explained the role of positive attitudes towards tourists in determining a tourist visitation to a destination (Hoffman and Low, 1978; Ritchie and Zins, 1978) and evaluation of tourist destination (Gearing et al., 1974). Pleasant attitudes to tourists ranked second in a list of ten tourism attributes of a holiday destination (Goodrich, 1978).

Limitations of the attitude studies

The major limitation of the past studies is that most of them are descriptive in nature and focus on differences in attitudes. Also, there has been little attention paid to explanations of these differences. In addition, most of the studies have small sample sizes and focus on students rather than tourists. Moreover, the concepts of an attitude and perception have been used interchangeably, often mistakenly. Many researchers have not acknowledged the differences between these two concepts.

Further, the use of an attitude concept might be limited in the analysis of tourist–host contact. Firstly, it is difficult to predict behaviour from attitudes (Cialdini et al., 1981; Fishbein and Ajzen, 1975, 1980; Fridgen, 1991; Robertson, 1985). For instance, what people did do and what they said they would do is not the same thing (LaPiere, 1934). Secondly, a stay-at-home control sample is needed to evaluate the effect of contact on attitudes (Campbell and Stanley, 1966). Finally, travel motivations should be analysed to understand attitudes and their effect on social contact, clarify its purpose and its meanings for the participants (Triandis and Vassiliou, 1967).

Image

The importance of image has been recognized in the tourism literature (Ashworth and Goodall, 1988; Ahmed, 1991; Britton, 1979; Baloglu and McCleary, 1991; Bojanic, 1991; Bignon *et al.*, 1998; Baloglu and Mangaloglu, 2001; Crompton, 1979b; Chon, 1990, 1991, 1992; Choi *et al.*, 1991; Chen and Kerstetter, 1999; Chaudhary, 2000; Dimanche and Moody, 1998; Echtner and Ritchie, 1991, 1993; Fakeye and Crompton, 1991; Goodrich, 1978; Hunt, 1975; Hall *et al.*, 1999; Jenkins, 1999; Lubbe, 1998; Mayo, 1973, 1975; McLellan and Foushee, 1983; Moutinho, 1984; MacKay and Fesenmaier, 1997; Pearce, 1982a; Phelps, 1986; Schmoll, 1977; Telisman-Kosuta *et al.*, 1989; Woodside and Lysonski, 1989). It was noted that image determines destination choice, successful tourism development, tourism marketing strategies, and travel decision-making. Further, image plays an important role in evaluating tourist behaviour and satisfaction. Therefore, image is a useful concept in analysing social interaction between tourists and hosts, and satisfaction with this interaction.

The most common method for measuring image is to ask the respondents to choose adjectives from a given list that best describe various national groups or destinations (Katz and Braly, 1933). However, this method has been criticized for forcing respondents to choose from a given list. Another method requires respondents to judge how far apart different groups are on a scale from very similar (1) to very different (9).

Attribution

Attribution is a process of ascribing characteristic qualities to people or things. Tourists and hosts attribute certain qualities to their behaviour and try to explain what causes their behaviour. The process of attribution is not only important for an understanding of social interaction between tourists and hosts but also their satisfaction with each other. According to Valle and Wallendorf (1977), tourist behaviour may be attributed either to the tourist (an internal attribution such as personality), or the situation or environment (an external attribution such as cultural environment). Tourists who attribute their dissatisfaction to the external environment can be more dissatisfied than tourists who attribute their dissatisfaction to themselves (Francken and Van Raaij, 1981). However, Bochner (1982) noted that hosts and tourists might be biased in their attributes because they have less knowledge about those who are perceived than about them. This particularly applies to culturally different tourists and hosts who have little access to information about each other. Therefore, since people attribute differently, misunderstanding may occur (Triandis, 1975). The scope for misunderstanding may be particularly great when tourists and hosts from different cultures make different attributions.

Stereotyping

The concept of perception is also related to the concept of stereotype (Fridgen, 1991; Lippman, 1965; Pool, 1978; Triandis, 1972). Stereotyping refers to the attribution of certain traits, labelling, and perceptions of people on the basis of common characteristics. Jandt (1988) referred to stereotyping as judgments about others on the basis of their ethnic group membership. Stereotypes can also be developed in the basis of culture, occupation, age, or sex. Scollon and Scollon (1995) noted that stereotyping is simply another word for overgeneralization. Stereotypes generalize about a group of people on the basis of a few individuals belonging to only that group. People use stereotypes when they face a new situation and lack deep knowledge of each other.

Importance of stereotypes
Stereotypes are important for the study of tourist–host contact because they are useful in the description of tourists (Brewer, 1984) as well as hosts. Brewer (1984) made the distinction between general and specific stereotypes. Stereotypes often form the core of the perceptions tourists and hosts use to interact with each other. MacCannell (1984) noted that tourists and hosts are vulnerable to stereotypes that can easily influence perceptions tourists and hosts hold of each other, and even decide about tourist visitation. Positive stereotypes may attract tourists. For example, stereotypes of Tahitian women as beautiful helped to attract many tourists (Petit-Skinner, 1977). Stereotypes are also useful in distinguishing various categories of tourists (Pi-Sunyer, 1978). They can be used to explain tourist and host behaviour, and guide hosts and tourists in their mutual interaction. They can show a convenient way of how to interact during superficial and short-term relationships, and can establish a base for later understanding (Frankowski-Braganza, 1983). They provide a model for the tourist–host interaction (Frankowski-Braganza,

1983) because they provide an effective way of dealing with unknown people and managing unfamiliar interactions (Lippman, 1922).

Stereotypes studies

Numerous studies have investigated the stereotypes of national groups and different types of stereotypes have been identified (Brewer, 1978, 1984; Boissevain and Inglott, 1979; Buchanan and Cantril, 1953; Callan and Gallois, 1983; Chandra, 1967; Jahoda, 1959; Laxson, 1991; Nunez, 1977; Pi-Sunyer, 1978; Pi-Sunyer and Smith, 1989; Triandis, 1972; Triandis and Vassiliou, 1967; Turner and Ash, 1975). In many destinations residents have been found to have specific stereotypes of the tourists by nationality. Tourism industry employees also suggested that tourists of different nationality behave differently. For instance, the Japanese were always described as travelling in groups, bowing to everybody they meet, spending, and photographing heavily (Cho, 1991). Ritter (1989) described the Japanese as those who prefer to travel in groups for a short time only, because a long holiday and being away from a group and family means painful separation and psychological lack of well-being. Koreans were portrayed as being proud of their own identity, willing to accept everything that has similarities to the Korean way of life, insisting on going to Korean restaurants, preferring to travel in groups, and proud of travelling to Asian countries with Confucian philosophy (Business Korea, 1991). According to Kitano (1981), Asians were perceived as exotic people, who all looked alike. 'Koreans were mistaken for Japanese, who in turn were taken for Chinese, who in turn were seen as still another nationality' ... 'even though their languages and cultures may be totally different' (Kitano, 1981, p. 126). American tourists were stereotyped according to the general traits, which Mexicans assigned to all Americans such as being cautious, calculated, purposeful, and careful with money (Brewer, 1984). Americans were also described as loving originality and being close to nature, desiring freedom, and social acceptance (Ritter, 1987). Swedish tourists were characterized by the Maltese residents as being misers, and French and Italians as excessively demanding (Boissevain and Inglott, 1979). Catalans stereotyped English tourists as stiff, honest, dependable, and socially conscious (Pi-Sunyer, 1978).

Weaknesses of stereotyping

Although stereotypes have a 'kernel of truth' in their description of the characteristic of the group, they are in many cases inaccurate (Brislin, 1981). 'Stereotyping is a way of thinking that does not acknowledge internal differences within a group and does not acknowledge exceptions to its general rules' (Scollon and Scollon, 1995, p. 156). This results in a tendency to regard all members of a particular group in a similar way without acknowledging the differences between them. Many stereotypes are wrong and exaggerated. Often the negative attributes are emphasized, while the positive are ignored (Lustig and Koester, 1999). As a result, stereotyping leads to errors in interpretation and the judging of human behaviour. This has harmful consequences for the labelling of a group of people and interpreting their behaviour (Lustig and Koester, 1999). Stereotyping limits the understanding of human behaviour (Scollon and Scollon, 1995). Stereotypes may promote prejudice and discrimination of members from cultures other than one's own (Lustig and Koester, 1995).

Further, stereotypes develop without any proof in reality (Katz and Braly, 1933; LaPiere, 1936; Pepitone, 1986). For example, hosts develop stereotypes from gossip, government propaganda, observing tourists, and personal past experience in dealing with tourists. Tourists develop stereotypes of hosts from tourist literature, the media, educational sources, prior travel experience, or other holidaymakers.

Negative stereotypes

A large number of stereotypes are negative and refer to unfavourable traits (Pepitone, 1986). For instance, the common stereotype of the tourist is one who is rich, loud and insensitive to host community needs, being devoid of human qualities, and faceless strangers (Pi-Sunyer, 1978). The classic stereotype of the host is one who is poor and has power to exploit guests during economic transactions (Frankowski-Braganza, 1983). Negative stereotypes are harmful because they create distrust, lead to discrimination and rude and hostile behaviour (Fridgen, 1991), and impede social interaction (Jandt, 1998). It is difficult to foster interaction if stereotypes are negative. Negative stereotypes are usually maintained when social contact is minimal. When social contact is prolonged, stereotypes may be adjusted. They can be adjusted in accordance with observed behaviour (Frankowski-Braganza, 1983). However, it was also argued that stereotypes are reciprocal and difficult to change. They are inflexible and long lasting.

Positive stereotypes

Although a large number of studies describe negative stereotypes (Kitano, 1981) there have also been a few studies on positive stereotypes. For example, the Chinese and Japanese were perceived as hard-working, quiet, achievement oriented, and with a minimum number of social problems. Australians were perceived (by the Japanese) as significantly more friendly, good, pleasant, beautiful, trustworthy, kind, powerful, and strong (Pittam *et al.*, 1990). The Japanese were perceived (by the Australians) as significantly more gentle, educated, rich, powerful, successful, and ambitious than themselves. The Japanese were also perceived to be progressive, alert, scientifically minded, courteous, and artistic. Australians perceived themselves as happy-go-lucky and pleasure loving (Callan and Gallois, 1983; Kippax and Bridgen, 1977). Australians were also perceived to be materialistic and ambitious. The Japanese perceived themselves as reserved, formal, cautious, and evasive (Barnlund, 1975). Iwawaki and Cowen (1964) suggested that the Japanese are suppressive, cautious, and meticulous.

Ethnocentrism

Ethnocentrism is a belief in one's own cultural superiority; that the customs, traditions, beliefs and behavioural practices of one's own culture are better to those of other cultures. The concept of ethnocentrism comes from the Greek words *ethos*, people or nation, and *ketron*, centre, which mean being centred on one's cultural group. Judgments of others and interpretation of others is done according to the categories of one's own culture. Those from other cultures who behave and do things differently are perceived as being bad mannered and wrong. Assessment of others and what is right or wrong often creates negative responses to those who are culturally different. Their cultures are treated as deviations from normality.

Ethnocentrism generates emotional reactions to cultural differences and reduces people's willingness to understand different cultures (Lustig and Koester, 1999). People who believe in cultural superiority are not able to objectively assess other cultures and those who are different, and interpret and judge others' behaviour. Ethnocentrism limits peoples' ability to understand the symbols and meanings used by other cultures. Ethnocentrism also tends to exaggerate cultural differences by highlighting the most distinct differences in beliefs and practices and ignoring others. Ethnocentrism blocks effective intercultural interaction and communication because it does not allow for understanding those who are different. Ethnocentrism leads to cultural arrogance, avoidance, withdrawal, faulty attribution, and faulty categorization (Dodd, 1995). It can also lead to prejudice and discrimination. Extreme ethnocentrism may lead to conflict and even warfare (Rogers and Steinfatt, 1999).

Summary

Perception refers to the process of attributing meanings to the environmental stimuli, internal experience, impression, and interpretation of others' behaviour. Perceptions are subjective and they differ from reality. Perceptions are selective, involve categorization and don't recognize individual variations. The concept of perception is important for social interaction. Perceptions of others may be positive or negative. The positive perceptions of others encourage social interaction and affect satisfaction with this interaction. There is a relationship between culture, social interaction and perception. Perceptions are determined by culture. Differences in culture create barriers to social interaction. Cultural similarity generates positive perceptions, dissimilarity results in perceptual mismatches. Knowledge of the others' culture and its influence on social behaviour is necessary to avoid negative perceptions of others. There are several techniques for measuring perceptions. Perceptions of people are more difficult to measure than perceptions of physical objects as they may be subject to more bias. The tourists' perceptions of hosts are an important part of holiday perception. They may determine tourist holiday satisfaction and attract or deter tourists from a destination. There are studies that show the vital role of tourists' perceptions of hosts. Many studies have been done on hosts' perceptions of tourists. The importance of tourists' nationality for differentiating tourists was acknowledged. More studies on hosts' perceptions of tourists have been done in developed countries than in developing countries.

The concept of perception is also related to the concept of an attitude, image, and attribution. The use of an attitude is limited in the analysis of tourist–host contact. Stereotyping leads to errors and limits the understanding of human behaviour. Ethnocentrism is a belief of cultural superiority and limits people's ability to understand other cultures.

Discussion points and questions

1. Explain why the concept of an attitude is less effective in the analysis of tourist–host contact than the concept of perception.
2. Identify major characteristics of the perception concept.

3. Give three examples of the international tourists' perceptions of the locals at the destination visited. Compare these perceptions with the locals' perceptions of the international tourists at the same destination.
4. Explain the ways culture influences perceptions.
5. Do you agree with the statement that perceived cultural similarity and familiarity enhances social interaction? Give three examples of the cultural differences between people that make them attractive to each other and enhance their social interaction.
6. Identify five objections to using nationality as a variable for differentiating tourists from different cultural backgrounds.
7. Give five examples of the positive and negative stereotypes of international tourists. Do you agree that these stereotypes reflect the real characteristics of these tourists?
8. Why do we use stereotypes? Why are stereotypes often inaccurate? Why are stereotypes helpful? Why are stereotypes dangerous? Can we modify and/or eliminate stereotypes?
9. Why is ethnocentrism a problem in a tourism context? Why do we cling to ethnocentrism? How can we overcome ethnocentrism: (a) why learn about others? (b) Why learn about us?

Since perceptions affect satisfaction, the last part of the literature review examines the concept of tourist satisfaction in reference to tourist–host contact.

Further reading

Allport, G. (1954/1979) *The Nature of Prejudice*. New York: Doubleday Anchor; Reading, MA, Addison-Wesley.

Brewer, M. and Campbell, D. (1976) *Ethnocentrism and Intergroup Attitudes*. New York: Wiley.

Brislin, R. (1981) *Cross-Cultural Encounters: Face-to-Face Interaction*. New York, Pergamon.

Macrae, N., Stangor, C. and Hewstone, M. (1996) *Stereotypes and Stereotyping*. New York: Guilford.

Robinson, J. and Nemetz, L. (1988) *Cross-Cultural Understandings*. UK: Prentice-Hall International.

Van Dijk, T. (1987) *Communicating Racism: Ethnic Prejudice in Thought and Talk*. Newbury Park, CA: Sage Publications.

6

Satisfaction

Objectives

After completing this chapter the reader should be able to:

- understand the multi-faceted nature of satisfaction and difficulties in defining satisfaction

- identify dimensions of satisfaction

- understand the concept of service and service quality

- identify dimensions of service quality

- understand the relationship between service quality and satisfaction

- understand the importance of the interpersonal element of service

- identify major techniques for measuring satisfaction and the difficulties involved in this process.

Introduction

The aim of this chapter will be to explain the concept of satisfaction. Reference will be made to satisfaction with service, in particular, satisfaction with the quality of interpersonal interaction between a tourist and a service provider in the process of service delivery. The techniques for measuring satisfaction will be introduced.

Concept and definitions

Although the literature review indicates that some efforts have been made to analyse the concept of satisfaction (e.g. Allen *et al.*, 1988; Bowen, 2001; Cho, 1998; Chon, 1987; Dorfman, 1979; Geva and Goldman, 1991; Hughes, 1991; Lewis and Pizam, 1982; Lopez, 1980; Loundsbury and Hoopes, 1985; Mayo and Jarvis, 1981; Mossberg, 1995; Pearce, 1980a, 1984; Pizam *et al.*, 1978, 1979; Pizam, 1994; Pizam and Milman, 1993; Qu and Li, 1997; Rimmington and Yuksel, 1998; Ryan, 1991, 1995; Weber, 1997; Whipple and Thach, 1998; Zalatan, 1994), this concept is still 'undefined and methods of measurement are not provided' (Engledow, 1977, p. 87). There is a lack of research in forming a definition of satisfaction (Swan and Combs, 1976) and ignorance of consumer satisfaction studies in general (Pizam *et al.*, 1978). The definitions of satisfaction (given below) show the difficulty of defining satisfaction.

Expectations versus experiences

According to the normative standard definition (Cadotte *et al.*, 1982), satisfaction refers to the comparison of expectations with experiences in terms of performance: when experiences differ negatively from expectations, dissatisfaction occurs. In tourism, satisfaction is primarily referred to as a function of pre-travel expectations and post-travel experiences (LaTour and Peat, 1980; Moutinho, 1987; Swan and Martin, 1981; Whipple and Thach, 1988). Tourist satisfaction has been defined as the result of the comparison between expectations about the destination and a tourist's experience at the destination visited (Pizam *et al.*, 1978). When experiences compared to expectations result in feelings of gratification, the tourist is satisfied; when they result in feelings of displeasure, the tourist is dissatisfied (Pizam *et al.*, 1978). Similarly, Hughes (1991) noted that tourists whose expectations are fulfilled by their experiences report satisfaction, while those whose expectations are not fulfilled report dissatisfaction. 'The greater the disparity between expectations and experiences, the greater the likelihood of dissatisfaction' (Hughes, 1991, p. 168). According to Shames and Glover (1988), satisfaction results only when the expectations are met or exceeded. According to Knutson (1988), the best way to satisfy customers is to exceed their expectations. Knutson (1988) cited ten laws that help to achieve customer satisfaction such as focusing on customers' perceptions, creating positive first impressions, and fulfilling guests' expectations.

Relativity of the satisfaction concept

Hughes (1991) and Olander (1977) reported the relativity of the satisfaction concept. Hughes (1991) found that even though experiences did not fulfil tourists' expectations, tourists might still be satisfied. He distinguished three levels of positive satisfaction: very satisfied, quite satisfied and satisfied. Hughes (1991) noted that those who rate their expectations and experiences as very similar express high satisfaction; those who rate their expectations and experiences as only somewhat alike report a lower level of satisfaction. The level of satisfaction decreases when expectations are not fulfilled. Pearce (1988) suggested that satisfaction or fulfilment of expectations might also depend on how much people value the outcome or result of those expectations. In other words, satisfaction depends on people's values or beliefs. This notion was supported by Olander (1977) who pointed out that satisfaction should be assessed in relation to certain standards such as values or beliefs.

Expectations versus performance

Satisfaction was also defined as differences between expectations and (experiences of) performance (Oliver, 1989; Van Raaij and Francken, 1984). However, this definition was criticized for assuming that expectations are adequate predictors of satisfaction. In fact, the most satisfying experiences are those not expected. Therefore, the definitions of satisfaction based on experiences and expectations are regarded as inadequate.

Expectations versus perceptions

Many scholars agreed that satisfaction derives from the differences between expectations and perceptions (Nightingale, 1986; Parasuraman et al., 1985). Moutinho (1987) and Van Raaij and Francken (1984) referred to satisfaction as the degree of disparity between expectations and perceptions of performance. Chon (1989) defined tourist satisfaction as the fit between expectations and perceived outcome of the experience. Hughes (1991) noted that satisfaction is primarily determined by tourists' perceptions.

Input versus output of social exchange

Satisfaction is also referred to as the process of comparison between what one expects with what one receives (Oliver, 1989). If one gets what one expects, then one is satisfied, and vice versa. The equity definition of satisfaction (Swan and Mercer, 1981) compares perceived input-output (gains) in a social exchange: if the gains are unequal, the larger is dissatisfaction. For instance, if tourists receive less than they pay for, the input-output balance is inequitable, and tourists are dissatisfied. Satisfaction is, therefore, a 'mental state of being adequately or inadequately rewarded ...' (Moutinho, 1987, p. 34). However, as it was pointed out before, satisfaction depends on how much people value the result of such exchange (Pearce, 1988).

Fit between expectations and environment

Tourist satisfaction is related to the fit between expectations and fit to the environment (Hughes, 1991). The degree of fit depends on the tourists' expectations and the ability of the environment to meet these expectations. For instance, the fit between tourists and hosts increases when hosts are able to meet tourists' expectations. As the degree of fit increases, tourist satisfaction also increases. According to Hughes (1991, p. 166), the optimal fit between individuals' expectations and the environment occurs when the attributes of the environment are congruent with the individuals' beliefs attitudes, and values. In other words, the optimal fit between tourists and their environment is achieved when the host environment reflects the values of its visitors (Hughes, 1991).

Fit between the tourist and the host value system

According to Pearce and Moscardo (1984), tourist satisfaction is higher if the value system of the tourist fits into the value system of the host. Where values and value orientations do not fit, mismatch can lead to feelings of stress, anxiety, uncertainty, and result in dissatisfaction. Therefore, one condition of tourist satisfaction with hosts is the match between tourists' and hosts' value systems.

Satisfaction versus attribution

The process of attribution has also explained the satisfaction concept. An attribution definition of satisfaction refers to positive or negative disconfirmation of expectations. 'A negative disconfirmation (when actual is not as expected) results in dissatisfaction. A positive disconfirmation (when actual is better than expected) results in satisfaction' (Hunt, 1991, p. 109). A disconfirmed expectation can be attributed to external forces (e.g., specific situation) or internal forces (e.g., characteristics of an individual) (Pearce and Moscardo, 1986).

Internal and external attribution

Tourist satisfaction may be attributed either to the tourist (an internal attribution) or the situation and environment (an external attribution) (Valle and Wallendorf, 1977). Tourists who attribute their dissatisfaction to external factors (e.g., facilities, service) can be more dissatisfied than tourists who attribute their dissatisfaction to internal factors (e.g., themselves) (Van Raaij and Francken, 1984). Consequently, those tourists and hosts who attribute their dissatisfaction to external attribution (e.g., differences in cultural values) can be more dissatisfied than those who attribute their dissatisfaction to internal attribution (e.g., own personality).

One can argue that cultural values could be seen as internal attributes. However, since culture belongs to the external environment that influences tourist behaviour it is assumed that the influence of cultural differences on the tourist experiences is attributed to external forces. Understanding the attribution process is extremely important in explaining the concept of tourist dissatisfaction because it allows for gaining more insight into its causes.

Pre-travel favourability versus post-travel evaluation

It was also noted that tourist satisfaction is dependent on the pre-travel favourability toward the destination visited, which contributes to the post-travel evaluation of the destination (Pearce, 1980a). If the pre-travel favourability is initially high, tourist post-travel evaluation is positive (Pearce, 1980a). In other words, positive pre-travel perceptions result in satisfaction and positive post-travel evaluation. This observation supports Hughes' (1991) view that satisfaction depends on perception. However, according to Pearce (1980a), the initial favourability is not always a guarantee of satisfaction, since the pre-travel perceptions can change due to travel experience. In addition, the holidays that leave the tourist a little unsatisfied, generate more return visits than holidays with the highest satisfaction scores. Although Japanese tourists were dissatisfied with some areas of service, they wished to come back to Australia for a holiday (Reisinger, 1990).

Satisfaction as a multi-faceted concept

There is an assumption by many researchers that satisfaction is a uni-faceted concept. However, this is mistaken because satisfaction is a multifaceted concept that consists of a number of independent components (Hughes, 1991; Pizam *et al.*, 1978). Thus, holiday satisfaction is also a multi-faceted concept that consists of many independent aspects of the holiday experiences such as facilities, natural environment or services, and which needs to be analysed separately. The identification of satisfaction with separate components of a total tourist holiday can indicate the dissatisfying aspects of the holiday experiences. It can also reduce misunderstanding of which component causes dissatisfaction within the whole product (Whipple and Thach, 1988).

Satisfaction with hosts

The vital component of tourist holiday satisfaction is satisfaction with hosts. In this book hosts are referred to as service providers. Service providers are part of a tourist holiday and they are the first contact point for tourists, and remain in direct contact with tourists through an entire visit. Consequently, the tourist' satisfaction with service providers may significantly affect total holiday satisfaction. Satisfaction with hosts can increase international visitation, generate repeat purchases of the same tourism product, increase tourist expenditures, and extend the tourist stay.

Dimensions of satisfaction

In order to assess tourist satisfaction it is necessary to analyse different dimensions of satisfaction (Pizam *et al.*, 1978). The two major dimensions of satisfaction are the *instrumental* dimension that represents satisfaction with physical performance (e.g., loudness) and *expressive* dimension that represents satisfaction with psychological performance (e.g., comfort) (Swan and Combs, 1976). Satisfaction with hosts should be analysed by measuring satisfaction with both the hosts' physical (e.g., appearance, promptness) and psychological (e.g., hospitality) performance.

Importance of psychological dimension of satisfaction

By identifying various performance dimensions of satisfaction, it is possible to analyse the causes of dissatisfaction (Ojha, 1982). According to Ojha (1982, p. 23), there are tourists who are satisfied in spite of the problems with physical product, and there are tourists who are dissatisfied in spite of the best product. The best physical product may not compensate for psychological dissatisfaction. Therefore, the psychological dimension of satisfaction is extremely important. As Ojha (1982, p. 24) pointed out, satisfaction 'does not come only from good sights but from the behaviour one encounters, the help one receives, the information one gets and the efficiency with which his needs are served'. Similarly, Pizam *et al.* (1978) emphasized the vital role of the psychological dimension of satisfaction such as hospitality of the host community, which was defined as willingness to help tourists, friendliness, and courtesy toward tourists. The procedural fairness definition of satisfaction (Goodwin and Ross, 1989) indicates that satisfaction derives from the perceptions of being treated fairly. Therefore, the expressive dimension of satisfaction (satisfaction with psychological performance) should be measured when analysing tourist satisfaction with hosts.

Outcomes of dissatisfaction

The outcomes of dissatisfaction may be various. According to Moutinho's (1987) theory, tourists may either change destination or continue visitation, with or without interaction with hosts. Extremely dissatisfied tourists may choose to change a destination for their holiday. The dissatisfied tourists may either change a destination or decide to continue visitation with no intention for further interaction with hosts. Satisfied and extremely satisfied tourists may either continue visitation with the intention of further interaction or may change a destination. According to Pearce's (1988) theory, the satisfied tourists may return to a destination, recommend it to other tourists, or express favourable comments about it. The dissatisfied tourists may not return to a destination and may not recommend it to other tourists. They may also express negative comments about a destination and damage its market reputation.

Satisfaction versus customer service quality

The concept of satisfaction is often discussed in relation to satisfaction with social relationships (Dorfman, 1979) and customer services (Whipple and Thach, 1988). It seems that tourist satisfaction can also be explained in terms of satisfaction with service. As Urry (1991) pointed out, services offered to tourists are high contact services and are characterized by a direct person-to-person interaction. The satisfaction with service depends on the quality of services offered to tourists (Urry, 1991). Therefore, the concept of service quality and satisfaction with service is discussed below.

The concept of service

The concept of service has received substantial attention in the fields of tourism (Fick and Ritchie, 1991; Ostrowski *et al.*, 1993; Augustyn and Ho, 1998; Lam *et al.*, 1999), hospitality (Lewis and Chambers, 1989; Saleh and Ryan, 1991; Bojanic and Rosen, 1994), and recreation (MacKay and Crompton, 1988). Service has been defined as 'any activity or benefit one party can offer to another that is essentially intangible and does not result in the ownership of anything. Production may or may not be tied to a physical product' (Kotler *et al.*, 1989, p. 725).

Characteristics of service

The unique characteristics of services such as intangibility, perishability, inseparability of production and consumption, and heterogeneity are constantly acknowledged in the services marketing literature (e.g., Berry, 1980; Eiglier and Langeard, 1975; Lovelock, 1991). These characteristics make it difficult to evaluate services (Zeithaml, 1981). The marketing and consumer behaviour literature provides discussion on the differences between goods and services.

Service encounter

Within the service industry the focus of activities and operations is on the service process or encounter. Service encounter has been defined as the moment of interaction between the customer and the provider, or the dyadic interaction between customer and service provider (Czepiel *et al.*, 1985; Shostack, 1985; Solomon *et al.*, 1985; Surprenant and Solomon, 1987). Shostack (1985) defined the service encounter as a period of time during which a consumer directly interacts with a service. The extent of personal interaction and time involved in service provision greatly varies among services.

Moments of truth

Norman (1984) reported that a service encounter represents several consecutive and simultaneous 'moments-of-truth' in an interpersonal environment, which are assessed by how closely expectations are met. Consequently, service quality is delivered over several 'moments-of-truth' or encounters between service staff and customers, and depends upon the interpersonal skills and the environment in which the service is delivered.

Service classification

There are numerous classification schemes and definitional frameworks for analysing services (Cowell, 1984; Lovelock, 1991; Shostack, 1987). Different service types have been distinguished depending on the extent of personal contact required in the service encounter. Mills' (1986) work is often cited in this regard. He divides services into three primary categories: (1) maintenance-interactive, (2) task-interactive, and (3) personal-interactive. *Maintenance-interactive* services are of a simple nature and are characterized by little uncertainty in transactions (e.g., fast food restaurant services). *Task-interactive* services are characterized by greater risk in transactions, depend upon the service providers for information and expertise (e.g., banking services, brokerage firms) and, consequently, require a more intense interaction between the service provider and the customer. *Personal-interactive* services represent the most intense interaction of the three types. As Mills noted (1986), these services are characterized by professionalism, a transaction binding contract, a high degree of customization, information exchange, and trust underlying the service encounter. Tourism and hospitality services are characterized by a very intense personal contact between service providers and a customer, which determines the quality of services offered to tourists and is the focus of service quality analysis.

Service quality

Many theorists discussed the concept of service quality (e.g. Gronroos, 1978, 1982, 1984; Lehtinen and Lehtinen, 1982; Lewis and Booms, 1983; Sasser and Arbeit, 1978; Sasser *et al.*, 1978; Parasuraman *et al.*, 1985, 1986, 1988). Parasuraman *et al.* (1985) noted service quality is an elusive construct, not precisely defined, and not easily expressed by consumers. The criteria of service quality are still not adequately determined. Defining service quality and providing techniques for its measurement is a major concern of service providers and researchers. This becomes a particularly complex issue in a high contact service industry such as tourism and hospitality.

Dimensions of service quality

There are many dimensions of service quality. According to Lehtinen and Lehtinen (1982), there are three distinct service quality dimensions:

1. *physical* that includes the physical aspects of the service
2. *corporate* that involves the service organization's image or profile, and

183

3. *interactive* that derives from the interaction between contact personnel and the customer.

Researchers agree that the interactive dimension of service quality is central to service. Service quality occurs during the interaction between a consumer and a service provider, or the service encounter. The quality of the customer-provider interaction is vital in the assessment of overall quality of service (Crosby and Stephens, 1987; Parasuraman *et al.*, 1985, 1988; Solomon *et al.*, 1985; Urry, 1991).

Gronroos (1984) distinguished technical and functional service quality. *Technical* quality represents what the consumer receives from the service as a result of the interaction with the service provider. *Functional* quality represents the manner (or performance) in which a service provider delivers service to a customer. Gronroos (1984) also stressed the vital role of the service providers in service delivery.

Martin (1987) distinguished two other dimensions of service quality: procedural and convivial. The *procedural* dimension is mechanistic in nature and deals with systems of selling and distributing a product to a customer. The *convivial* dimension is interpersonal in nature and emphasizes the service provider's positive attitudes to customers, behaviour, and appropriate verbal and non-verbal skills. It also deals with the service provider's personal interest in the customer, being friendly, appreciative of the customer, suggestive, being able to fulfil the customer's psychological needs and meet expectations, naming names, gracious problem solving, appreciating of the customers' needs, tactfulness, courtesy, attentiveness, guidance, and tone of voice. This dimension stresses the customer's need to be liked, respected, relaxed, feel comfortable, important, pampered, and welcomed (Martin, 1987).

Importance of service providers' attributes

The service providers' attributes are the vital elements of service quality. Callan (1990, p. 48) referred to service quality as 'a responsive, caring and attentive staff', 'staff who get things done promptly and provide honest answers to problems', 'treating others in a kindly fashion', 'hospitality which leads the guest to feel at home, well cared for and anxious to return', 'the elimination of all criticism', 'making the recipient feel thoughtful, efficient, correct and magnanimous'. According to Hochshild (1983), service also requires the need to smile, in a pleasant and involved way to customers. Pizam *et al.* (1978) emphasized the role of the hospitality factor in service provision: (a) employees' willingness to help tourists, courtesy toward tourists, and friendliness; and (b) residents' willingness to help, be courteous, and hospitable. Knutson (1988) indicated prompt and courteous service as important for clients' satisfaction with service quality. Saleh and Ryan (1992) noted that staff appearance is even more important than the range of facilities being offered.

Importance of service providers' perceptions

Perceptions of service providers are part of the overall perceptions of a tourism product quality. These perceptions determine the success of the tourism and hospitality operations, which rely very heavily on the development of positive perceptions of service providers. Pearce (1982b) illustrated the important role of many people associated with the travel and hospitality industry such as restaurateurs, salesmen, and hoteliers who contribute to the overall tourist perceptions of services offered to tourists. Sutton (1967) reported that competency in providing services is an important element influencing tourist perceptions of service quality. Pearce (1982b) indicated that annoyance by not being able to achieve a certain standard of service, impoliteness, or feelings of discontent create negative tourist perceptions of service. The positive perceptions of the service such as the service providers' friendliness, responsibility, or courtesy encourage repeat visitation of the host region and repeat purchase of the same tourism product. Negative perceptions of service deter visitation and discourage repeat purchasing. Therefore, the way tourists perceive service quality influences the success of a tourist destination. Mossberg (1995), who investigated tourist satisfaction with tour leaders and their importance in charter tours in Rhodes, Bulgaria/Turkey and Sri Lanka, found that the tour leader was important to the tourist's perceptions of the tour, and different performances and duties of the guide influenced the tourist's perceptions. The service that a tour guide offered depended on his/her experience that influenced the tourist's level of satisfaction.

Subjectivity of service quality

Service quality is a multidimensional concept. Each dimension of service quality can be perceived differently depending whether it is perceived by a customer/tourist, a provider or management. The subjective nature of service quality makes it difficult to evaluate. Lewis and Booms (1983) highlighted the subjective nature of service quality by noting that there is an element of 'appropriateness' about service quality. They noted that evaluation of service quality depends upon 'what is acceptable and what is not' (p. 100). This idea was supported by Parasuraman et al. (1988) who reported that service quality is determined by a subjective customer perception of service. Consequently, service quality is often related to the perception of service by a customer.

Service quality versus expectations

Gronroos (1982) reported that consumers compare service expectations with perceptions of the service they receive in evaluating service quality. Lewis and Booms (1983) noted that delivering quality service means conforming to customer expectations. Eiglier and Langeard (1987) stated that service quality is the capacity to meet customers' expectations. When customer expectations are not met, service quality is perceived as poor. When customer expectations are met or exceeded, service quality is perceived as high. However, according to Lewis (1987), the differences between perceptions and expectations can measure the existence or non-existence of quality regardless of what quality is.

Parasuraman et al.'s SERVQUAL model of service quality

Parasuraman et al. (1985, 1986, 1988, 1990) and Berry et al. (1990) conducted important research that resulted in the development of the SERVQUAL model of service quality. The SERVQUAL model contributed to service quality theory in two ways. Firstly, it incorporated aspects of consumer behaviour into the concept of service quality. Secondly, it identified and explained specific dimensions or factors that both consumers and service providers use to assess and evaluate service performance and quality standards. From the standpoint of consumer behaviour, the Parasuraman et al. (1985, 1988) model defines service quality as the differences between one's expectations from the service provider compared to the perceptions of the outcomes of the service performance. Parasuraman et al.'s (1985) conceptual model of service quality was based on the gaps in service quality between perceptions and expectations on the part of management, consumers, and service providers. They identified five gaps in service quality:

- management perceptions of consumer expectations and consumer expectations
- management perceptions of consumer expectations and service quality specifications
- service quality specifications and service delivery
- service delivery and service quality communicated externally to customers, and
- consumer perceptions of service and consumer expectations from service.

The above five gaps have an impact on the consumer's evaluation of service quality (Parasuraman *et al.*, 1985). Service quality as perceived by a consumer depends on the size and direction of the fifth gap, which by itself, is a function of the other four gaps.

Since it is a consumer who defines quality, the evaluation of service quality largely depends on the consumer. It is a challenge for the service providers to understand the process by which service quality is evaluated by customers.

Criteria of service quality

The ten most important criteria of service quality were distinguished by Parasuraman *et al.* (1985, 1986) in his SERVQUAL model, namely, reliability, responsiveness, competence, access, courtesy, communication, credibility, security, understanding and knowing the customer, and tangibles. These criteria are used by consumers in assessing service quality. Since many of these criteria were dependent they were reduced to five dimensions of service quality: tangibles, reliability, responsiveness, assurance, and empathy. The reliability dimension was assessed by consumers as the most important criterion in assessing service quality. However, the importance attached by consumers to the service quality dimensions may differ prior to and after service delivery. Evaluation of service quality is not only based on the outcome of a service, but also on the process of service delivery (Parasuraman *et al.*, 1985, 1988). Therefore, the significance of the service quality dimensions lies in the fact that they apply to the process by which the service is delivered rather than an outcome of a service.

SERVQUAL application

The SERVQUAL model has been widely applied in empirical studies in various disciplines and been shown to be highly valuable and appropriate for a wide range of services (e.g., retail, securities, brokerage, product repair and maintenance). Fick and Ritchie (1991) tested the SERVQUAL instrument with customers in four tourism service sectors: airline, hotel, restaurant, and skiing. They found that the measurement scale was useful to compare between travel sectors, or across firms within the same sector. However, the scale did not appear to be entirely valid for all tourism service sectors. Saleh and Ryan (1991) applied a modified version of the SERVQUAL to the hotel industry. In both studies it was shown that experiences with service transactions in the service encounter depended upon the perceptions of the quality of service offered by the hospitality and tourism industry employees (hosts) who were responsible for creating and delivering service. Particularly, the quality of services depended on the ability of hosts to assess the tourist's needs and satisfaction, and to deliver individualized service.

SERVQUAL criticism

Despite its growing popularity and widespread application SERVQUAL has been subjected to a number of criticisms. SERVQUAL has been criticized for being based on a disconfirmation model rather than an attitudinal model. In the first model customer satisfaction is operational-ized in terms of the relationships between expectations and outcomes. Cronin and Taylor (1992) claimed that perceived quality is best concep-tualized as an attitude. They criticized Parasuraman *et al.* (1988) for their hesitancy to define perceived quality in attitudinal terms, even though they had claimed that service quality was similar in many ways to an attitude.

The SERVQUAL has also been criticized for: (a) little evidence that customers assess service quality in terms of perception-expectation gaps; (b) focusing on the process of service delivery, not the outcomes of the service encounter; (c) an unstable and contextual number of dimensions (the number of dimensions comprising service quality vary across situa-tions and industries); (d) items that do not always load on to the factors which one would *a priori* expect; (e) inappropriate operationalization of the term expectations; (f) its four to five item scale that does not capture the variability within each dimension; (g) a standardized clustered item order that generates a systematic order bias; (h) assessing services that are delivered during only one encounter; (i) the reversed polarity of items in the scale that causes respondent error; (j) a 7-point scale, lack of verbal labelling for points 2 through to 6, for problems with interpretation of the meaning of the midpoint of the scale; (k) double administration of the instrument that causes boredom and confusion; and (l) the overall SERVQUAL score that accounts for a disappointing proportion of item variances (Buttle, 1996). This criticism should be of concern to users of the instrument. However, SERVQUAL undoubtedly has had a major impact on business and academic communities, and it may be useful in a revised form depending on the situation.

Properties of consumer goods

Nelson (1974) distinguished two categories of properties of consumer goods:

1. *Search properties* that are attributes a consumer can determine prior to purchasing a product (e.g., size, colour, feel)

2. *Experience properties* that are attributes that can be assessed only after purchase or during consumption (e.g., taste, wearability).

Darby and Karni (1973) added to Nelson's properties a third category *credence properties* that the consumer finds impossible to evaluate even after purchase and consumption (e.g., medical care, education).

These properties facilitate the evaluation of service quality and define the degree of difficulty of service evaluation. Those services that are high in experience properties are difficult to evaluate; and those services that are high in credence properties are the most difficult to evaluate. Since most services contain a high percentage of experiences and credence properties, service quality is more difficult to evaluate than the quality of goods (Zeithaml, 1981) that contain a high percentage of search properties. Most of Parasuraman *et al.*'s (1985, 1988) ten service quality criteria, except tangibles and credibility, contain a high percentage of experience properties and, therefore, can be evaluated only after the purchase. Two of the service quality criteria, those of competence and security, contain a high percentage of credence properties and thus cannot be evaluated even after purchase.

Service quality versus satisfaction
The services marketing literature indicates that there is a difference between the concepts of service quality and satisfaction with service. Service quality is concerned with the attributes of the service itself (Crompton and MacKay, 1989). Satisfaction is a psychological outcome deriving from an experience. It is an 'emotional state that occurs in response to an evaluation of the interactional experiences' (Westbrook, 1981, p. 68). Service quality is related to customer satisfaction and is a way of thinking about how to satisfy customers so that they hold positive perceptions of the service (Ostrowski *et al.*, 1993). Satisfaction depends on the quality of service attributes (Crompton and MacKay, 1989). Usually a high quality of service attributes results in high satisfaction.

Service quality is essential in the determination of customer dissatisfaction (Bitner *et al.*, 1990). Service quality depends vastly on the interpersonal element of service performance (Bitner *et al.*, 1990). The quality of interpersonal interaction between customer and service provider is an important element in the assessment of overall satisfaction with service quality (Crosby and Stephens, 1987; Parasuraman *et al.*, 1985, 1988). Therefore, the quality of the interpersonal interaction between a tourist and a service provider is an important determinant of tourist dissatisfaction with services. According to Jacinto *et al.* (1999), holiday satisfaction is positively influenced by the intercultural interaction and the quality of services.

Positive and negative disconfirmation

Since service quality depends on the customer perception of service, the positive perception of service quality enhances customer satisfaction, and a negative perception creates dissatisfaction with the service. Parasuraman *et al.* (1985) reported that the perception of service quality could range from ideal through satisfactory to totally unacceptable quality. The range depends on the discrepancy between the service expectations (ES) and service perceptions (PS) so that when ES > PS, perception of service quality is less than satisfactory and tends toward totally unacceptable quality; when ES = PS, perception of service quality is satisfactory; and when ES < PS, perception of service quality is more than satisfactory and tends toward ideal quality. Similarly, Smith and Houston (1982) claimed that when expectations from service are not fulfilled, dissatisfaction with service results (negative disconfirmation); when expectations are met or exceeded, satisfaction with service results (positive disconfirmation). Thus, customer satisfaction (CS/D) typically is modelled as a function of disconfirmation arising from discrepancies between prior expectations and actual performance (Cardozo, 1965; Oliver, 1989).

Importance of interpersonal dimension of service

It is possible that a perceived high quality service may result in low satisfaction. The mechanistic system of service delivery may be of high quality, however, the interpersonal dimension of service may be of a low quality and result in low satisfaction with total service. On the other hand, the service provider's attitudes, behaviour and verbal skills may give the customer more satisfaction than the pure mechanistic system of delivery of service. As Crompton and MacKay (1989) indicated, the positive social interaction between a consumer and a service provider may compensate even the low quality of service and result in high satisfaction. The high quality convivial dimension of service (interpersonal) may compensate the low quality procedural dimension of service (Martin, 1987). Therefore, the perception of the interpersonal element of service delivery is an essential element in the determination of tourist satisfaction with service.

Importance of understanding the customer's needs

Service quality and satisfaction depend on the differences between the customer's and the provider's perceptions of the customer experiences and specifically, the extent to which the service provider accurately understands the nature of the tourist's needs. Saleh and Ryan (1991) found that hotel providers and their guests evaluated service performance much the same way. However, they reported differences between providers and guests for gaps between expectations and performance. Vogt and Fesenmaier (1995) found that service providers did not understand the level at which customers evaluated their experiences. They reported that it is important *who* delivers the service as opposed to *what* is delivered. They argued that it is vital to consider both the customer and the provider in defining service quality, be more aware of the tourists' needs, and include all types of employees involved in delivering services to tourists.

Cultural influences on service satisfaction

Culture determines expectations and perceptions of service quality that, in turn, determine satisfaction with service. For example, Mok and Armstrong (1998) found significant differences in expectations from hotel service quality among guests from the UK, USA, Australia, Japan and Taiwan. Tourists from these countries had different expectations for two of the service quality dimensions, namely tangibles and empathy. The Japanese tourists, for instance, had the lowest expectation for the tangibles. Both the Japanese and Taiwanese tourists also had significantly lower expectations for the empathy dimension than western tourists. The findings implied that tourists from different cultures might have different expectations of the physical facilities, equipment, and appearance of the tourism and hospitality industry's personnel. Therefore, understanding the differences in cultural orientations would help to determine the type of services expected.

Choi and Chu (2000) investigated Asian and Western travellers' perceptions of service quality in Hong Kong hotels. The results suggested that Asian travellers' satisfaction derived from the value factor, whereas Western travellers' satisfaction was influenced by the room quality factor. Choi and Chu (2000) concluded that the differences in the perceptions could be explained by cultural factors.

Furrer *et al.* (2000) argued that cultural orientations determine perceptions of service quality. They tested a conceptual link between all five cultural dimensions developed by Hofstede (1980, 1991) and Bond

(1987), and variations in the relative importance of all five service quality dimensions developed by Parasuraman *et al.* (1985, 1988), Parasuraman *et al.* (1991) and Zeithaml *et al.* (1988, 1993). They developed a Cultural Service Quality Index (CSQI) that evaluates the relative importance of each SERVQUAL dimension as a function of the five cultural dimensions and that can be used to segment multicultural markets.

Feather (1982) noted that cultural values influence satisfaction. Winsted (1999) analysed the importance of service dimensions to consumer satisfaction in two different countries: the United States and Japan. Formality was found to be more important in status-conscious societies than in egalitarian societies, and personalization was more important in individualistic countries than in collectivistic countries. Authenticity was more important for professional services, while courtesy and promptness were more important for generic services. Caring and courtesy received the highest ratings as most important to satisfaction with service encounters.

Service perception and satisfaction studies

Service perceptions and, in particular, the perceptions of a customer-service provider interaction in the process of service delivery and satisfaction with this interaction have still not received enough research attention in the area of tourism. There is a need to analyse the tourists' perceptions of services in their host destinations. Such analysis would provide valuable information for hospitality and marketing strategists, particularly if the differences in perceptions are observable and they are generated by the differences in cultural background. Differences in cultural values would help to identify the factors contributing to differences in perceptions, and in turn, to assess the effectiveness of the service providers' performance from the perspective of the culturally different customer. The examination of the tourist perceptions of the service performance would also enable detection of negative perceptions and change or modify them if necessary, and therefore better respond to culturally different tourists' needs.

Measurement of satisfaction

There are two distinct approaches to the measurement of satisfaction (Maddox, 1985): (1) measurement of overall satisfaction, and (2) measurement of satisfaction with its various dimensions.

Measurement of overall satisfaction

The first approach is to measure the overall satisfaction with the object or person. Such measurement is normally easy and requires a minimum respondents' effort (Maddox, 1985). However, the problem is in choosing from among a number of techniques measuring overall satisfaction. Usually a scaling technique is used. However, there are many discussions about the appropriateness of measuring scales. Pizam *et al.* (1978) argued that satisfaction should be measured on an interval scale. Dann (1978) criticized this type of measurement for being highly skewed because tourists may express various degrees of satisfaction with various components of their holiday experiences. The other measurement techniques such as interviewing or asking direct questions related to satisfaction were also criticized for being responsible for skewed answers. Dann (1978) argued that indirect rather than direct techniques are more useful. Maddox (1985) examined the construct validity of several methods and scales measuring satisfaction. Respondents were asked to indicate their satisfaction on graphic, face, and delighted-terrible (DT) scales. The DT (verbal) appeared to be better than graphic and face scales (non-verbal scales).

Measuring overall satisfaction with people appears to be more complex than measuring satisfaction with physical objects. The physical characteristics such as size or volume can be directly observed and quantified. The psychological characteristics such as intelligence or hospitality must be inferred. As a result, the measurement of people's psychological traits vastly depends on the perceptions of these traits by observers. Personal biases may occur due to the different assessment of the inferred qualities by observers. These biases are threats to the accuracy of measurement.

Measuring satisfaction with a tourism product is difficult because the tourism product consists mostly of services that are intangible and perishable in nature. In addition, the measurement of satisfaction with the expressive performance of services (e.g., atmosphere of hospitality, reputation) is even more difficult than with the instrumental performance of service (e.g., speed, correctness).

Measurement of satisfaction with various dimensions

The second approach to measuring satisfaction is to measure satisfaction with various dimensions contributing to overall satisfaction (Maddox, 1976; Smith *et al.*, 1969). In addition, since the tourism product is a composite of many interrelated components, the measurement of satisfaction with the tourism product requires first of all the identification of individual components of this product and measurement of satisfaction with each component (Pizam *et al.*, 1978). For instance, satisfaction with the total tourism product can be analysed by measuring satisfaction with facilities, natural environment or services offered. Satisfaction with services can be evaluated by measuring satisfaction with the interpersonal element of service. The interpersonal element of a service can be further analysed by measuring satisfaction with individual service providers such as tour guides, shop assistants, waitresses, and customs officials, and their attributes such as politeness, friendliness, and professionalism. For instance, satisfaction with a tour guide can be measured by the satisfaction with the tour guide's knowledge of the historical, geographical and cultural environment (Almagor, 1985), knowledge of the culture being visited and the visitor culture, organizational and communication skills (Hughes, 1991; Pearce, 1984). As Hughes (1991) noted, satisfaction is a multifaceted concept.

Importance of satisfaction with tourism components

Measuring tourist satisfaction with a particular component of the tourism product is important because this measurement has a significant impact on tourist satisfaction with the total tourism product. If the individual components of a tourism product are not identified and satisfaction with the total product only is measured, a 'spill over' effect may occur. This means that dissatisfaction with one component may lead to dissatisfaction with the total product. The measurement of separate components of satisfaction can help to develop an understanding of which component of tourism product creates dissatisfaction and which one should be changed or modified. More adequate definition of the satisfaction concept can also be developed.

Complaints

One of the common measures of dissatisfaction is complaint. However, this measure is very subjective and may present a biased view due to high dissatisfaction rates that may not lead to many complaints (Gronhaug, 1977). According to Roth *et al.* (1990), the most frequent consumer response to dissatisfaction is to 'do nothing' (Roth *et al.*, 1990). However, complaints should be monitored because dissatisfied guests complain widely to friends (Maddox, 1985), and the consequences of such complaints can be very negative. The complaints from the 'matched' tourists (whose expectations can be met by tourism management) (Pearce and Moscardo, 1984, p. 23) are easier to handle, and the needs of the 'matched' tourists can be satisfied quickly. The expectations and needs of the 'mismatched' tourists are more difficult to meet and satisfy (Pearce and Moscardo, 1984, p. 23). Such 'mismatched' tourists can be tourists from different cultural backgrounds.

Another reason why complaints should not be used as a measure of satisfaction is because they do not always indicate real dissatisfaction. Complaints can be caused by misunderstandings arising out of intercultural differences encountered during an overseas trip (Hanningan, 1980). International tourism more than any other area is affected by cross-cultural differences (Hanningan, 1980). Thus, the complaints of international tourists do not always express tourist dissatisfaction. Many complaints often express the intercultural difficulties encountered in a foreign country rather than dissatisfaction. Therefore, an understanding of the cultural factors that influence the international tourists' dissatisfaction is vital for any international tourism study.

Criticism of satisfaction measurement

Some researchers question the usefulness of satisfaction measurement at all. Some argue that the measurement of satisfaction with actual experiences is not useful. Instead satisfaction should be measured on the basis of expectations. 'The expectations indicators are three times as powerful in explaining satisfaction than objective conditions' (Gauthier, 1987, p. 1). Others argue that satisfaction should be measured over time. However, the lack of a stable technique for satisfaction measurement makes the measurement over time difficult. Pizam et al. (1978) highlighted many difficulties in measuring tourist satisfaction. Pizam et al. (1979) questioned Dann's (1978) approach to satisfaction measurement and, in particular: (a) overlooking the measurement of various elements of tourism satisfaction; (b) confusing the terms of motivation to travel, objective of travel and satisfaction from travel; (c) not providing information about the 'push factors' that greatly influence the tourist's experiences; (d) assuming that tourism satisfaction is not a function of satisfaction with the services but a function of overall life satisfaction; and (e) ignoring Likert type scales as appropriate instruments for measuring tourism satisfaction.

Importance of satisfaction measurement

Despite the difficulties and criticism of satisfaction measurement, tourism managers should be concerned with measuring tourist satisfaction. 'Vacation dissatisfaction ... underlines the vacationer's decision process' (Van Raaij, 1986; Van Raaij and Francken, 1984, p. 105) and influences the purchase intention (Moutinho, 1987). Satisfaction determines whether the tourist becomes a repeat visitor. Monitoring tourist satisfaction can provide invaluable information for detecting problems that cause dissatisfaction with holidays and have negative impact on future visitation. 'Remedial action could be initiated before a crisis occurs' (Maddox, 1985, p. 2). It is important to know the possible consequences of tourist dissatisfaction.

Summary

There are many definitions of satisfaction. However, none of the definitions gives a clear explanation of the concept of satisfaction. Satisfaction was defined as an outcome of the comparison between expectations and experiences; a difference between expectations and perceptions of performance; a fit between expectations and the environment; a fit between the tourist and the host value systems; and input-output of social exchange. Satisfaction was explained by the attribution process. Satisfaction is a relative, subjective and multifaceted concept. Total holiday satisfaction should be assessed by measuring satisfaction with the individual components of the holiday experiences. Satisfaction with hosts is an important element of the total holiday satisfaction and should be measured with the host's physical and psychological performance.

The concept of tourist satisfaction can be analysed in terms of satisfaction with the service offered to tourists. Satisfaction with service depends on the quality of service that is determined by the quality of the interpersonal interaction between a service provider and a customer. Major dimensions of service quality have been identified of which the majority are related to the interpersonal element of service. The positive perceptions of the interpersonal element of service are extremely important because they may compensate for the low mechanistic process of service delivery, and result in high satisfaction.

There are two approaches for measuring satisfaction: measurement of overall satisfaction and measurement of satisfaction with various elements contributing to overall satisfaction. Measuring satisfaction with people requires the observer to infer the psychological traits of people and is very subjective. Measuring satisfaction with a tourism product is complex because the tourism product consists mostly of intangible services, requires the identification of individual components of service, and measurement of satisfaction with each component. There are various techniques for measuring satisfaction. Many of these techniques have been criticized. Indirect rather than direct techniques were found to be more useful. Complaints are not good measures of dissatisfaction as they often express intercultural difficulties rather than dissatisfaction. Tourist satisfaction should be measured because such measurement can detect the causes of tourist dissatisfaction and predict its consequences.

Discussion points and questions

1. Explain why is it difficult to define the concept of satisfaction.
2. Identify major causes and outcomes of tourist dis/satisfaction with their holidays.
3. Why is tourist satisfaction with service providers a vital component of the overall holiday satisfaction?
4. Identify the major criteria of service quality. Which criteria appear to be the most important in assessing service quality in tourism? Why?
5. Explain the relationship between service quality and satisfaction.
6. What is the influence of culture on service quality and tourist holiday satisfaction?
7. Which technique of satisfaction measurement does appear to be the most adequate; why should international tourist complaints not always be used in assessing holiday satisfaction?

Further reading

Bitner, M. J., Booms, B. H. and Tetreault, M. (1990) The service encounter: diagnosing favourable and unfavourable incidents. *Journal of Marketing* 54: 71–84.

Gronroos, C. (1982) Service quality model and its marketing implications. *European Journal of Marketing* 18(4): 36–44.

Parasuraman, A., Zeithaml, V. A. and Berry, L. L. (1985) A conceptual model of service quality and its implications for future research. *Journal of Marketing* 49: 41–50.

Parasuraman, A., Zeithaml, V. A. and Berry, L. L. (1986) *SERVQUAL: A Multiple-Scale Item for Measuring Consumer Perceptions of Service Quality*. Cambridge, MA: Marketing Institute.

Parasuraman, A., Zeithaml, V. and Berry, L. L. (1988) SERVQUAL: A multiple-scale item for measuring consumer perceptions of service quality. *Journal of Retailing* 64: 12–40.

Parasuraman, A., Zeithaml, V. and Berry, L. (1990) *An Empirical Examination of Relationships in an Extended Service Quality Model.* Cambridge, MA: Marketing Science Institute.

Pizam, A., Neumann, Y. and Reichel, A. (1978) Dimensions of tourist satisfaction with a destination area. *Annals of Tourism Research* 5(3): 314–322.

Pizam, A., Neumann, Y. and Reichel, A. (1979) Tourist satisfaction: uses and misuses. *Annals of Tourism Research* 6(1): 195–197.

Shostack, G. L. (1985) Planning the service encounter. In Czepiel, J. A., Solomon, M. R. and Surprenant, C. F. (eds) *The Service Encounter.* Lexington, MA: Lexington Books: pp. 243–254.

Surprenant, C. F. and Solomon, M. R. (1987) Predictability and personalization in the service encounter. *Journal of Marketing* 51: 73–80.

Part 2

Methods for Cross-Cultural Analysis in Tourism

The methods detailed in this part are selected as a combination of scientific techniques that provide a wide and sophisticated inter-related set of analysis tools that can be applied to cross-cultural research. Although non-quantitative methods are useful, in particular as theory building exploratory tools, researchers working in the field of cross-cultural research need and should be able to use hypothesis testing scientific method. It is insufficient to say that the issues of cross-cultural research are too complex for analysis by rigorous statistical methods. The modern techniques described and applied in Part 2 are suitable for studying the complexities of cross-cultural interaction, while at the same time providing both exploratory theory-building tools and in depth investigative processes.

The particular advantage of such an approach is that it is replicative and comparative. Given sufficient research the results can be tested in different scenarios and meaningfully compared over time, aiding in a specific manner, with the general building of one research outcome upon another.

The use of non-quantitative methods are not specifically included, partly because they are well documented elsewhere and partly because they are relatively well known. Although the quantitative methods described here have been well used before, their precise mathematical foundation and detailed application is not contained elsewhere in the tourism literature. Furthermore, the application of these methods to studies in cross-cultural analysis in tourism provides a new approach.

- **Chapter 7** introduces factor analysis for cross-cultural structural analysis. It explains the basic terminology, stages of analysis and the difference between Factor Analysis and Principal Components Analysis. An example of the application of Factor Analysis in the area of cross-cultural behaviour is provided.
- **Chapter 8** defines and explains the concept of structural equation modelling (SEM), its objectives, application in cross-cultural tourism behaviour, types and stages of SEM modelling, and interpretation of its statistical results.

7

Principal components and factor analysis for cross-cultural analysis

Objectives

After completing this chapter the reader should be able to:

■ understand the difference between Principal Components and Factor Analysis

■ understand the process by which factor analytic methods operate

■ define the meaning of the statistics produced by factor analytic methods

■ understand the different forms of Factor Analysis

■ use factor analytic methods correctly for analysing cross-cultural tourism research data.

Introduction

Factor Analysis was developed to specifically test a hypothesis of complete independence of dimensions, commonly termed 'simple structure'. Principal Components Analysis on the other hand, while developed for the same reasons as Factor Analysis is less specific and does not test a hypothesis of simple structure or any other hypothesis. Principal Components merely finds the dimensions of a large data set on the basis of dividing total variance into as many distinguishable groups as possible and in this regard it is essentially descriptive.

Therefore, Factor Analysis differs from Principal Components Analysis in both computation and more importantly in the objective of the analysis. Whereas Principal Components is useful for determining dimensions among the total variability of a data set (which can be divided between unique variance to one variable and common variance shared by several variables), Factor Analysis focuses on the variance common (shared) to several variables. The distinction between shared and common variance is discussed in more detail in the section on the differences between Principal Components Analysis and Factor Analysis. Moreover, Factor Analysis has the added capability of testing hypotheses that can be stated in the form of intercorrelations between variables.

It is not possible to discuss just one method completely in a realm divorced from the other technique. The processes of one method are similar to the other. This has led to considerable confusion in the literature and sometimes the confusion of each technique labelled as the other method, most usually Principal Components Analysis is mistakenly called Factor Analysis. In order to attempt a clear presentation an effort has been made to totally divide the techniques with Principal Components Analysis discussed first, followed by Factor Analysis. At the beginning of the discussion on Factor Analysis the difference between the two methods is discussed in more detail. Also, in the Factor Analysis discussion where rotation of factors is discussed, the question of rotating principal components (not strictly part of Principal Components Analysis) is discussed. At the end of the chapter some common variations of the input of data into both Principal Components and Factor Analysis are outlined.

Factor analytic methods are particularly useful in cultural analysis because of the questions raised by cultural differences. Do differences exist and in what form? To what degree do tourists perceive cultural differences and how important are these differences to their motivations to travel and satisfaction with travel experiences? Factor Analysis and Principal Components Analysis can be used to measure cultural attitudes and to help in assessing the existence and extent of such differences.

Principal Components Analysis

Principal Components Analysis is a method of classification that derives dimensions among a set of variables measuring the same population (using samples of the same size). Thus it takes a group of variables measured over a sample or population of observations, and examines the interrelationships among them. The result of the analysis is a new set of variables (which replace the original variables) and which show a set of interrelated variable (meaning original variable) relationships. Hence the new set of variables becomes the focus of interpretation. The reasons for searching out the possible combinations of original variables to create the new variables are three-fold:

1. To remove collinearity.

The new variables could be generated in such a manner as to reorganize the original variables into groups having as little collinearity as possible.

2. To reduce the number of original variables.

If significant collinearity exists among a set of variables, a reduction in the number of meaningful variables may be possible. Collinearity suggests that two or more variables are measuring the same characteristic. The new variables generated can be used to indicate a reduced set of variables (since the new variables are generated stepwise in order of significance) eliminating redundancy and aiding in the identification of the most useful variables for prediction.

3. To identify dimension or classes (groups) among the set of observations on the basis of a set of variable measures.

The analysis can be used to search for order (dimensions) in a large data set. Each new variable forms a dimension in the data set upon which each original variable loads to varying degrees. The meaning of the dimensions can then be considered.

If the dimensions were predicted in advance of the analysis the meaning of the dimensions would exist prior to the analysis. Such a process is possible and is called Factor Analysis.

Tests of significance

Although Factor Analysis and Principal Components Analysis are essentially statistical techniques, they are also essentially descriptive rather than statistically inferential. Hypotheses can be generally tested and detailed description can be formed into inference, but not statistical inference in the sense that a statistical test of significance is applied. Factor analytic techniques do not rely upon a statistical test of significance. There is an assumption that a representative sample will be analysed (a requirement of research design) but the requirement of a normal distribution is rarely met. Tests on the statistical significance of component loadings are rarely used.

A rudimentary precaution is to use the sphericity test on the correlation matrix. This tests the null hypothesis that the population correlation matrix is an identity matrix (diagonal terms equal 1 and off diagonal terms equal 0), which means that the variance for each variable are uncorrelated in the population from which the sample was drawn, and the observed correlations differ from zero only by chance. The name of the test derives from the notion that the population space of the standardized variables will be spherical. The test therefore assumes the sample population is distributed as a multivariate normal distribution. Bartlett (1950) originated the test, which is a Chi-square test of the null hypothesis. The consequence is that a nonsignificant Chi-square at 95 per cent indicates the correlation matrix should not be analysed.

Another measure of sample adequacy is the Kaiser-Meyer-Olkin (KMO) measure that is expressed as an index between zero and one. This index uses the measure of partial correlation, which is the correlation between two variables when the influence of the other variables is eliminated. The index is calculated by dividing out the simple correlation coefficient squared between all variable pairs, by the sum of the squared partial correlation coefficients between all variable pairs. If the partial correlation effect is small relative to the total correlation the KMO measure will be close to one, and this is the better outcome because this means correlations between pairs of variables are explained by other variables, that is, meaningful factors (components) are likely. The level of KMO required is somewhat subjective but logically should exceed 0.5 because a point beyond a 50 per cent index would normally be accepted as more likely than not to derive useful factors (components). Hair *et al.* (1995) suggests 0.7 as the bottom level of acceptability, 0.7 to be middling, above 0.8 to be meritorious, and above 0.9 marvellous.

Yet another indicator is to examine the partial correlation coefficients. The SPSS program produces the negative image of the partial correlations in an 'anti-image correlation' matrix. The proportion of large coefficients should be small. The diagonals of the matrix are the equivalent of the KMO for each individual variable (as opposed to all variable pairs) and SPSS terms these diagonals the measures of sampling adequacy (MSA). Large MSA values are expected for the development of useful factors (components). When it is necessary to reduce the number of variables those variables with a small MSA are the first to consider removing. However, the theory for the inclusion of particular variables must be considered as equally important.

Because SPSS now outputs the above statistics, they are commonly used. However, factor analytic techniques are mathematical and not statistical, so that they do not depend upon such tests for their use. It is also necessary to remember that the tests above depend upon large samples, subjectively above 100 or more directly defined as the number of cases (N) minus the number of variables (X) being greater than 30.

Segmental correlation

The basis of both Principal Components and Factor Analysis is that each variable can be divided into several independent parts in terms of its association with other variables and, therefore, that each correlation coefficient can be segmented similarly into independent parts.

Hence it is possible to identify groups of variables within each of which correlations are high but between which correlations are nearly zero. For example, in the level of service quality there may be three major measurable components: responsiveness to guests, confirmation of quality, and cultural awareness. However, none of the indicators is all dominant at any one time. In fact, we could possibly categorize three types of combination: factors A, B and C:

	Per cent		
X	A	B	C
Responsiveness	50 +	10 +	30
Confirmation	60 +	·5 +	30
Awareness	70 +	10 +	15

The new hybrid distribution is type A to C. Notice that for each of the original variables the sum is not 100 per cent. This indicates that there is a residual (error) in the distribution of quality indicators that is not related to any of the three general types.

Each general type is called a *segment* (S). Hence for each original variable (X) we have a regression model:

$X_n = f(S_1, S_2, \ldots, S_n) \pm \varepsilon.$

We have, in fact, three variables:

$X1 = f(S_1, S_2, \ldots, S_n) \pm \varepsilon$

$X2 = f(S_1, S_2, \ldots, S_n) \pm \varepsilon$

$X3 = f(S_1, S_2, \ldots, S_n) \pm \varepsilon$

The objective is to determine the contribution of each segment to each variable.

In Principal Components Analysis the error terms become segments. Thus each original variable becomes related to a series of components, one of which may well be a residual term. The components analysis is thus a closed model with all variance in the original variables assigned. This results in a set of components (new X variables) whose number equals the number of original variables.

In Factor Analysis the residual forms unique variance, which is not accounted for. The remaining common variance is divided into a set of factors (which are similar to components). The total variance in Factor Analysis is standardized to 1.0, so that unless the residuals sum to zero (highly unlikely) the sum of the variances of each variable must be less than 1.0. Therefore, the number of factors must be less than the number of variables.

Simple representation of correlation and component extraction

The most readily understood method of representing correlations between dimensions of data in multi-dimensional space is geometrical. In addition, the most readily understood method for extracting components (or factors) is the centroid method, which is not used today with the development of computers, and has been replaced by matrix algebra. Consequently, in representing the correlations geometrically and using the centroid method, the objective is to provide a relatively easy understanding of the processes involved.

Correlations

The product-moment correlation (r) is the square root of the proportion of the variance in X1 related to the variance in X2, and vice versa. Looking at just two variables (X1 and X2), the perpendicular from the three quarters point (correlation of 0.75) on X1 must meet the end of the line representing X2, and a perpendicular from the three-quarters point on X2 must meet the end of the line representing X1. Thus, each variable casts a shadow on the other, and the length of the shadow represents the correlation between them (Figure 7.1).

Basic trigonometry is used to find the angle between the two variables. The cosine of the angle between the lines representing two variables equals the correlation between those two variables. Cosines vary between −1 and +1 like correlation coefficients. A cosine of zero is equal to 90° and r of zero. So lines at right angles represent uncorrelated variables and this is termed an *orthogonal* relationship. Therefore, it follows that a cosine of 180° is equal to a correlation of −1.0, so that negative correla-

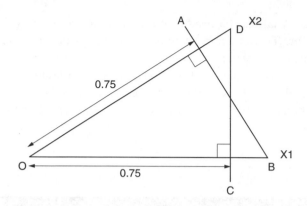

Figure 7.1 Geometric correlation between two variables X1 and X2

tions are shown by obtuse angles and a −1.0 correlation by a straight line passing through the origin.

Looking now at a two-dimensional scatter diagram (refer to Figure 7.2) the form of a set of normally distributed values varies according to the correlation between X1 and X2. In Figure 7.2A the two variables X1 and X2 are completely uncorrelated and the bivariate distribution is circular. In Figure 7.2B the variables are correlated positively (positively because of the elongation on the positive axes) and the scatter of values is elliptical rather than circular. The axes of the ellipse are separated by the angle (Θ), which has a cosine of 0.58 (hence $r_{12}=0.58$) and the shape of the ellipse is defined by the correlation between the two variables. In Figure 7.2C the correlation is greater and the ellipse much more elongated.

Correlation matrix

It is impossible to display correlation matrices in two-dimensional space. For example:

	Correlations				*Angles*		
	X1	X2	X3		X1	X2	X3
X1	1.00	0.64	0.83	X1	0	50	34
X2	0.64	1.00	0.21	X2	50	0	78
X3	0.83	0.21	1.00	X3	34	78	0

Having drawn the correlation $r_{12}=0.64$ as 50 it would then be impossible to locate a vector for X3 which is both 78° from X2 and 34° from X1. A

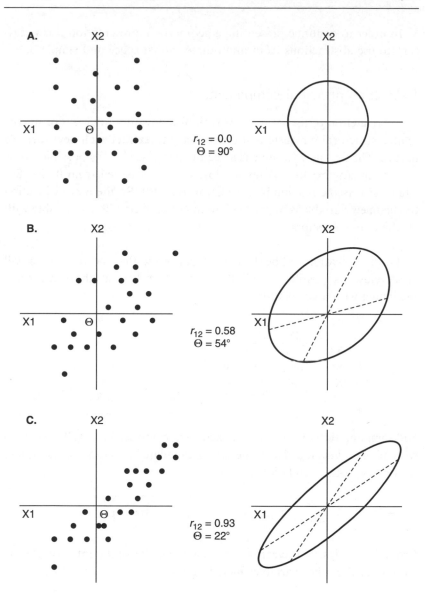

Figure 7.2 Two-dimensional presentation of correlation

three-dimensional diagram would be required. The number of dimensions required is equal to the number of variables. Thus, four variables at right angles to each other (uncorrelated) would be all orthogonal forming a four-dimensional space.

In order to continue presenting a geometric representation it is necessary to use abstractions from multi-dimensional space and simple data.

Extracting principal components

In the reduction of the total set of variables down to a new set of uncorrelated structural dimensions it is necessary to extract each new variable in turn. The first new variable is a vector that is as close as possible to the vectors already existing. Angular closeness is measured from 0° to 180° where 180° is the maximum correlation of −1.0. So the aim in locating the first new variable is to get as close to either 0° or 180° as possible with all the original vectors.

The best location will be the mean location, so that the new vector will be as close as possible to all the original vectors at the same time. Beginning with a correlation matrix:

	X1	X2	X3		
X1	1.00	0.64	0.83		
X2	0.64	1.00	0.21		
X3	0.83	0.21	1.00		
SUM	2.47	1.85	2.04	6.36	= Total Sum

and summing the correlations for each variable to see how well correlated with all the others it is. Next, the sum is calculated as a ratio of the square root of the total correlations:

	X1	X2	X3
$\text{Sum}/\sqrt{\text{Total Sum}}$ =	0.98	0.73	0.81

From this analysis it is clear that X1 has the highest total intercorrelation with all of the other variables including itself.

If every correlation were 1.00 the maximum value of the total sum (TS) of the correlations would be n^2 or in our example TS $= 9$ (3^2). The square root of this value ($\sqrt{\text{TS}} = 3$) is the maximum correlation sum possible for one variable. Hence $\sqrt{\text{TS}}$ is the maximum sum possible for any one variable and as such is the new variable or principal component. The ratio of the sum of the correlations for each variable to $\sqrt{\text{TS}}$ is thus the correlation of each variable with the principal component. Thus, (rounded):

	X1	X2	X3	TS
Sum of Correlations	2.47	1.85	2.04	6.36
Sum/$\sqrt{TS}$	0.98	0.73	0.81	
Angles	11°	43°	36°	

For each component three separate indices can be calculated concerning the relationship of the component to each of the original variables:

1. the correlation (cosine of the angle);
2. the angle between the component and each original variable;
3. the correlation squared (coefficient of determination) or the proportion of the variance associated with the component.

For example, given Figure 7.3:

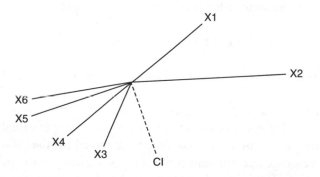

Figure 7.3 Geometric relationship between six variables and one principal component

representing six original variables and the first principal component; the following indices could be derived for Figure 7.3 (refer to Table 7.1):

Table 7.1   Correlations, correlations squared and angles for the component in Figure 7.3

Variable	Correlation(r)I	Angle	r^2
X1	0.4732	140	0.2239
X1	0.3722	85	0.1385
X3	0.9615	5	0.9245
X4	0.9051	47	0.8192
X5	−0.2043	107	0.0417
X6	−0.5000	111	0.2500
		Σ =	2.3978

The correlations are known as component *loadings* and are inter-preted in the same way as Pearson product-moment correlation coeffi-cients. Hence the r^2 values are coefficients of determination, which indicate the proportion of the variance in the original variable, which can be associated with the component: for X3, 92.45 per cent of its variance is associated with the variance of CI. Consequently, the sum of the squared loadings indicates the total variance accounted for by the component. This sum value is known as the *eigenvalue* (λ). Therefore:

$$\lambda_i = \sum_{j=1}^{n} L_{ij}^2 \tag{1}$$

where: L_{ij} is the loading for variable j on component i.

In the example above, lambda $= 2.3978$.

The eigenvalue alone says little; however when it is related to the total variance in the correlation matrix it becomes a measure of relative importance for each principal component. The total variance in the matrix is $n \times 1.0^2 = n$, given n variables each with a standardized variance of 1.0 (that is the case if the component accounted for the total variance of each variable, and consequently each correlation ± 1.0). In order to compare each eigenvalue it is merely calculated as a percentage of n. For the data in Table 7.1:

$$100(\lambda 1/n) = 100(2.3978/6) = 39.96.$$

The example data suggests that the first component accounts for 40 per cent of the total variance, which is related to variables X3 and X4 to a considerable degree. This is confirmed by looking back to the angles (Figure 7.3) presented earlier. This analysis leaves some 60 per cent of the variance in the data unac-counted for and raises the question of whether there is some general pattern to the residuals, in those por-tions of the variables not related to the mean pattern. To answer this question the *second component is extracted.*

This process requires: all the proportions of the inter-correlations, which are a function of the correlations of the individual variables with the component, are subtracted from the original correlations.

Thus for our example of six variables discussed previously, if we have an assumed correlation of

$r_{12} = 0.6381$ and take $LI_1 = 0.4732$ (the first loading X1 for the first component) and $LI_2 = 0.3722$; with $LI_1^2 = 0.2239$ as part of the correlation r_{11} associated with the component, LI_2^2 as part of r_{22} associated with the component, and $(LI_1)(LI_2)$ as part of r_{12} associated with the component, then:

$$r_{12} = 0.6381$$

and:

$$(LI_1)(LI_2) = (0.4732)(0.3722) = 0.1761$$

so that: $r_{12} - (LI_1)(LI_2) = 0.6381 - 0.1761 = 0.4620$.

Therefore, the correlation between X1 and X2, once the influence of the first component has been removed is 0.4620, and is the partial correlation, $(r_{12}.I.)$.

The first component is extracted in the above manner to produce a new correlation matrix made up of partial correlations $(r_{ij} - (LI_i)(LI_j)$, where i and j are variables). A second principal component can now be extracted as an average vector from this partial correlation matrix in the same manner as the first component was extracted from the original correlation matrix.

In this process variables that have loaded highly on a previous component will have little remaining variance to be loaded highly on subsequent components, while variables that have not loaded highly and have remaining variance are candidates for loading highly on subsequent components.

Furthermore, the second and subsequent components will be orthogonal to the first or previous components because the residuals from the previous component are uncorrelated with the first component (otherwise they would not be residual; they would have loaded onto the previous component and increased the correlation). Since zero correlation is shown by orthogonal vectors in our diagrams the second component when added into Figure 7.3 becomes right-angular with the first component (see Figure 7.4). The indices shown in Table 7.2 could be derived for Figure 7.4.

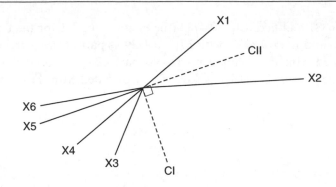

Figure 7.4 Geometric relationship of Figure 7.3 with a second principal component

Table 7.2   Correlations, correlations squared and angles for the second component in Figure 7.4

Variable	Correlation(r)II	Angle	r^2
X1	0.9658	45	0.9328
X2	0.9830	3	0.9663
X3	−0.3416	107	0.1167
X4	−0.1210	132	0.0146
X5	−0.2132	170	0.0455
X6	−0.3101	161	0.0962

$$\Sigma = 2.1721 = \text{II (eigenvalue)}$$

As a proportion of total variance: $(2.1721/6)100 = 36.2020$ or 36 per cent. This value is below the 40 per cent accounted for by LI, which is always the case as the second mean vector component is extracted from the residual variance, which is less important than the original variance. Hence successive eigenvalues become smaller and the amount of total variance they explain is less.

Adding the two eigenvalues: $2.3978 + 2.1721 = 4.5699$ we have a large proportion of the total variance $(n=6)$ accounted for. However, at least a third component would need to be extracted from the remaining variance to complete the analysis.

Communality

A set of loadings is derived once all the principal components have been extracted:

Loadings

Variable	CI	II	III	IV	V	VI	h²
X1	0.4732	0.9658	–	–	–	–	–
X2	0.3722	0.9830	–	–	–	–	–
X3	0.9615	−0.3416	–	–	–	–	–
X4	0.9051	−0.1210	–	–	–	–	–
X5	−0.2043	−0.2132	–	–	–	–	–
X6	−0.5000	−0.3101	–	–	–	–	–

Eigenvalue $= \sum$

The communality (h^2) is the sum of the squared loading for each variable:

$$h_j^2 = \sum_{i=1}^{k} L_{ij}^2 \tag{2}$$

where: L_{ij} is the loading for variable j on component i

k is the number of components.

Therefore, it is the proportion of the variance for each variable accounted for by all the components. The communality must equal 1.0 when the number of components used in its calculation equals the number of variables.

Scores

In Principal Components Analysis it is desirable to have a measure of the relationship of each original data case to each of the linear principal components. These measures are called the *component scores* and are calculated by:

$$Sc_{ik} = \sum_{j=1}^{n} D_{ij} L_{jk}$$

where: Sc_{ik} = the component score of observation (case); on component k, summed over all n original variables.

D_{ij} = the standardized value for observation i on variable j.
L_{jk} = the loading of variable j on component k.

Hence, the components are determined on the basis of the original variable loading with the component. So, if a case has a high value for the variable with a large component loading then it has a high value on the component.

Each original measure for each original variable is standardized to become a Z score (refer to Hypothesis Testing in the Web support material), and these measures are represented as D_{ij}. So, if the original data that generated our previous example in Figure 7.4 and Tables 7.1 and 7.2, for the first case were as Z scores:

	X1	X2	X3	X4	X5	X6
Case One (D_{ij})	−1.32	+0.08	−2.31	+1.52	−0.80	+0.93

and given the component loadings previously listed for CI:

| Component One (L_{jk}) | 0.4732 | 0.3722 | 0.9615 | 0.9051 | −0.2043 | −0.5000 |

then:

$$Sc_{iI} = (-1.32)(0.4732) + (0.08)(0.3722) + (-2.31)(0.9615)$$
$$+ (1.52)(0.9051) + (-0.80) - (0.2043) + (0.93) - (0.5000) = 1.7417$$

which is the first component score of the first case value for the first component.

There will be as many scores as original case values (N) times components K, or N × K component scores, represented in a matrix. Each matrix of component scores is usually termed a raw component score matrix. This is because the standard deviations of the scores for each component vary, although the mean does not, being equal to zero. The variation in the raw scores, like the variation of residuals around a line of best fit, will reflect how closely the component (line of best fit) accounts for the scatter of cases. Since this measure of explained variance in Principal Components Analysis is given as the eigenvalue for each component, it is not surprising that the standard deviation of the raw scores for each component is the same as the eigenvalue for each component.

Since the objective of producing a components scores matrix is to examine how the individual data cases are related to each of the components, the differing standard deviations interfere with interpretation. The scale of each component's scores varies. Consequently, it is considered desirable to rescale all the raw scores to have not only a mean of zero but the same standard deviation of one (the mean has remained zero because the raw data used for each component score calculation was standardized as a Z value (D_{ij}). Z scores have a mean of zero and standard deviation of one. However, the standard deviations vary because of the multiplication of D_{ij} by component loadings of different sizes (L_{jk}). The rescaling can be achieved by converting the raw scores to Z values. However, it is more common to divide each raw score by the eigenvalue for the respective component on which it is listed, having the effect of expressing each raw score as a proportion of the total variance explained and reducing the scores to a common base.

The result of the standardizing procedure is to produce a new matrix of standardized component scores to replace the matrix of raw component scores.

Factor Analysis

Factor Analysis is a term that stands for several different types of analysis including Principal Axes Factor Analysis, Alpha Factor Analysis, Image Factor Analysis, and Direct Factor Analysis, each of which may be rotated in an orthogonal or oblique manner. In addition the target of rotation may be either 'simple structure' or defined in advance of the analysis. These latter subjects will be discussed in more detail below, suffice it to point out that there are several possible analytic processes covered under the general title Factor Analysis and each has a particular advantage in particular problem situations.

The most commonly used Factor Analysis is the Principal Axes method, which is identical to Principal Components Analysis except for the use of communality estimates in the diagonal of the correlation matrix and the rotation normally applied in the analysis. Because of the similarities in name and calculation between Principal Components Analysis and Principal Axes Factor Analysis the two have often been confused. Additionally, the current literature discussing the methods in text form rarely manages to give any adequate distinction between the two methods. Moreover, some books list Principal Components Analysis as a subsection of Factor Analysis to make the confusion complete.

The difference between Principal Components Analysis and Factor Analysis

The major difference between the two methods is the diagonal in the correlation matrix. In Principal Components Analysis the diagonals of the matrix are one:

	X1	X2	X3
X1	1.00	0.50	0.60
X2	0.50	1.00	0.70
X3	0.60	0.70	1.00

In this model the components derived account for all the variance in each variable, including that 'shared' with other variables. Hence the total variance = 1.0 is accounted for. Since, at least theoretically, each variable will have some variance unique to itself, apart from any shared variance, in order to account for all the variance, there must be as many components as variables. Given the stepwise calculation of components whereby the first component accounts for the most variance and subsequent components for the most remaining variance, the last components are likely to have only one variable loaded significantly on them, representing the unique variance for that variable.

The terms used to divide the variance are *unique* variance, which is composed of individual variation of a given variable including sampling error, and *common* variance, which refers to the shared variance between variables (see Figure 7.5).

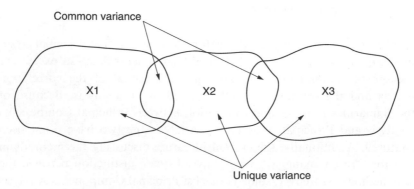

Figure 7.5 The relationship between unique and common variance

Factor Analysis accounts for the common variance as opposed to Principal Components Analysis, which accounts for total variance. Hence the diagonal of the correlation matrix must become some measure of the common variance between each set of variables and not one. Since the factors derived from Factor Analysis account for only part of the total variance there is no theoretical expectation that the number of factors will equal the number of variables. In fact, the number of factors may well be fewer than the number of variables, which is a most desirable trait of Factor Analysis, aiding in the reduction of the number of variables.

Unfortunately, Factor Analysis has got a problem in the measurement of common variance for the diagonals of the correlation matrix. It is the solution of this problem, determining the common variance, which is the major reason for the different types of Factor Analysis techniques. The most common method (Principal Axes Factor Analysis) employs the squared multiple correlation coefficient of each variable against all the other variables in the analysis. The diagonal calculated in this way is a good guess of the communality. The sum of these principal diagonal ('trace') values is the total common variance to be analysed.

This procedure weights the importance of each variable in the Factor Analysis by the strength of its correlation with all the other variables. As a result of this weighting of each variable the factors are pulled closer to the variables with the larger communalities. For example, given:

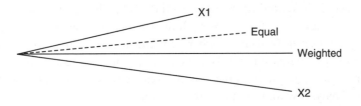

where there are two variables X1 and X2, and X2 is longer than X1 because of the weighting process, the factor will not lie at *equal* distances between the two variables but will be pulled toward the more heavily weighted variable, X2. Principal Components Analysis treats all variables equally (they all have the same length); the diagonal trace is equal to 1.0 in all cases, whereas Factor Analysis does not. Hence Principal Components Analysis would extract the line '*equal*' whereas a Factor Analysis would extract the line '*weighted*'.

The main question that arises from the difference between Principal Components Analysis and Factor Analysis is how important the difference is. In short, the importance of the difference is all encompassing, so much so, that Principal Components Analysis should not be considered simply one of several Factor Analysis models, but a separate technique. The components derived from Principal Components Analysis identify inter-relationships among groups of variables and unique variance, so that some components consist of both unique and common variance; while others consist only of unique variance. The mixture of variance remains largely indecipherable, although the component loadings hint at the relationship. Some components have several variables loaded thereon (often variables showing some inter-correlation in the correlation matrix), while some components have only one variable loading highly on them.

Factor Analysis removes the confusion by accounting only for common variance by the weighting of variables according to their inter-relationships in the correlation trace.

Therefore, the choice of method depends upon the problem to be solved. If the researcher wants to classify all the variation in the data set – for example, to draw dimensions of movement in a matrix of the travel of people from a set of source origins to all destinations in the set – then Principal Components Analysis is the appropriate method. The fundamental total dimensions of travel (such as dimension one movement to sunny, seaside leisure resorts) will be drawn out, as will movement that is unique to one place and less easily explained. On the other hand, if the researcher is attempting to understand only the inter-relationships between variables – for example how socio-economic status can be defined from several variables, where it is the inter-relationship (common variance) that defines the nebulous concept of socio-economic status and not just unique variance associated with one variable – then Factor Analysis would be more appropriate.

As a result of the above it could be argued that Factor Analysis is the best method for determining whether groups of variables exist. If groups do exist they will have shared common variance. These groups can be induced from an experimental analysis – although it is not necessary in using Factor Analysis to have hypothesized the groups' existence as is often stated in literature. However, if an inductive process is used the interpretation of the resulting dimensions may be difficult. This is equally true for Principal Components Analysis except that the wider range of variance (resulting in diversity of component loadings) may allow for easier classification in some situations.

Factor rotation

There are several methods for rotating the factors around the origin so as to increase the 'fit' of the factors to groups of variables. This rotation is necessary because the first factor located (using the Principal Axes method) is a mean location between variables, and in many cases this may not distinguish groupings to the best extent. For example, see Figure 7.6a.

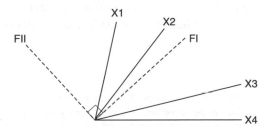

Figure 7.6a Factors for rotation among four variables. *Note:* The variables are given as equal lengths to maintain a simple explanation. In fact, with a Factor Analysis method each variable would be weighted by the communality and the lines would be different lengths to represent the weighting process

given the four variables X1 to X4, in the above relationship, there appear to be two groups: (X1 and X2) and (X3 and X4); however, Factor One divides the two groups in order to achieve a mean location. Ideally, the rotation of the factors around the origin would move the factors into a position that would locate them as close as possible to each group but as far away from each other as possible (see Figure 7.6b).

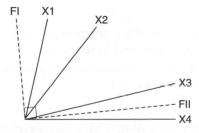

Figure 7.6b Factors for rotation among four variables

Before a method was derived to achieve this result, analysts produced graphical representations of the factors and visually selected the best possible rotations. The problem was, of course, that no two analysts would select exactly the same rotation. The problem was solved by Thurstone in 1947 when he developed the concept of a *simple structure* which is a normative (ideal) model toward which the rotation can aim, although it would never be achieved because of the unreal normative definition. The concept of simple structure gave Factor Analysis a mathematical rigidity so that two people conducting the same analysis on the same data would now come to the same result.

Simple structure is defined by a factor loadings matrix where every variable has a loading of either +1.0 or −1.0 on one factor, and 0.0 on all others. The actual factor, which has the loading of ±1.0, is not specified. For example, see Table 7.3.

Table 7.3   Example loadings matrix for simple structure in Factor Analysis

	Factor loadings		
Variable	*I*	*II*	*III*
X1	+1.0	0.0	0.0
X2	−1.0	0.0	0.0
X3	0.0	0.0	+1.0
X4	0.0	+1.0	0.0
X5	0.0	0.0	−1.0
X6	0.0	−1.0	0.0

The factors are rotated around the origin to get as close as possible to this ideal norm. In order for the ideal to be attained, the variables would have to be perfectly correlated or uncorrelated in a given pattern and the trace estimates would all have to be 1.0.

Of the several rotation methods that have been developed, two general types have stood the test of time: orthogonal and oblique rotation.

Orthogonal rotation

Orthogonal rotation is way and above the most commonly used method. It retains the notion of right-angles between factors, that is, the factors are always kept at the maximum degree (90°) for an uncorrelated state. As said earlier, when factors are separated by a right-angle they are uncorrelated and said to be *orthogonal* to each other.

Using our previous example in Figures 7.6a and b, an orthogonal rotation is shown where the dotted factor lines rotate clockwise from their position in Figure 7.6a to their location in Figure 7.6b. Such an orthogonal rotation maintains the right-angle and improves the delineation of the two groups.

The most commonly used method of orthogonal rotation is *Kaiser's varimax rotation*, which maximizes the variance in the cosines.

The number of factors extracted is vital to a rotation, since this determines the number of groups of variables defined. Every rotation is unique to each number of factors rotated. If only three factors from a possible total of 10 are rotated, the opportunity to closely define these groups is more enhanced than if say six factors are rotated. As each additional factor is added into the rotation, more groups must be distinguished, and the difference between the groups becomes more blurred. If only one factor is rotated, the object of the analysis is lost (to distinguish groups), and there is no need to rotate. In fact rotation may reduce the loadings for the first factor in favour of other factors.

Once the factors have been rotated, the sum of the squared loadings on any factor is no longer termed the eigenvalue. The term eigenvalue refers to that specific mean vector in the correlation matrix determined *prior* to rotation.

The question within Factor Analysis becomes: how many factors should be rotated? Kaiser suggested that the number of factors should be equal to the number having eigenvalues greater than one. The idea is sensible since the sum of all n roots (eigenvalues) is equal to n, so that a value of one is par, and surely if another factor is to be added, it would be preferable to have it account for more than an average contribution. From the experience of many analyses, and quite apart from any mathematical justification in theory, factors retained that exceed an eigenvalue of one are known to be more readily interpretable than factors with less than or equal to an eigenvalue of one.

Other proposals have been made for selecting the number of factors, for example, Cattell (1966) suggested a graphical method called the scree test, which is based on plotting the sizes of the eigenvalues and taking only those factors whose eigenvalues fall above the evening out point (scree slope) in the decreasing eigenvalue plot. These alternative proposals offer no more or less than Kaiser's test of an eigenvalue greater than one. The interpretation of the resulting factors is discussed in the example later in 'Cultural analysis using Principal Components Analysis'. There are other methods of orthogonal rotation (see Mulaik, 1972) including transvarimax methods (equamax and ratiomax) described in Saunders (1962), parsimax (Crawford, 1967), and simultaneous orthogonal varimax and parsimax (Horst, 1965).

Oblique rotation

Oblique rotation is used only when orthogonal rotations are not suited to identifying group structure. An assumption has to be made that the factors that result are independent (orthogonal), which may well not be the case in any given analysis. In the case of oblique rotation the angle between the factors can be other than 90° (see Figure 7.7).

The simple structure now changes and it is hypothesized that every variable has one loading of $+1.0$ or -1.0, but the other loading no longer needs to be 0.0. Of course, an orthogonal result could theoretically be reached if the groups are in fact unrelated.

A similar problem to orthogonal rotation occurs in defining an appropriate number of factors to rotate. Kaiser's test of an eigenvalue greater than one is normally used.

An additional problem occurs with the degree of obliqueness that can be allowed. Each additional factor added could divide already existing groups, especially for the last factors rotated. The more factors that were incorporated the closer the solution to one variable per factor would be the ultimate result, if all factors were rotated.

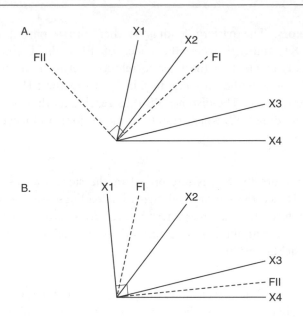

Figure 7.7 Oblique factor rotation

Unlike orthogonal rotation, two factor loadings are obtained from an oblique rotation, the *structure loading* and the *pattern loading*. The following diagram shows the difference between the two loadings.

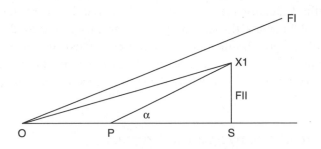

Only one variable X1 is shown for simplicity. The structure loading is obtained in the same way as orthogonal rotation; the X1 line casts a shadow reflecting its correlation onto the factor giving the line O, S. The pattern loading line is drawn parallel to other factors, in this case, FI, bisecting the FII line at P. The distance OP is called the pattern loading, for X1 on Factor II. The pattern loading shows the correlation between the variable and the factor, independent of the effects of the other factors. The pattern loading is therefore a partial correlation between X1 and FII when the effect of FI is held constant. The angle α is equivalent to the inter-correlation between the factors, and the line X1 − P is the only one to join X1 to factor FII, which would produce this angle. The distance PS thus represents that portion of the structure loading, OS, which results from the joint influence of factors I and II on X1.

The structure loading is interpreted in the same way as orthogonal loadings. Hence the factors and structure loadings are really the main focus of interpretation. The pattern matrix gives all the partial correlations between variables and factors when the influence of the other factors is held constant.

No communalities, eigenvalues or sums of squared loadings are output from an oblique rotation because they cannot be interpreted. Joint variance can be double counted or omitted in these measures.

The Oblimin method is probably the most commonly used method of oblique rotation because it is available in SPSS, Carroll (1960). Other methods include Kaiser's (1970) second generation Little Jiffy, the Oblimax method (Saunders, 1961), promax (Hendrikson and White, 1964) and Maxplane (Cattell and Muerle, 1960). Use of the Oblimin direct method (Jennrich and Sampson, 1966) requires a setting of the degree of obliqueness through a specific parameter named delta. For delta equal to zero the factors are highly correlated and they become less correlated as delta becomes negative. For most problems delta should be set between zero and −5 (where the factors become less oblique).

Rotation to alternative 'simple structure'

If the Factor Analysis is to be used to test a hypothesis, that hypothesis concerning group structure could be stated in the form of an alternative 'simple' structure, to which the Factor Analysis could rotate.

The hypothesis to be tested must state the expected distribution of common variance between factors for a set of variables, so that each variable is hypothesized to associate with a particular factor.

Rotation and Principal Components Analysis

Principal components with eigenvalues greater than one (using Kaiser's test) are commonly rotated using an orthogonal rotation, such as varimax. However, unlike Factor Analysis there is no relevant 'simple structure' to which such a rotation can aim, or a norm against which rotated loadings can be compared. Simple structure as a hypothesis refers to common variance only and does not allow for the unique variance distributed among principal components.

Consequently, the rotation of a Principal Components Analysis cannot result in a Factor Analysis, although, as it so happens, the difference between the two methods is often not great. Rotated components with eigenvalues greater than one are usually better group identifiers than unrotated components. However, rotated components cannot be used to test for a hypothesis of structure the way rotated factors can. Rotation of components is not in itself a hypothesis testing procedure, but merely an attempt to more clearly identify components.

Factor scores

Factor scores are the equivalent of principal component scores, discussed earlier, for Factor Analysis. Unlike component scores that are directly calculable, factor scores can only be estimated. This is because Factor Analysis concerns only common variance, and each observed value has a combination of common and unique variance in unknown proportions.

The estimation process involves regressing the data matrix onto the loadings matrix, and thus assuming that the average proportions of common and unique variance in the loadings are the same for each observation. Such an assumption is quite a major draw-back to Factor Analysis. Moreover, the further away from simple structure any loadings matrix is, the more difficult it is to interpret such estimated scores.

This problem of estimating useful factor scores has not been overcome, and until it is, the factor score estimates if used, could be highly misleading.

However, the obvious solution to the problem of mixed variance in the basic data values is to begin the analysis knowing the proportion of unique and common variance for the observations. A multiple regression can provide this information, where the residual measures unique variance and the predicted value common variance. Hence *Image Factor Analysis* has developed as an alternative Factor Analysis method based upon the correlations among the common variance elements only, after the unique variance elements (measured by the residuals from multiple regression) have been removed. In this way the factor scores can be computed directly and do not have to be estimated.

The problem faced by a user of Image Factor Analysis, who has chosen this method to obtain useable factor scores, is that the original data has been transformed prior to the Factor Analysis (by removal of unique variance) and the loadings which result, and even the factors generated, are different from what would have been obtained using a conventional Factor Analysis. Image Factor Analysis is best used only when it is essential to use Factor Analysis to test the hypothesis of simple structure, and it is also essential to derive useful and accurate factor scores for the purpose of the study in hand.

Controlling the input matrix in both Principal Components and Factor Analysis

Most modern analysis procedures allow the analyst to vary the nature of the input matrix into both Principal Components and Factor Analysis. That is, the input matrix does not have to be in the two forms already discussed: a correlation matrix for Principal Components with diagonals of 1.0, and a correlation matrix with communalities as the trace for Factor Analysis. The eigenvalues and eigenvectors of factor analytic methods can be extracted from any square symmetric matrix.

Two common alternative matrices can be used, and possibly some other forms. The most common alternative input matrix is a covariance matrix, and the second alternative is a binary matrix.

Covariance matrix input

In cases where the observations have magnitude, which is essential to the derivation of meaningful factors or components, a covariance matrix of cross-products can be used. Because cross-products do not, like the correlations, vary between ±1.0, the loadings emphasize the absolute size of the original values.

For example, where the data for the analysis is the movement of tourists between regions, the volume of flow is essential to the observation of components or factors of grouped tourist movement. Such an analysis would draw out groups of regions that are linked by their in (or out) flow of tourists by volume flow.

The data used in such an analysis must be measured on a uniform scale to be meaningful. If, for example, the volume of tourism were measured in various ways (for example by residence versus nationality) for each region, the results could not be interpreted.

The choice between using a Principal Components Analysis or a Factor Analysis with a covariance matrix input would seem to be unimportant and if the factor method is the Principal Axes method there should be no difference in results.

Binary matrix input

In a binary matrix a value of one indicates a direct connection between two variables and a value of zero no direct connection. The components or factors that result group the variables on the basis of their interconnections.

For example, a network (of roads, airways, wires, etc.) is made up of nodes and lines linking the nodes. The nodes are the variables of the analysis. In the situation where two nodes are connected, the input matrix shows a one and for a disconnection a zero. Hence, given the network below:

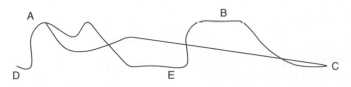

the matrix becomes:

		Nodes				
		A	B	C	D	E
	A	0	0	1	1	1
Nodes	B	0	0	1	0	1
	C	1	0	0	0	0
	D	1	0	0	0	0
	E	1	1	0	0	0

Factor and Principal Components Analysis of such a matrix will identify the major linkage patterns. In a truly complex network, where such linkages are not obvious, such an analysis may be used to either describe the system, or to test a hypothesis about the nature of the linkages. In the particular case of a binary matrix, the difference between using a Factor Analysis and Principal Components Analysis merely lies in the nature of the eigenvectors of the loading matrix; they are standardized in Principal Components Analysis, and unstandardized in Factor Analysis.

Alternative input matrix modes for both Principal Components and Factor Analysis

Apart from the inputting of different correlation matrices there is another question concerning the choice of data matrix structure. In fact, there are six modes (Table 7.4) or six different ways, in which a data matrix can be extracted from a body of data (refer to Figure 7.8).

The original data body is normally represented in the fashion displayed in Figure 7.8. The data body has *n* variables for N observations over *t* time periods.

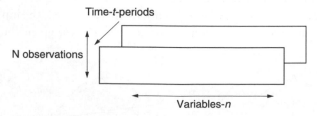

Figure 7.8 Data body for the description of the six matrix modes for data input into Principal Components and Factor Analysis

Table 7.4   Six modes of data matrix for input into Principal Components or Factor Analysis

1.	R-Mode	Most common form and the one used for discussion throughout Chapter 8.
		The n variables form columns.
		The N observations form rows.
		Time held constant.
2	Q-Mode	The N observations form columns.
		The n variables form rows.
		Time held constant.
3.	O-Mode	The t time periods form columns.
		The n variables form rows.
		Observations held constant.
4.	P-Mode	The n variables form columns.
		The t time periods form rows.
		Observations held constant.
5.	S-Mode	The N observations form columns.
		The t time periods form rows.
		Only one variable studied.
6.	T-Mode	The t time periods form columns.
		The N observations form rows.
		Only one variable studied.

Care must be taken in using the various modes. All can be used for descriptive purposes; however, for inferential purposes the number of rows should exceed the number of columns. Preferably the rows should equal $20 \times P$ (where P is the number of columns) if a hypothesis is to be tested.

Example   **Cultural analysis using Principal Components Analysis**

The following example analysis is part of a paper titled 'Importance and expectations of destination attributes for Japanese tourists to Hawaii and the Gold Coast compared' by L. Turner and Y. Reisinger reprinted from the *Asia Pacific Journal of Tourism Research*, Vol. 4, No. 2, 1999, pp. 1–18 with permission from the publisher. This study provides a good example of the use of Principal Components Analysis in a tourism-based cross-cultural setting.

Japan is a good example of a market supplying growth for numerous world destinations including Hawaii in the US and the Gold Coast in Australia. Both of these destinations are potential competitors for Japanese tourists for several reasons: (1) they are about equal travel time away from Japan; (2) they are both tropical resort destinations offering 'sun, sand and relaxation'; (3) they are both western, English speaking destinations; (4) they are both modern destinations having similar history and culture, and offering modern environments that are not steeped in cultural heritage; (5) the cultural heritage in both destinations dates back to endogenous native populations; (6) they both offer a marketing profile, which includes wild environments and scenic landscapes; and (7) the population of both destinations can reasonably be expected to offer similar levels of service quality.

An interesting question that arises is how do Japanese tourists view these two potentially competing destinations? What differences can be found in the levels of expectations, and ultimate satisfaction with the destination attributes? These questions are answered using, in part, Principal Components Analysis.

The specific destination attributes selected for this study were adopted from previous destination attractiveness and image studies (Echtner and Ritchie, 1991; Gearing et al., 1974; Ritchie and Zins, 1978; Sirakaya et al., 1996). Twenty-seven ideographic questions were asked in the general form: 'How satisfied are you with'. A seven-point scale ranged between 'extremely satisfied' (1) through 'satisfied' (4) to 'extremely dissatisfied' (7). It was considered that a seven-point scale would allow for a wide range of answers to enhance the statistical variability of responses. A sample of 607 Japanese tourists visiting Hawaii and 663 visiting the Gold Coast has been collected, giving a total sample of 1270 tourists. In Hawaii 300 arriving tourists, and separately on the Gold Coast, 307 arriving tourists were sampled. On departure from Hawaii 300 tourists and 363 from the Gold Coast were sampled.

The samples were collected over the period August 1998 to March 1999. Two separate survey instruments were devised, one for arriving tourists and one for departing tourists. Only departing tourists were asked the satisfaction questions, and only arriving tourists were asked the expectation questions. The sample of arriving and departing tourists in each of the two locations were the same individuals.

The instruments were translated into the Japanese language via a process of original and back translation. The surveys were distributed and collected using Japanese speaking interviewers. Pilot testing of thirty-four Japanese tourists was conducted on the instrument to ensure all questions could be understood and did not contain ambiguous questions or interpretive problems.

There is a potentially significant difficulty in asking the Japanese to directly indicate levels of satisfaction, as it is often the case in eastern cultures and the Japanese culture in particular, to keep criticism private in order to avoid conflict or loss of face. This was not considered a major concern in this survey because the respondents marked their own survey instruments on a seven-point scale. They were not required to verbalize their comments or express their feelings with the interviewer.

A simple individual attribute analysis is insufficient to make conclusions about the relative merits of the two destinations. The question is how do these attributes combine to create an image of expectation and satisfaction? More importantly, how do these images compare? The literature on tourism decision-making clearly indicates that travellers do not simply compare individual attributes in making their destination choices, but rather react to the overall image of destinations. Tables 7.5 to 7.12 provide

Table 7.5 Total variance explained and significance tests. Expectations on arrival on the Gold Coast

Component	Extracted communality	Initial eigenvalue	Percentage of explained variance	Rotated eigenvalue	Percentage of explained variance
1	0.564	8.912	33.008	4.326	16.022
2	0.666	3.192	11.821	3.337	28.383
3	0.656	1.862	6.896	3.029	39.602
4	0.639	1.507	5.583	2.850	50.158
5	0.661	1.285	4.759	2.659	60.006
6	0.667	1.235	4.575	1.791	66.641

Kaiser-Meyer-Olkin Measure of Sampling Adequacy	0.874
Bartlett's test of Sphericity: Approx Chi-Square	4665.775
d.f.	351
Significance	0.000

Table 7.6 Principal Components Analysis of expectations on arrival for the Gold Coast

Dimension	1	2	3	4	5	6
Characteristic	*Exotic place*	*Transport*	*Cleanliness*	*Cost*	*Social*	*Assistance*
Popular image of the destination		0.605				
Safety of the destination		0.655				
Ease of getting there		0.774				
Ease of local transportation		0.706				
Architecture/buildings		0.694				
Quality of accommodation						
Unpolluted environment			0.821			
Clean facilities			0.696			
Rest and relaxation						
Exotic environment	0.729					
Opportunity for adventure	0.825					
Availability of tourist information						0.615
Assistance with foreign language						0.656
Nightlife and entertainment	0.674					
Sport activities	0.715					
To visit national parks						
To visit historic sites/museums	0.609					
To see the wildlife			0.675			
Shopping opportunities						
To experience a different culture and customs						
To experience different food and drink					0.715	
Opportunity to socialize with locals					0.689	
Friendliness of the local people					0.732	
To improve your social standing in Japan	0.630					
The cost of airfare				0.757		
Local prices				0.858		
The exchange rate				0.853		
Percentage variance explained – Total [66.64]	33.01	11.82	6.90	5.58	4.76	4.58

Table 7.7   Total variance explained and significance tests. Expectations on arrival at Hawaii

Component	Extracted communality	Initial eigenvalue	Percentage of explained variance	Rotated eigenvalue	Percentage of explained variance
1	0.621	10.742	39.786	4.241	15.706
2	0.647	2.263	8.382	3.842	14.228
3	0.720	1.687	6.248	3.192	11.823
4	0.736	1.275	4.721	2.823	10.454
5	0.634	1.079	3.996	2.151	7.968
6	0.682	1.020	3.779	1.818	6.732

the results from four Principal Components Analyses of expectation and satisfaction for the Gold Coast and Hawaii. For the purpose of this study a Principal Components Analysis was run using SPSS 10.1 for each of the characteristic matrices for the Gold Coast and Hawaii. The objective of the analysis is exploratory, to see whether there are different dimensions of expectation and satisfaction in each location, and also to see whether any like dimensions are in a similar or dissimilar order of significance. It may be that combinations of characteristics as opposed to individual measures are more informative about differences between the two destinations.

An eigenvalue of one is used as the cut-off value to determine the number of components to be rotated. In this case the scree test would be less useful as it is more difficult to determine the cut-off point of the scree slope because the eigenvalues tend to scale down evenly (refer to Table 7.5). The KMO is very high at 0.87 and the sphericity test is rejected well beyond 95 per cent statistical significance indicating high sample adequacy in Table 7.5. The KMO is particularly high at 0.92, 0.94 and 0.90 and the sphericity test hypothesis is also rejected indicating sample adequacy in Tables 7.7, 7.9 and 7.11, respectively. In each of the four analyses the anti-image matrix is not given because of size. However, the diagonals all show high negative partial correlations.

Only dimensions that load two or more variables (at 0.6 or higher) are accepted for interpretation because fewer than two variables do not allow for an adequate description of the dimension (refer to Tables 7.6, 7.10 and 7.12).

Table 7.8 Principal Components Analysis of expectations on arrival for Hawaii

Dimension	1	2	3	4
Characteristic	Socials	Safety	Cleanliness	Cost
Popular image of the destination		0.681		
Safety of the destination		0.710		
Ease of getting there		0.775		
Architecture/buildings		0.742		
Quality of accommodation			0.672	
Unpolluted environment				
Clean facilities			0.729	
Rest and relaxation			0.722	
Exotic environment				
Opportunity for adventure				
Availability of tourist information				
Assistance with foreign language				
Nightlife and entertainment				
Sport activities				
To visit national parks	0.723			
To visit historic sites/museums	0.809			
To see the wildlife	0.722			
Shopping opportunities				
To experience a different culture and customs	0.608			
To experience different food and drink				
Opportunity to socialize with locals	0.656			
Friendliness of the local people				
To improve your social standing in Japan				
The cost of airfare				0.823
Local prices				0.879
The exchange rate				0.860
Ease of local transportation				
Percentage variance explained – Total [59.14]	39.79	8.38	6.25	4.72

Table 7.9 Total variance explained and significance tests. Satisfaction on departure from the Gold Coast

Component	Extracted communality	Initial eigenvalue	Percentage of explained variance	Rotated eigenvalue	Pecentage of explained variance
1	0.680	12.405	45.945	5.057	18.729
2	0.681	2.244	8.313	4.363	16.158
3	0.708	1.259	4.663	4.259	15.776
4	0.595	1.239	4.587	3.468	12.846

Table 7.10   Principal Components Analysis of satisfaction on departure for the Gold Coast

Dimension	1	2	3	4
Characteristic	Safe	Social	Cost	Adventure
Popular image of the destination	0.735			
Safety of the destination	0.745			
Ease of getting there	0.770			
Ease of local transportation	0.620			
Architecture/buildings	0.691			
Quality of accommodation	0.661			
Unpolluted environment				
Clean facilities				
Rest and relaxation				
Exotic environment				
Opportunity for adventure				0.610
Availability of tourist information				
Assistance with foreign language				
Nightlife and entertainment				
Sport activities				
To visit national parks				0.684
To visit historic sites/museums			0.623	
To see the wildlife				
Shopping opportunities				
To experience a different culture and customs		0.689		
To experience different food and drink		0.695		
Opportunity to socialize with locals		0.698		
Friendliness of the local people		0.714		
To improve your social standing in Japan			0.657	
The cost of airfare			0.683	
Local prices			0.734	
The exchange rate			0.770	
Percentage variance explained – Total [66.9]	45.95	8.31	4.66	4.59

Table 7.11   Total variance explained and significance tests. Satisfaction on departure from Hawaii

Component	Extracted communality	Initial eigenvalue	Percentage of explained variance	Rotated eigenvalue	Pecentage of explained variance
1	0.582	9.874	36.572	3.306	12.243
2	0.621	2.428	8.993	3.243	12.012
3	0.741	1.728	6.401	3.070	11.371
4	0.642	1.326	4.910	2.760	10.224
5	0.681	1.222	4.526	2.379	8.810
6	0.615	1.115	4.131	2.060	7.631
7	0.670	1.004	3.718	1.879	6.960

Table 7.12 Principal Components Analysis of satisfaction on departure for Hawaii

Dimension	1	2	3	4	5	6
Characteristic	*Exotic*	*Social*	*Sites*	*Safe*	*Cost*	*Adventure*
Popular image of the destination						
Safety of the destination				0.638		
Ease of getting there				0.810		
Ease of local transportation				0.745		
Architecture/buildings						
Quality of accommodation	0.603					
Unpolluted environment	0.749					
Clean facilities	0.789					
Rest and relaxation	0.630					
Exotic environment	0.620					
Opportunity for adventure						0.696
Availability of tourist information						
Assistance with foreign language						
Nightlife and entertainment						
Sport activities						
To visit national parks			0.837			
To visit historic sites/museums			0.836			
To see the wildlife			0.805			
Shopping opportunities						0.631
To experience a different culture and customs		0.631				
To experience different food and drink		0.665				
Opportunity to socialize with locals		0.755				
Friendliness of the local people		0.766				
To improve your social standing in Japan						
The cost of airfare					0.683	
Local prices					0.850	
The exchange rate					0.842	
Percentage variance explained – Total [65.53]	36.57	8.99	6.40	4.91	4.53	4.13

Example	Component interpretation

The interpretation of the components can be described as logically subjective, and is based upon the nature of the variables loading on each component.

There are four dimensions of expectations for Hawaii and six for the Gold Coast (refer to Tables 7.6 and 7.8). The interpretation is as follows:

1. The first dimension of expectation for Hawaii is based upon attractions and wildlife, culture, and socializing. For the Gold Coast the main expectations are exotic, adventurous, sporting, and nightlife/entertainment attributes.
2. The second dimension for Hawaii is ease of transport, architecture, safety, and popular image that is the same for the Gold Coast.
3. The third dimension for Hawaii is quality of accommodation, cleanliness and rest, whereas for the Gold Coast it is a clean, unpolluted wildlife environment.
4. The fourth dimension for Hawaii is low cost, which is the same for the Gold Coast.
5. There is a fifth dimension for the Gold Coast of food and socializing.
6. There is also a sixth dimension for the Gold Coast of information and language assistance.

There are six dimensions of satisfaction for Hawaii and four for the Gold Coast (refer to Tables 7.10 and 7.12). The interpretation is as follows.

1. Dimension one for Hawaii is quality accommodation, in a restful, exotic, clean, and unpolluted environment. For the Gold Coast the first dimension is ease of transport in a safe destination with a popular image.
2. The second dimension for Hawaii is culture, food and socializing, and it is the same for the Gold Coast.
3. The third dimension for Hawaii is visiting natural and historical sites and wildlife, whereas for the Gold Coast it is low cost and improving social standing.
4. The fourth dimension for Hawaii is safety and ease of transport, and for the Gold Coast, it is adventure and visiting national parks.
5. The fifth dimension for Hawaii is cost.
6. The sixth dimension for Hawaii is adventure and shopping.

Discussion of the dimensional differences

The issue of interest in comparing the dimensions is how much the dimensions of expectation are met by final satisfaction. In this regard Hawaii performs very well. The first and most important dimension of expectation for Hawaii is the natural environment, wildlife, and socializing, which come out in the first three dimensions of satisfaction for Hawaii along with culture, food and an exotic, clean and unpolluted environment. Hawaii does not do quite so well for the expectation of safety and ease of transport, which are a second dimension of expectation and a fourth dimension of satisfaction. Hawaii also does less well on cost, which is the fourth dimension of expectation, and a lowly fifth dimension of satisfaction.

For the Gold Coast there are significant problems. The first dimension of expectation (exotic, adventurous, sporting, nightlife) is not met by satisfaction. The most important expectations are simply not met on the Gold Coast, and an unexpected result for the Gold Coast is ease of transport, safety, socializing, and low cost. The surprise areas of satisfaction may be considered good in themselves, but they are also boring and at the whim of financial change (exchange rates) compared with exotic and adventurous expectations.

In conclusion, it would seem that Hawaii outperforms the Gold Coast in terms of satisfaction for the tourist, based on the analysis from this study.

Summary

Factor Analysis can be used to study cultural differences. There are major differences between Factor Analysis and Principal Components Analysis. The primary aims include removing collinearity between variables, reducing the number of variables, and identifying groups of variables. Tests of significance can be performed. The process of calculation can be explained graphically. There are different ways to extract relevant components. Two main forms of rotation are orthogonal and oblique rotation. There are several ways to enter data into a factor analytic analysis. The example with an application to tourism cultural analysis using Principle Components Analysis was presented.

Discussion points and questions

1. Explain the difference between the objectives of Factor Analysis and Principal Components Analysis.
2. State three aims of Principal Component Analysis.
3. Create an example problem that could be analysed by Principal Components Analysis.
4. Describe the difference between oblique and orthogonal rotation.
5. Define the following terms: factor loadings, communality, eigenvalue and factor score.
6. How do you determine how many factors should be rotated?
7. How do you use the rotated loadings matrix to describe the nature of the components?
8. Why is a good KMO closer to one?

Further reading

Ap, J. and Crompton, J. (1998) Developing and testing a tourism impact scale. *Journal of Travel Research* 37(2): 120–130.

Cai, L. and Combrink, T. (2000) Japanese female travellers – a unique outbound market. *The Asia Pacific Journal of Tourism Research* 5(1): 16–24.

Cooley, W. and Lohres, P. (1971) *Multivariate Data Analysis.* New York: Wiley.

Harman, H. (1976) *Modern Factor Analysis*, 3rd edition, Chicago: University of Chicago Press.

Johnston-Walker, R. (1999) The accommodation motivations and accommodation usage patterns of international independent pleasure travellers. *Pacific Tourism Review* 3(2): 143–150.

Keng, K. and Cheng, L. (1999) Determining tourist role typologies: an exploratory study of Singapore vacations. *Journal of Travel Research* 37(4): 382–390.

Lindeman, R., Merenda, P. and Gold, R. (1980) *Introduction to Bivariate and Multivariate Analysis.* London: Scott, Foresman and Co.

Morrison, D. (1976) *Multivariate Statistical Methods*, 2nd edition, New York: McGraw-Hill.

Rummel, R. (1967) Understanding factor analysis. *Conflict Resolution* 11: 444–480.

Turner, L. and Reisinger, Y. (1999) Importance and expectations of destination attributes for Japanese tourists to Hawaii and the Gold Coast compared. *Asia Pacific Journal of Tourism Research* 4(2): 1–18.

8

Structural equation modelling for cross-cultural analysis

Objectives

After completing this chapter the reader should be able to:

- understand the concept of structural equation modelling (SEM)

- identify research problems that can be solved using SEM

- understand the application of SEM in tourism.

Introduction

During the last decade structural equation modelling (SEM) has increasingly been applied in the marketing discipline, particularly in the US. In the tourism discipline this technique has not been applied widely. The concept of SEM is difficult to understand due to its statistical complexity and non-user-friendly computer manuals.

This chapter introduces the basic concepts associated with SEM using LISREL in a comprehensive and non-technical manner. It is based upon the article 'Structural equation modelling with LISREL: application in tourism' by Y. Reisinger and L. Turner published in *Tourism Management*, Vol. 20, No 1, 1999, pp. 71–88, reprinted with permission from Elsevier Science. The purpose of this chapter is to: (1) explain the concept of SEM modelling, its major objectives and advantages; (2) show how useful structural models are in solving research problems within the tourism discipline; (3) present the major steps involved in the formulation and testing of a LISREL model through an application of LISREL modelling to test an hypothesis about the relationship between the tourist perceptions of a beach resort and their satisfaction with the resort; and (4) draw attention to potential limitations associated with the LISREL approach.

What is structural equation modelling?

Structural equation modelling is a multivariate technique that combines (confirmatory) factor analysis modelling from psychometric theory and structural equations modelling associated with econometrics. The term 'structural' assumes that the parameters reveal a causal relation. However, the technique does not 'discover' causal relations. 'At best, it shows whether the causal assumptions embedded in a model match a sample of data' (Bollen, 1989, p. 4).

Objectives of structural equation modelling

The primary aim of SEM is to explain the pattern of a series of inter-related dependence relationships simultaneously between a set of latent (unobserved) constructs, each measured by one or more manifest (observed) variables.

The measured (observed) variables in SEM have a finite number of values. Examples of measured variables are distance, cost, size, weight or height. The measured (manifest) variables are gathered from respondents through data collection methods, or collected as secondary data from a published source. They are represented by the numeric responses to a rating scale item on a questionnaire. Measured variables in SEM are usually continuous.

On the other hand, latent (unobserved) variables are not directly observed, have an infinite number of values, and are usually continuous. Examples of latent constructs are attitudes, customer satisfaction, and perception of value or quality. Latent variables are theoretical constructs that can be determined to exist only as a combination of other measurable variables. As such they are similar to principal components and are sometimes theoretically justified from a previous factor analysis.

In this primary form of analysis SEM is similar to combining multiple regression and factor analysis. As such, the SEM expresses the linear relationship between two separate sets of latent constructs (which may have been derived by two separate factor analyses). When using SEM these latent constructs are termed exogenous (independent) constructs and endogenous (dependent) constructs. Figure 8.6 shows that endogenous latent constructs such as repeat visitation and satisfaction depend on independent exogenous latent constructs such as culture and perception.

The SEMs include one or more linear regression equations that describe how the endogenous constructs depend upon the exogenous constructs. Their coefficients are called path coefficients, or sometimes regression weights.

However, there is an important difference between factor analysis modelling and SEM modelling. In factor analysis the observed variables can load on any and all factors (constructs). The number of factors is constrained. When using SEM, confirmatory factor analysis is used and the observed variables are loaded onto particular constructs. The loadings are free or fixed at particular values, and the independence or covariance of variables is specified.

Although the primary purpose of SEM is the analysis of latent constructs and in particular the analysis of links between latent constructs, SEM is also capable of other forms of analysis. SEM can be used to estimate variance and covariance, test hypotheses, conventional linear regression and factor analysis. In complex analysis frameworks SEM may be preferable to conventional statistical methods, for example, where it is required to test whether factor analysis on data from several populations yields the same factor model simultaneously. Another example is where a multiple regression is required to test for several dependent variables from the same set of independent variables simultaneously, particularly if it is possible for one dependent variable to simultaneously determine another. The SEM is a powerful method for effectively dealing with multicollinearity (when two or more variables are highly correlated), which is one of the benefits of SEM over multiple regression and factor analysis.

All aspects of SEM modelling must be directed by theory, which is critical for model development and modification. A clear misuse of SEM can occur when data is simply fitted to a suitable SEM and theory is then expanded from the analytic result.

There are three components in general structural equation models: 1) Path analysis; 2) the conceptual synthesis of latent variable and measurement models; and 3) general estimation procedures (Bollen, 1989).

Application of structural equation modelling

SEM modelling has been widely used in a number of disciplines, including psychology (Agho et al., 1992; Shen et al., 1995), sociology (Kenny, 1996), economics (Huang, 1991), criminology (Junger, 1992), cross-national (Mullen, 1995; Singh, 1995), cross-cultural research (Riordan and Vandenberg, 1994), healthcare (Babakus and Mangold, 1992; Taylor, 1994a; Taylor and Cronin, 1994), gerontology (Russell, 1990), human resources management (Medsker et al., 1994), environmental studies (Nevitte and Kanji, 1995), family studies (Fu and Heaton, 1995), religious studies (Legge, 1995), migration studies (Sandu and DeJong, 1995), marketing, and many others. In the marketing discipline, LISREL has been used in a variety of applications, including consumer behaviour (Oliver and Swan, 1989; Singh, 1990; Fornell, 1992; Heide and Miner, 1992; Lichtenstein et al., 1993; McCarty and Shrum, 1993; Taylor and Baker, 1994; Spreng *et al.*, 1996), organizational buying behaviour (Michaels *et al.*, 1987), channel management (Schul and Babakus, 1988), product policy (DeBrentani and Droge, 1988), pricing strategy (Walters and MacKenzie, 1988), advertising (MacKenzie and Lutz, 1989), sales-force management (Dubinsky *et al.*, 1986), retailing (Good *et al.*, 1988), international marketing (Han, 1988), services marketing (Arora and Cavusgil, 1985; Crosby *et al.*, 1990; Hui and Bateson, 1991; Francese, 1991; Cronin and Taylor, 1992; Brown *et al.*, 1993; Price *et al.*, 1995; Taylor, 1994b), service quality in retail stores (Dabholkar *et al.*, 1996), and service satisfaction (Jayanti and Jackson, 1991). There are many other examples.

Reasons for popularity

The reason why SEM modelling has been applied in so many disciplines is its ability to solve research problems related to relationships between latent constructs, which are measured by observed variables. For example, such relationships can be found in educational research where the determinants of educational achievements and failure are analysed, or in consumer behavioural research where the reasons for purchasing various products and services are analysed. Many important marketing, psychological or cultural concepts are latent constructs, with unknown reliability, measured by multiple observed variables. The lower the measurement reliability the more difficult it is to observe relationships between the latent constructs and other variables. By using SEMs one can model important latent constructs while taking into account the unreliability of the indicators. Also, many latent constructs such as perceptions, evaluation, satisfaction, or behaviour measures have low reliability. By using regression one may get coefficients with unexpected signs: the predictors one would expect to be positively related to the dependent variable end up with negative coefficients, or vice versa. Regression analysis as opposed to SEM analysis does not eliminate the difficulties caused by unreliable measures. The SEMs consider unknown reliability of the measures and rank the measures in terms of their importance (Bacon *et al.*, 1998).

Application in tourism

SEM modelling has not been widely used in the tourism discipline, outside the US. However, the application of SEM in tourism is important as a tool for promoting better quality research. Tourism researchers are often faced with a set of interrelated questions. What variables determine tourist arrivals to a particular destination? How does demand as a latent variable combine with supply variables to affect tourist arrivals? How do demand and supply variables simultaneously affect tourist purchasing decisions and holiday satisfaction? How does tourist holiday satisfaction result in repeat visitation and loyalty to a destination? Many of the same independent variables affect different dependent variables with different effects. Other multivariate techniques do not address these questions within a single comprehensive method.

In the tourism discipline structural modelling has recently been used to assess traveller types (Nickerson and Ellis, 1991), hotel guest satisfaction (Gundersen *et al.*, 1996), service quality and satisfaction in the hotel/motel industry (Getty and Thompson, 1994; Thomson and Getty, 1994), tourists' and retailers' perceptions of service levels in a tourism destination (Vogt and Fesenmaier, 1995), factors that influence guest accommodation choice intentions (Richard and Sundaram, 1993), relationship between travel motivation and information sources in the senior travel market (Kim *et al.*, 1996), antecedents of customer expectations of restaurants (Clow *et al.*, 1996), resident attitudes toward tourism (Lindberg and Johnson, 1997), impact of tourism advertising on tourist spending (Butterfield *et al.*, 1998), response to wilderness recreation fees (Williams *et al.*, 1999), influence of tourists' experiences on holiday satisfaction and on the change of attitudes (Jacinto *et al.*, 1999), cultural differences between Asian tourists and Australian hosts (Reisinger and Turner, 1998a,b; 1999a,b; 2002b), importance and expectations of destination attributes (Turner and Reisinger, 1999), tourism flows from the UK to seven major destinations (Turner *et al.*, 1998), shopping satisfaction (Reisinger and Turner, 2002c; Turner and Reisinger, 2001), golf travellers' satisfaction (Petrick and Backman, 2002), and many others.

Gundersen *et al.* (1996) identified important factors for hotel guest satisfaction among business travellers. The analysis covered three departments of hotel operations (receptions, food and beverage, and housekeeping) and two dimensions of satisfaction (tangible and intangible). The structural model showed the relationships among the three departments and overall satisfaction with the hotel. The highest loadings were noted on the service aspects of all departments. The major explanatory variables for overall hotel guest satisfaction were tangible aspects of housekeeping and intangible aspects of reception service, suggesting that by focusing on these factors, high levels of satisfaction among business travellers can be achieved.

Getty and Thompson (1994) tested customers' perceptions of the lodging sector performance on multiple dimensions and the perceived level of overall quality possessed by the lodging property, satisfaction with the lodging experience, and customers' willingness to recommend the property. The customers' intentions to recommend the property were determined by their perceptions of the overall quality of the property, rather than their satisfaction with the stay. The specific quality and satisfaction dimensions, most responsible for willingness to recommend the property, included: the general appearance of the property, perceived value associated with the stay, willingness of employees to listen, and the degree to which the property provided a safe environment. Thompson and Getty (1994) suggested that customers' intentions to provide positive word of mouth are a function of their perceptions of the overall quality of the lodging property, rather than their expressed level of satisfaction with stay.

Vogt and Fesenmaier (1995) used four service quality dimensions (reliability, responsiveness, assurance, accessibility), measured by thirteen items, to evaluate service experiences as perceived by tourists and retailers. The results showed that tourists evaluated services differently to retailers.

Kim *et al.* (1996) tested a causal relationship between tourism motivation and information sources. They found that the more active travellers in the senior market were more likely to consult information sources before travel. Those who travelled to get rest and relaxation were less likely to search for travel information. Those who travelled to visit friends and families were not interested in searching for travel information.

Lindberg and Johnson (1997) tested two models to assess how the values people hold influence their attitudes toward tourism and what types of outcomes most affect attitudes. The value-attitude model showed that resident values regarding economic gains were better determinants of attitudes than values regarding disruption within the community. The expectancy-value model indicated that perceived economic and congestion impacts had greater influence on attitudes than perceived crime and aesthetic impacts.

Reisinger and Turner (1998a) determined which cultural differences between Asian tourists and Australian hosts are predictors of tourist satisfaction. The results indicated that differences in cultural values and rules of social behaviour between Asian tourists and Australian hosts directly influence tourist satisfaction, and differences in perceptions of service directly influence tourist social interaction. Perceptions of service providers only indirectly determine satisfaction through the mediating effect of interaction.

Turner and Reisinger (1999) determined the relationships between destination attributes importance and Japanese tourist expectations of those attributes on arrival, and confirmed that a study of satisfaction of destination attributes should be based upon a comparison of expectations on arrival against satisfaction on departure.

Reisinger and Turner (2002c) tested the theory that shopping satisfaction results from the importance of product attributes, which in turn, depend on the types of products purchased. They showed that the products considered important by Japanese tourists visiting Hawaii determine the importance of attributes, and the importance of attributes determine tourist satisfaction.

Petrick and Backman (2002) found that golf travellers' overall satisfaction was determined by information satisfaction and attribute satisfaction. Attributes related to the resort experience had more influence on overall satisfaction than attributes related to information provided and gold experiences.

Types of LISREL modelling

LISREL stands for LInear Structural RELationships and is a computer program for covariance structure analysis. It was originally introduced by Joreskog and Van Thillo in 1972.

The general LISREL model has many submodels as special cases. The mathematical notations are presented on the following page, followed by a presentation of the different submodels.

Abbreviations:

x – measured independent variable
y – measured dependent variable
ξ = latent exogenous construct explained by x-variables
η = latent endogenous construct explained by y-variables
δ – error for x-variable
ε – error for y-variable
λ – correlation between measured variables and all latent constructs
γ – correlation between latent constructs ξ (exogenous) and η (endogenous)
ϕ – correlation between exogenous latent constructs ξ
β – correlations between endogenous latent constructs η.

   Submodel 1 is the LISREL model, which is designed to measure observed variables. The model has only x, ξ, and δ-error variables. There are no y- and η-variables (see abbreviations). The data used measures only the correlation between the constructs (see Figure 8.1).

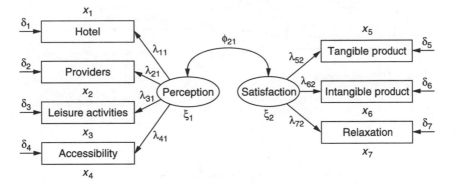

Figure 8.1 Hypothetical model: submodel 1

   Submodel 2 is the LISREL model, which is designed to estimate relationships among directly measured independent variables and the dependent variable(s). The model has no latent variables but there are two kinds of directly measured variables: x, y, and ζ-error variables. There are four types of LISREL Submodel 2: a single regression model, bivariate model, recursive model, and non-recursive model. The examples of these models are graphically presented in Figures 8.2–8.5.

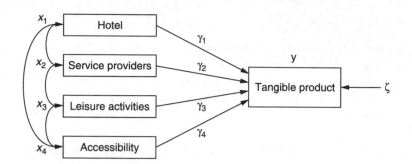

Figure 8.2 A single regression model

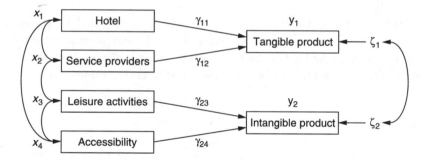

Figure 8.3 Bivariate model

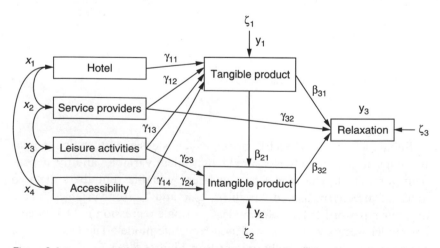

Figure 8.4 Recursive model

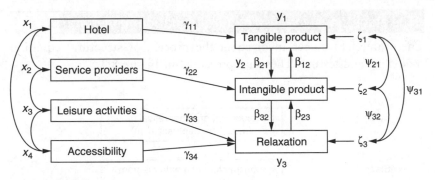

Figure 8.5 Non-recursive model

Full LISREL combines features of Submodel 1 and Submodel 2. It involves x, y, η, ξ, and ε, δ, ζ-variables (see Figure 8.6).

Submodel 3 is the LISREL model with no x-variables.
Submodel 3A involves only y, η, ξ, and ε, ζ-error variables.
Submodel 3B involves only y and η-variables with no ξ-variables.

The models 3A and 3B are not presented visually as they are parts of the full LISREL model. Since the full LISREL model has a large number of parameters, the advantage of using Submodel 3, rather than the full LISREL is that it has fewer parameter matrices, although each one is large, and it can handle models in which a δ correlates with an ε.

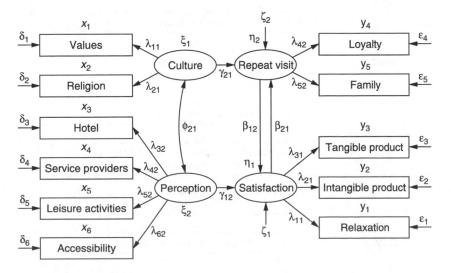

Figure 8.6 Full LISREL model

The stages involved in structural equation modelling

There are eight stages involved in the process of structural equation modelling and testing. These are presented in Figure 8.7.

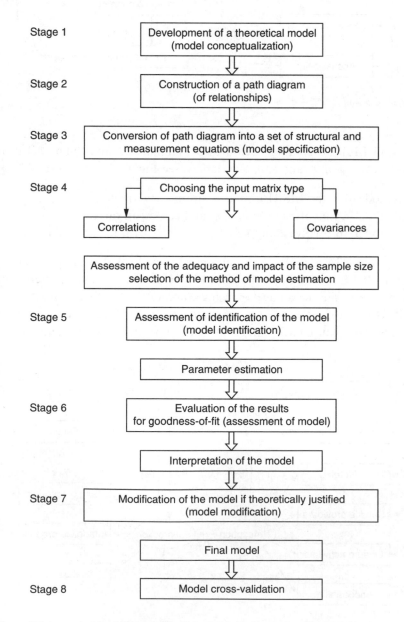

Stage 1 — Development of a theoretical model (model conceptualization)

Stage 2 — Construction of a path diagram (of relationships)

Stage 3 — Conversion of path diagram into a set of structural and measurement equations (model specification)

Stage 4 — Choosing the input matrix type — Correlations / Covariances

Assessment of the adequacy and impact of the sample size selection of the method of model estimation

Stage 5 — Assessment of identification of the model (model identification)

Parameter estimation

Stage 6 — Evaluation of the results for goodness-of-fit (assessment of model)

Interpretation of the model

Stage 7 — Modification of the model if theoretically justified (model modification)

Final model

Stage 8 — Model cross-validation

Figure 8.7 Stages involved in the application of structural equation modelling

Stage 1

The first part of stage 1 focuses on the development of a theoretical model with the linkages (defined relationships) between latent constructs and their measurable variables, reflecting proposed hypotheses. This part represents the development of a *structural model*.

For example: the hypothesized model consists of two dimensions (latent constructs): tourist perceptions of a beach resort and tourist satisfaction with the resort. The perception of a beach resort is measured by perceptions of: (1) a hotel, (2) service providers, (3) leisure activities, and (4) accessibility to the resort. The satisfaction with the resort is measured by satisfaction with (1) a tangible product, (2) an intangible product (service), and (3) degree of relaxation. It is hypothesized that there is a strong relationship (correlation) between the perception of a beach resort and tourist satisfaction with the resort (Submodel 1) (see Figure 8.1). It can also be hypothesized that tourist satisfaction is determined by tourist perceptions of this resort (full LISREL) (see Figure 8.6).

The second part of stage 1 involves the operationalization of the latent constructs via the measured variables and describing the way in which they are represented by empirical indicators (manifest variables). This part represents the development of a *measurement model*. The hypothetical measurement model is represented simply by a two-construct model (perception and satisfaction) as shown in Table 8.1.

The first part of stage 1 also provides information about the validities and reliabilities of the variables. The analysis is predominantly confirm-

Table 8.1 **Two-construct measurement model**

Variables/indicators	Indicators	Loadings on constructs	
	Perception	Satisfaction	
Hotel (x_1)	L1		
Service providers (x_2)	L2		
Leisure activities (x_3)	L3		
Accessibility (x_4)	L4		
Tangible product (x_5)		L5	
Intangible product (x_6)		L6	
Relaxation (x_7)		L7	

atory because it determines the extent to which the proposed model is consistent with the empirical data.

Critical points

The most critical point at this stage is to include all key predictive variables (multiple indicators of the latent variables) to avoid a specification error. The justification for inclusion of the specific latent constructs and their indicators in a model can be provided by factor analysis. However, this inclusion together must be theoretically sound and be weighted against the limitations of SEM and computer programs. A model should contain at most twenty variables (five to six constructs each measured by three to four indicators) (Bentler and Chou, 1987). The interpretation of the results and their statistical significance becomes difficult as the number of concepts becomes large (exceeding twenty).

Stage 2

Stage 2 involves the construction of a path diagram. In order to understand the geometric symbols represented in models and correctly draw a path diagram, LISREL requires familiarity with the Greek letters describing LISREL matrices. The Greek letters were presented previously.

In a path diagram all relationships between constructs and their indicators are graphically presented with arrows. They form a visual presentation of the hypotheses and the measurement scheme. A curved line indicates a correlation/covariance between constructs, e.g., between perceptions and satisfaction (Submodel 1) (see Figure 8.1). A straight arrow indicates a direct relationship from a construct to its indicators and direct effect relationship between constructs. The direct arrow from perceptions to satisfaction changes the Submodel 1 into a full LISREL analysis (with y-variables) by stating that perception determines satisfaction (see Figure 8.6).

All constructs fall into two categories: exogenous and endogenous. Exogenous constructs are independent variables and are not determined by any other variable in a model (there are no straight arrows pointing to these constructs, e.g., perception in full LISREL). Endogenous constructs are determined by other constructs and relationships contained in the model (there are arrows pointing to these constructs, e.g., satisfaction in full LISREL). They can also determine other endogenous constructs.

In order to avoid specification error, attention has to be paid not to omit any exogenous or endogenous constructs.

A path diagram should show all relationships. The number of paths should be theoretically justified. All relationships are to be linear.

Stage 3

Stage 3 involves the formal mathematical specification of the model by describing the nature and number of parameters to be estimated (which variables measure which constructs), translating the path diagram into a series of linear equations that link constructs, and translating the specified model into LISREL language in the form of matrices, indicating hypothesized correlations among constructs or variables. The coefficient matrices represent the paths in a model.

Because both constructs in the hypothetical path diagram are exogenous (Submodel 1), the measurement model and associated correlation matrices for exogenous constructs and indicators are needed. The appropriate LISREL notation is shown in Table 8.2.

Table 8.2   LISREL notation for the measurement model

Exogenous indicator		Exogenous construct		Error
x_1	$=$	$\lambda x_{11}\xi_1$	$+$	δ_1
x_2	$=$	$\lambda x_{21}\xi_1$	$+$	δ_2
x_3	$=$	$\lambda x_{31}\xi_1$	$+$	δ_3
x_4	$=$	$\lambda x_{41}\xi_1$	$+$	δ_4
x_5	$=$	$\lambda x_{52}\xi_2$	$+$	δ_5
x_6	$=$	$\lambda x_{62}\xi_2$	$+$	δ_6
x_7	$=$	$\lambda x_{72}\xi_2$	$+$	δ_7

Correlation among exogenous constructs (ϕ)

	ξ_1	ξ_2
ξ_1	$-$	
ξ_2	ϕ_{21}	$-$

λ – correlation between manifest variables and latent constructs ξ

At this stage a distinction must be made between fixed, constrained, and free parameters. Fixed parameters specify values a priori and they are not estimated as part of the model. An example of a fixed parameter would be to assign $\lambda_{11} = 1.00$ so that $\lambda_{21,}$ $\lambda_{31,}$ and λ_{41} would be compared against correlations when all parameters are free. Restricted (constrained) parameters are unknown and are estimated by the model. Example: when two independent variables (ξ_1 and ξ_2) have the same impact on a dependent variable (η_1) one can specify that $\gamma_{11} = \gamma_{12}$ (γ = correlation between latent constructs). In this case it is only necessary to estimate one parameter to determine the value of the other parameter. Free parameters have unknown values, are not constrained to be equal to any other parameter, and need to be estimated by the program.

The LISREL analysis run is based on control commands, which consist of several lines. The LISREL control lines and the input are explained in the LISREL SPSS manuals. Since there are five LISREL submodels different input files need to be requested for each model. The control commands for each submodel should be developed according to the instructions given in the LISREL manual. Also, the correct specification of each line depends on the research phenomena under study. Once the LISREL program is run it reproduces all command files. The matrix and the parameter specifications should be immediately inspected to make sure that no errors have been made.

Stage 4

Stage 4 considers whether the variance/covariance or correlation matrix is to be used as the input data, and this involves an assessment of the sample size. The covariance matrix is used when the objective is to test a theory, provide comparisons between different populations or samples, or to explain the total variance of constructs needed to test the theory. However, because the diagonal of the matrix is not one, interpretation of the results is more difficult because the coefficients must be interpreted in terms of the units of measure for the constructs. The correlation matrix allows for direct comparisons of the coefficients within a model. Therefore, it is more widely used. The correlation matrix is also used to understand the patterns of relationships between the constructs. It is not used to explain the total variance of a construct as needed in theory testing. Thus, interpretation of the results and their generalizability to different situations should be made with caution when the correlation matrix is used. The correlation matrix for the hypothesized model is presented in Table 8.3.

The most widely used method for computing the correlations or covariances between manifest variables is Pearson product-moment

Table 8.3   Correlation matrix for the hypothesized model

Variables	Hotel (x_1)	Service providers (x_2)	Leisure activities (x_3)	Access (x_4)	Tangible product (x_5)	Intangible product (x_6)	Relaxation (x_7)
x_1 Hotel	1.000						
x_2 Providers	−0.349	1.000					
x_3 Leisure	0.562	0.786	1.000				
x_4 Access	0.612	0.677	0.432	1.000			
x_5 Tangible	0.899	0.231	0.521	0.421	1.000		
x_6 Intangible	0.123	0.899	0.789	0.513	0.222	1.000	
x_7 Relaxation	0.433	0.335	0.788	0.188	0.111	0.654	1.000

correlation and the correlation matrix is computed using Prelis (Joreskog and Sorbom, 1988).

Sample size

Sample size plays an important role in estimating and interpreting SEM results as well as estimating sampling errors. Although there is no correct rule for estimating sample size for SEM, recommendations are for a size ranging between 100 to 200 (Hair *et al.*, 1995). A sample of 200 is called a 'critical sample size'. The sample size should also be large enough when compared with the number of estimated parameters (as a rule of thumb at least five times the number of parameters), but with an absolute minimum of fifty respondents. The sample size depends on methods of model estimation, which are discussed later.

After the structural and measurement models are specified and the input data type is selected, the computer program for model estimation should be chosen. There are many various programs available on the market. Although some offer different advantages, the LISREL computing program has been the most widely used program.

Stage 5

Stage 5 addresses the issue of model identification, that is, the extent to which the information provided by the data is sufficient to enable parameter estimation. If a model is not identified, then it is not possible to determine the model parameters. A necessary condition for the identification is that the number of independent parameters is less than or equal to the number of elements of the sample matrix of covariances among the observed variables.

For example: if t parameters are to be estimated, the minimum condition for identification is:

$$t \leq s$$

where $s = 1/2(p+q)(p+q+1)$
p = number of y-variables
q = number of x-variables

- If $t = s$ the set of parameters is *just identified* (there is only one and only one estimate for each parameter).
- If $t < s$, the model is *overidentified* (it is possible to obtain several estimates of the same parameter).
- If $t > s$, the model is *unidentified* (an infinite number of values of the parameters could be obtained).

In a just-identified model, all the information available is used to estimate parameters and there is no information left to test the model (df = 0). In an overidentified model there are positive degrees of freedom (equal to $s - t$), thus, one set of estimates can be used to test the model. In the unidentified model, one must either: (1) add more manifest variables; (2) set certain parameters to zero; or (3) set parameters equal to each other (Aaker and Bagozzi, 1979) to make all the parameters identified. However, all three steps can be applied if they are justified by theory.

The condition $t \leq s$ is necessary, but not sufficient, for the identification of a LISREL model. In fact, there are no sufficient conditions for the full structure model. The LISREL program provides warnings about identification problems.

Identification problems

The symptoms of potential identification problems are:

(a) very large standard errors for coefficients
(b) the inability of the program to invert the information matrix
(c) impossible estimates (e.g., negative and non-significant error variances for any construct)
(d) high correlations (±0.80 or above) among observed variables.

These symptoms must be searched out and eliminated.

Sources of identification problems

There are several sources of identification problems:

1. A large number of coefficients relative to the number of correlations or covariances, indicated by a small number of degrees of freedom – similar to the problems of overfitting, that is, insufficient sample size
2. The use of reciprocal effects (two-way arrows between the constructs)
3. Failure to fix the scale of a construct, that is, incorrect assignment of parameters as fixed or free
4. Skewness
5. Nonlinearity
6. Heteroscedasticity
7. Multicollinearity
8. Singularity
9. Autocorrelation.

It should be noted that heteroscedasticity, caused either by non-normality of the variables or the lack of a direct relationship between variables, is not fatal to an analysis. The linear relationship between variables is captured by the analysis but there is even more predictability if the heteroscedasticity is accounted for as well. If it is not, the analysis is weakened, but not invalidated.

Multicollinearity and singularity are problems with a correlation matrix that occur when variables are too highly correlated. For multi-collinearity, the variables are very highly correlated (0.8 and above); and for singularity, the variables are perfectly correlated and one of the variables is a combination of one or more of the other variables. When variables are multicollinear or singular, they contain redundant information and they are not all needed in the analysis.

Solutions to identification problems

The potential solutions for identification problems are to:

1. Eliminate some of the estimated coefficients (deleting paths from the path diagram)
2. Fix the measurement error variances of constructs if possible; if negative change to 0.005
3. Fix any structural coefficients that were reliably known, that is, eliminate correlations over one because of multi-collinearity of variables

4. Remove multicollinearity by using data reduction methods like Principal Components Analysis
5. Eliminate troublesome variables, e.g., highly correlated variables, redundant variables
6. Check univariate descriptive statistics for accuracy (e.g., out-of-range values, plausible standard deviations, coefficients of variation)
7. Check for missing values
8. Identify non-normal variables, e.g., check for skewness and kurtosis
9. Check for outliers
10. Check for non-linearity and heteroscedasticity
11. Reformulate the theoretical model to provide more constructs relative to the number of relationships examined.

Estimation methods

The LISREL program offers different kinds of parameter estimation methods:

- Instrumental Variables (IV)
- Two-stage Least Squares (TSLS)
- Unweighted Least Squares (ULS)
- Generalized Least Squares (GLS)
- Maximum Likelihood (ML)
- Generally Weighted Least Squares (WLS)
- Diagonally Weighted Least Squares (DWLS).

The most widely used are the Two-stage Least Square (TSLS) and Maximum Likelihood Estimation (MLE) methods. The TSLS method computes the initial estimates, and the MLE method computes the final solution. The TSLS method (as well as the IV method) of model estimation is non-iterative and fast. The MLE method (as well as ULS, GLS, WLS, and DWLS methods) is an iterative procedure and it successively improves initial parameter estimates. The MLE method may be used to estimate parameters under the assumption of multivariate normality and is robust against departures from normality. When using the MLE method the standard errors (SE) and Chi-square goodness-of-fit measures may be used if interpreted with caution. The MLE method is also more precise in large samples. The minimum sample size to ensure appropriate use of MLE is 100. As the sample increases the sensitivity of the method to detect differences among the data also increases. However, as the sample exceeds 400–500 the method becomes 'too sensitive' and almost any difference is detected, making all fit measures poor (Hair *et al.*, 1995). The initial and final estimates computed by TSLS and MLE methods for the hypothetical model are presented in Tables 8.4 and 8.5.

Table 8.4   Initial estimates (TSLS)

Variables	*Perception*	*Satisfaction*
Hotel	0.866	0.000
Service providers	0.847	0.000
Leisure activities	0.801	0.000
Accessibility	0.702	0.000
Tangible product	0.000	0.780
Intangible product (service)	0.000	0.923
Relaxation	0.000	0.930

	Perception	*Satisfaction*
Perception	1.000	
Satisfaction	0.664	1.000

Table 8.5   LISREL estimates (Maximum Likelihood)

Variables	*Perception*	*Satisfaction*
Hotel	0.863	0.000
Service providers	0.849	0.000
Leisure activities	0.805	0.000
Accessibility	0.695	0.000
Tangible product	0.000	0.775
Intangible product (service)	0.000	0.929
Relaxation	0.000	0.931

	Perception	*Satisfaction*
Perception	1.000	
Satisfaction	0.666	1.000

A comparison of the TSLS with those of the final ML estimates reveals that they are very accurate. No difference is larger than 0.02.

Types of solution
The LISREL program also offers three types of solution:

1. Non-standardized
2. Standardized
3. Completely standardized.

Non-standardized solution

In the non-standardized solution all latent and manifest variables are non-standardized. The non-standardized parameter estimates show the resulting change in a dependent variable from a unit change in an independent variable, all other variables being held constant. Non-standardized coefficients are computed with all variables in their original metric form and describe the effect that variables have in an absolute sense. Thus, they can be used to compare similar models in other populations. However, they are tied to the measurement units of the variables they represent. Any change in the measurement unit for an independent or dependent variable changes the value and comparability of parameters across populations (Bagozzi, 1977).

Standardized solution

In the standardized solution only latent variables (constructs) are standardized and the manifest variables (x and y) are left in their original metric.

Completely standardized solution

In the completely standardized solution both the latent and the manifest variables are standardized. The standardized parameters reflect the resulting change in a dependent variable from a standard deviation change in an independent variable. The standardized parameters are appropriate to compare the relative contributions of a number of independent variables on the same dependent variable and for the same sample of observations. They are not appropriate to compare across populations or samples (Bagozzi, 1980).

Stage 6

Stage 6 involves the assessment of the model fit using a variety of fit measures for the measurement and structural model (and supporting/rejecting the proposed hypotheses). However, before evaluating the goodness-of-fit between the data and model several assumptions of SEM must be met.

SEM assumptions

Assumptions of SEM are:

1. Independence of variables
2. Random sampling of respondents

3. Linearity of all relationships between variables, latent and observed
4. Multivariate normality of distribution (important in the use of LISREL)
5. No kurtosis and no skewness
6. Appropriate data measured on interval or ratio scale
7. Sample size 100–400
8. Exploratory purpose of the study.

The above assumptions can be tested through program PRELIS. The Generalized Least Squares (GLS), which is an alternative estimation method, can adjust for the violations of these assumptions. However, as the models become large and complex, the use of this method becomes more limited.

Additionally, if the use of SEM is associated with time-series data, considerable care is required to test for autocorrelation and stationarity, and where required the data transformed into a non-stationary series.

Offending estimates

Once the assumptions are met, the results must first be examined for offending estimates, which are coefficients that exceed acceptable limits. The common examples are:

- negative error variances or nonsignificant error variances for any construct
- standardized coefficients exceeding or very close to 1.0
- very large standard errors associated with any estimated coefficient.

These offending estimates must be resolved before evaluating the model results. In the case of negative error variances (Heywood case) the offending error variances can be changed to a very small positive value (0.005). If correlations in the standardized solution exceed 1.0, or two estimates are highly correlated, one of the constructs should be removed. Tables 8.6 and 8.7 present the Heywood case.

Tables 8.6 and 8.7 show that a loading for tangible product is greater than 1.0 (known as a Heywood case). A corresponding negative error measurement value for the same variable is derived (−0.325). Such estimates are inappropriate and must be corrected before the model can be interpreted and the goodness-of-fit assessed. In this case, the variable will be retained and the corresponding negative error variance will be set to a small value of 0.005 to ensure that the loading will be

Table 8.6   Initial results of the measurement model

Variables	Perception	Satisfaction
Hotel	0.644	0.000
Service providers	0.743	0.000
Leisure activities	0.564	0.000
Accessibility	0.432	0.000
Tangible product	0.000	**1.234**
Intangible product (service)	0.000	0.685
Relaxation	0.000	0.879

Table 8.7   Measurement error for indicators

Variables	Hotel	Service providers	Leisure activities	Accessi-bility	Tangible product	Intangible product	Relaxation
Hotel	0.585						
Service providers	0.000	0.572					
Leisure activities	0.000	0.000	0.453				
Accessibility	0.000	0.000	0.000	0.321			
Tangible product	0.000	0.000	0.000	0.000	−0.325		
Intangible product	0.000	0.000	0.000	0.000	0.000	0.422	
Relaxation	0.000	0.000	0.000	0.000	0.000	0.000	0.000

less than 1.0. The model is then re-estimated. Since in examining the new results, no offending estimates are found (a new loading on a tangible product is 0.996 and error variance is 0.005), the model can be assessed for its goodness-of-fit.

When assessing model fit, attention must be paid both to the measurement and the structural models. Fornell (1987) suggested simultaneous evaluation of both models. However, Anderson and Gerbing (1982) reported that proper evaluation of the measurement model (latent variables) is a pre-requisite of the evaluation of the structural model (the analysis of the relations among the latent variables). The LISREL program runs the assessment of both models simultaneously.

Types of fit measurement
There are three types of fit measurement:

■ *absolute fit measures* (assess the overall model fit, both structural and measurement together, with no adjustment for overfitting).

- *incremental fit measures* (compare the proposed model to a comparison model).
- *parsimonious fit measures* (adjust the measures of fit to compare models with different numbers of coefficients and determine the fit achieved by each coefficient). In order to achieve a better understanding of the acceptability of the proposed model multiple measures should be applied.

Absolute fit measures

The absolute fit measures provide information on the extent to which the model *as a whole* provides an acceptable fit to the data. They are evaluated by:

- Likelihood ratio of Chi-square to the degrees of freedom (the acceptable range is between 0.05 and 0.10-0.20). A large value of Chi-square indicates a poor fit of the model to the data; a small value of Chi-square indicates a good fit. The degrees of freedom judge whether the Chi-square is large or small. The number of degrees of freedom is calculated as:

$$df = 1/2[(p + q)(p + q + 1)] - t$$

where $p =$ the number of endogenous indicators
$q =$ the number of exogenous indicators
$p + q =$ number of manifest variables
$t =$ the number of independent parameters to be estimated.

- Goodness-of-fit index (GFI), which is an indicator of the relative amount of variances and covariances jointly accounted for by the model, shows how closely the proposed model comes to a perfect one (takes values between 0 and 1 and the closer to unity, the better the model fit). A marginal acceptance level is 0.90.
- Root mean square residuals (RMSR) reflect the average amount of variances and covariances not accounted for by the model. The closer to zero, the better the fit. A marginal acceptance level is 0.08. RMSR must be interpreted in relation to the sizes of the observed variances and covariances.
- Root mean square error of approximation (RMSEA).
- Noncentrality parameter (NCP).
- Scaled noncentrality parameter (SNCP).
- Expected cross-validation index (ECVI).

The NCP, SNCP and ECVI are used in comparison among alternative models.

Results in the hypothetical model:

Revised model	
Chi-square	15.87
Degrees of freedom	10
Significance level	0.08
Goodness-of-fit index (GFI)	0.949
Adjusted Goodness-of-fit index (AGFI)	0.889
Root mean square residual (RMSR)	0.056

The Chi-square value (15.87 with 10 df) has a statistical significance level of 0.08, above the minimum level of 0.05, but not above the more conservative levels of 0.10 or 0.20. This statistic shows some support for a notion that the differences between the predicted and actual matrices are non-significant and it indicates an acceptable model fit. The GFI of 0.949 is quite high, but not when adjusted for model parsimony (different number of coefficients). The RMSF indicates that the average residual correlation is 0.056, acceptable given strong correlations in the original correlation matrix.

Problems with Chi-square statistics

Since these statistics provide overall measures of fit they do not express the quality of the model. It has been argued that the Chi-square measure-of-fit should not be regarded as the best indicator of the model fit, particularly when there is data departure from normality. Lack of normality can inflate the Chi-square statistics and create upward bias for determining significance of the coefficients. Also, the use of Chi-square is not valid in most applications (Joreskog and Sorbom, 1989a). Although the Chi-square measure may be treated as a test of the hypothesis, the statistical problem is not one of testing a hypothesis (which a priori might be considered false), but one of fitting the model to the data, and deciding whether the fit is adequate or not. Joreskog and Sorbom (1989b) explain that in most empirical work, models are only experimental and regarded as only an approximation to reality, and for this reason the Chi-square should not be used. Other reasons for not using a Chi-square as criteria for judging the adequacy of the model include sample size and problems related to the power of the test. Large samples tend to increase the Chi-square due to specification error in the model. Thus, Chi-square statistics should be interpreted with caution.

GFI, AGFI and RMSR measures

Measures such as GFI, AGFI and RMSR also do not express perfectly the quality of the models. According to Joreskog and Sorbom (1989b), quality should be judged by other internal and external criteria such as theoretical grounding. For instance, these measures can show poor fit because of one relationship only being poorly determined. Thus a fit of 0.5–0.6 does not precisely state whether the model *is* or *is not* supported by the data. In practice, it can suggest that some of the poorly described relationship paths should be eliminated from the model to make it more sound, and the model should be run again to see if an improved fit could be obtained. These measures also do not indicate what is wrong with the model (Joreskog and Sorbom, 1989b). As to the RMSR, they work best if *all* observed variables are standardized.

The incremental fit measures

While all the absolute measures might fall within acceptable levels, the incremental fit and parsimonious fit indices are needed to ensure acceptability of the model from other perspectives. The incremental fit measures assess the incremental fit of the model compared to a null model (the most simple model that can be theoretically justified, e.g., a single construct model related to all indicators with no measurement error). These are:

1. Tucker-Lewis measure (TL);
2. Normed fit index (NFI).

These incremental fit measures should exceed the recommended level of minimum 0.90 to support acceptance of the proposed model.

Results in the hypothetical model:

Null Model	
Chi-square	210.876
Degrees of freedom	15
Significance level	0.000
Tucker Lewis (TL)	0.9414

Both incremental fit measures exceed the recommended level of 0.90 and support acceptance of the proposed model.

Parsimonious fit measures

Parsimonious fit measures determine the model fit in comparison to models of differing complexity. The fit is compared versus the number of estimated coefficients (or degrees of freedom) needed to achieve the level of fit (fit per coefficient). The two most appropriate parsimonious fit measures are:

- Normed Chi-square (Chi-square/df) (the level recommended by Carmines and McIver (1981) is between 1.0 and 3.0)
- Adjusted for the degrees of freedom goodness-of-fit index (AGFI) (takes values between 0 and 1; and the closer to unity, the better the model fit). If there is a drop in AGFI as compared to GFI, the overall fit of the model can be questioned.

Results in the hypothetical model show that the normed Chi-square (Chi-square divided by degrees of freedom) is 1.587 (15.87/10). This falls within the recommended levels of 1.0 to 3.0. The AGFI value of 0.889 is close to the recommended level of 0.90. These results show support for model parsimony.

In summary, the various measures of overall model goodness-of-fit gave support to the results of an acceptable representation of the hypothesized constructs.

The other parsimonious fit measures are:

- Parsimony normed fit index (PNFI)
- Parsimonious goodness-of-fit index (PGFI)
- Comparative fit index (CFI)
- Incremental fit index (IFI)
- Relative fit index (RFI)
- Critical N (CN).

Squared multiple correlation coefficients

The fit of the *measurement model* is assessed by examining squared multiple correlation coefficients (SMC) for the y- and x-variables, which indicate how well the y- and x-variables measure the latent construct, the largest amount of variance accounted for by the constructs, and the extent to which the individual variables are free from measurement error. They also represent the reliabilities (convergent validities) of these measures. These coefficients lie between 0 and 1 (the closer to 1, the better the variable acts as an indicator of the latent construct).

Results in the hypothetical model:

Squared multiple correlations for x-variables

Hotel	Providers	Leisure	Access	Tangible	Intangible	Relaxation
0.745	0.720	0.648	0.483	0.600	0.863	0.867

The results show that all x-variables are good measurements of both constructs.

The total coefficients of determination (TCD) (R^2) for all y- and x-variables provide measures of how well the y- and x-variables *as a group* measure the latent constructs. The closer to 1, the better. Results in the hypothetical model show that total coefficient of determination for x-variables is 0.981. All x-variables as a group measure the latent constructs very well.

The fit of the *structural model* is assessed by the squared multiple correlations (SMC) for structural equations, which indicates the amount of variance in each endogenous latent variable accounted for by the independent variables in the relevant structural equation, and the total coefficient of determination (TCD) (R^2) for structural equations, which shows the strength of the relationships for all structural relationships together. Results in the hypothetical model show that the R^2 for the total structural equations is 0.788.

Multi-collinearity

The results of structural equation modelling can be affected by multi-collinearity as in regression. If large values of correlation for the observed variables appear the deletion of one variable, or reformulation of the relationships should be considered. Although there is no limit on what defines high correlation, values exceeding 0.90 and even 0.80 can indicate problems, values below 0.8 can be compensated for by declaring covariance paths between independent variables. That is, it is possible to model multicollinearity within the SEM analysis.

271

Each of the constructs can also be evaluated separately by examining:

- *T*-values
- Correlations between the latent constructs
- Standard errors (SE)
- Fitted residuals (FR).

T-values

The examination of the *t*-values is associated with examining the indicators' loadings (*t*-values for the paths) for statistical significance. If the *t*-values associated with each of the loadings for the path coefficients are larger than 2, the parameters are significant and variables are significantly related to their specified constructs, thus verifying the relationships among indicators and constructs.

The examination of the *t*-values associated with each of the loadings in the hypothetical model indicates that for each variable they exceed the critical values for the 0.05 significance level (critical value = 1.96) and the 0.01 significance level as well (critical value = 2.576). Thus all variables are significantly related to their specified constructs, verifying posited relationships among indicators and constructs (see Table 8.8).

Table 8.8 Construct loadings (*t*-values in parentheses)

Variables	Perception	Satisfaction
Hotel	0.644	0.000
	(6.543)	
Service providers	0.788	0.000
	(7.899)	
Leisure activities	0.655	0.000
	(8.999)	
Accessibility	0.566	0.000
	(6.888)	
Tangible product	0.000	0.877
		(12.435)
Intangible product (service)	0.000	0.899
		(11.456)
Relaxation	0.000	0.901
		(12.345)

Correlation between the latent constructs

The examination of the correlation between the latent constructs is associated with examining the ϕ values and t-values.

Example: correlation among latent constructs (t-value in parentheses)

	Perception	Satisfaction
Perception	1.000	
Satisfaction	0.899	1.000
	(14.567)	

The examination of the correlation between the latent constructs and the t-value show that the correlation is very high and the t-value exceeds the critical value of 1.96, indicating that the latent constructs are significantly correlated with each other.

Standard errors

The examination of standard errors is associated with assessing the standard errors (SE) for each coefficient and construct. Standard errors show how accurately the values of the parameters are estimated. The smaller the standard errors, the better the estimation. However, what is small or large depends on the units of measurement in latent constructs and the magnitude of the parameter estimate itself. The standard errors are correct under assumptions of multivariate normality. They should be interpreted with caution if the condition of normality does not hold. Therefore, t-values are better to be used as independent units of measurement.

Fitted residuals

The model fit can also be examined by assessing the fitted residuals (FR), which represent the differences between the observed and the fitted correlations calculated from the model. They should be relatively small to the size of the elements of the correlation matrices to indicate that the fit of the models is acceptable. However, since the fitted residuals depend on the metric of the observed variables (the unit of measurement), they can vary from variable to variable, and are difficult to use in the assessment of fit. The problem is avoided by evaluating the standardized residuals (SR) (fitted residuals divided by their standard errors), which are independent of the metric of the observed variables and can be interpreted as standard normal deviations. An SR that exceeds the value of 2.58 in absolute terms indicates substantial specification and prediction error for a pair of indicators.

Q-plot

The best picture of fit is obtained by looking at the Q-plot, which plots the standardized residuals (horizontal axis) against the quartiles of the normal distribution (vertical axis). The best possible fit is obtained when all residuals lie in a straight vertical line; the worst is when the residuals lie in a horizontal straight line. An acceptable fit is indicated when the residuals lie approximately along the diagonal, with steeper plots (greater than 45°) representing better fits (see Figure 8.8). If the pattern of residuals is non-linear this indicates departure from normality, linearity and/or specification errors in the model.

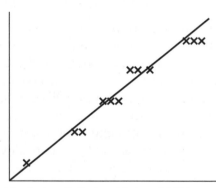

Figure 8.8 The Q-plot for the hypothetical model. A model fit is acceptable as the residuals lie along the diagonal

Stage 7

Stage 7 considers whether modifications to the model have to be made in the light of the results obtained at the previous stage. At this stage the analysis becomes exploratory in nature and results from previous analysis are used to develop a better fitting model. The aim is to identify specification errors and produce a new model that fits the data better. This new model has to be verified on a second independent sample.

Examination of the standardized residuals

The first modification to the model may be done through examination of the standardized residuals and the modification indices. The standardized residuals (normalized) are provided by the program and represent the differences between the observed correlation/covariance and the estimated correlation/covariance matrix. Residuals values greater than ±2.58 are considered statistically significant at 0.05 level. Significant residuals indicate substantial error for a pair of indicators. The acceptable range is one in twenty residuals exceeding 2.58 by chance. In the hypothetical model only one value exceeded 2.58. Thus, only one correlation from the original input matrix has a statistically significant residual. This falls within the acceptable range.

Deleting or adding parameters

The other two ways in which modification to a model can be made is by deleting or adding parameters. In both cases, deleting or adding parameters should be guided by theory. Non-significant *t*-values can give insight as to which parameters should be eliminated. However, if a theory suggests that particular parameters should be included in the model, even non-significant parameters should be retained because the sample size may be too small to detect their real significance (Joreskog and Sorbom, 1989b).

The effect of the deletion on the model fit can be assessed by comparing the Chi-square values of the two models, particularly the differences in Chi-squares.

When to use modification indices

The modification indices (MI) can be used to decide which parameters should be added to the model. The MI are measures of the predicted decrease in the Chi-square that results if a single parameter (fixed or constrained) is freed (relaxed) and the model reestimated, with all other parameters maintaining their present values. The improvement in fit from relaxing the parameters is acceptable under the condition that only one parameter is relaxed at a time. The model modification should never be based solely on the MI. Modification of the models must be theoretically justified. Consideration should be given to whether some of the parameters are not necessary to measure the latent constructs. According to Darden (1983), achieving a good fit at all costs is not always recommended because a good fit for a model may theoretically be inappropriate. There are many models that could fit the data better. In fact, a poor fit tells more, that is, the degree to which the model is not supported by the data.

Comparison of nested models

If the best fitting model cannot be found using the confirmatory strategy (where the researcher specifies a single model and SEM to assess its significance), then the best fitting model can also be determined by comparison of competing or nested models. Firstly, a number of alternative models are compared to find a model which comes closest to a theory. Differences between models are indicated by the differences in the Chi-square values for the different models. These differences can be tested for statistical significance with the appropriate degrees of freedom. The objective is to find the best fit from among the set of models. Secondly, an initial model goes through a series of model respecifications in order to improve the model fit.

Stage 8

Stage 8 involves the cross-validation of the model with a new data set. This is done by dividing the sample into two parts to conduct a validation test. The LISREL multisample analysis can be used for this purpose. The cross-validation test is performed when modification indices are used and the model did not provide an acceptable fit. This test should also be performed when the model shows an acceptable fit in the first analysis. In addition, cross-validation can be used to compare competing models in terms of predictive validity and facilitate the selection of a model; to compare the difference between samples belonging to different populations and assess the impact of moderating variables (Sharma *et al.*, 1981).

However, cross-validation has its limitations: (1) it requires access to the raw data and a new data set; (2) the sample must be large enough to divide it into sub-samples and generate reliable estimates (minimum sample size should be between 300–500 observations); and (3) bias may occur if sample splitting is done randomly.

Summary

SEM modelling is a powerful tool enabling researchers to go beyond factor analysis into the arena of determining whether one set of unobserved constructs (dimensions) can determine (be seen to be likely to determine) another set of dimensions. In tourism studies, it is often the case that the variables under study cannot be directly observed or measured (for example, motivation, satisfaction, importance, perception) yet these unobserved variables might be hypothesized to determine one another. SEM analysis is a methodology capable of handling this type of analysis, along with more conventional regression models, and simultaneous regression models, while accounting for multicollinearity and, with appropriate care, other assumptions of regression modelling.

Discussion points and questions

1. What are the objectives of structural equation modelling?
2. How can structural equation models be used to solve problems within the tourism discipline? Give examples.
3. What steps are involved in formulation and testing of models?
4. What is the difference between a structural and measurement model?
5. What does the model identification mean?
6. What are the sources of identification problems and how can they be avoided?
7. Explain the differences between various kinds of parameter estimation.
8. What is the difference between a standardized and non-standardized solution?

Further reading

Bagozzi, R. (1980) *Causal Models in Marketing*. New York: Wiley.
Bollen, K. A. (1989) *Structural Equations with Latent Variables*. New York: Wiley.

Carmines, E. G. and McIver, J. P. (1981) Analyzing models with unobserved variables: Analysis of covariance structures. In Bohrnstedt G. W. and Borgatta, E. F., (eds). *Social Measurement*: Current Issues, Beverly Hills, CA: Sage Publications, pp. 65–115.

Hox, J. (1995) AMOS, EQS, and LISREL for Windows: a comparative review. *Structural Equation Modeling* 2(1): 79–91.

Joreskog, K. and Sorbom (1989a) *LISREL 7: User's Reference Guide*. Mooresville. Scientific Software Inc.

Joreskog, K. and Sorbom (1989b) *LISREL 7: A Guide to the Program and Applications*. Chicago, IL: SPSS Inc.

For more detailed information readers should refer to specialized literature such as the journal *Structural Equation Modeling*.

Part 3

Applications of Cultural Analysis in Tourism

Part 3 provides an example of the application of quantitative methodology to cross-cultural analysis utilizing factor analysis and structural equation modelling to identify the differences between the Asian and Australian cultures. Five Asian cultural groups (Indonesia, Japan, Korea, Mandarin speaking and Thai) of tourists are analysed and the implications for marketing and management of their cultural differences are outlined.

The focus of the analysis is to determine the main relationships between cultural differences and Asian tourist satisfaction. From these relationships the analysis develops cultural models providing insight into the factors influencing Asian tourist and western host interaction.

A major finding from the analysis is that marketers cannot rely just on perceptions of service to generate satisfaction by visiting Asian tourists. Satisfaction can also be influenced by cultural values, rules of social behaviour and social interaction.

9

Cultural analysis: marketing and management implications

Objectives

After completing this chapter the reader should be able to

- learn about the application of Principal Components Analysis to the cultural analysis of tourism

- learn about the application of structural equation modelling to the cultural analysis of tourism

- identify cultural differences between Asian and western populations

- identify cultural differences between Asian tourist markets

- understand the relationships between cultural factors and their impact on tourist holiday satisfaction

- identify the key cultural differences that influence Asian tourist satisfaction with international hosts.

Introduction

This chapter begins with a very brief summary of the literature review presented in previous chapters, followed by the presentation of a tourist satisfaction model and its variables. This model is used in the subsequent example of cross-cultural analysis applied to tourism. The factor analysis and structural equation modelling are used for the purpose of this analysis to identify cultural differences between Asian tourists and Australian hosts. Five Asian cultural groups of tourists are analysed, and the implications for marketing and management of their cultural differences are outlined.

Brief conceptual summary

The previous chapters reviewed existing literature on the cultural differences that influence the social interaction between international tourists and their hosts. It was suggested that in the cross-cultural context the cultural background of tourists and hosts, specifically the cultural similarities and differences in their background, mostly determine this interaction. The cultural values, the most important variables in differing cultures, determine the similarities and differences in cultural backgrounds (Hall, 1976, 1977; Hofstede, 1980; Kluckhohn and Strodtbeck, 1961; Rokeach, 1973). Cultural values determine rules of social behaviour, which vary across cultures and generate interaction difficulties. Rules of social interaction influence the development of social perceptions, which also differ across cultures. The cultural similarities in perceptions develop positive perceptions and encourage social interaction. Cultural dissimilarities create misperceptions and discourage interaction.

Further, tourist and host social interaction can be explained within the context of the service encounter (Riley, 1995). The cultural differences between tourists and service providers may affect their social experiences. The quality of services offered to tourists by service providers decide about tourist satisfaction with hosts. The positive perceptions of service providers create positive perceptions of service quality and result in satisfaction with service, and vice versa.

Cultural model of conceptual relationships

The findings of the literature review show that it is possible to draw a diagram that represents and clarifies the relationships among the theoretical concepts that have been described in the previous chapters. Figure 9.1 shows the relationships among these concepts.

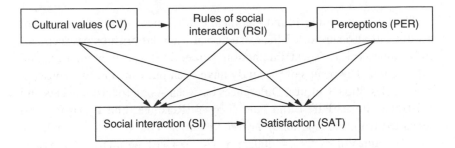

Figure 9.1 Cultural model of conceptual relationships

The major dependent variables (criteria) in the model are tourist-host social interaction (SI) and satisfaction with tourist-host interaction (SAT). The independent variables are cultural values (CV), rules of social interaction (RSI), and perceptions (PER). The rules of social interaction and perceptions may also be treated as dependent variables since they depend on cultural values. Also, perceptions may depend on rules of interaction. Figure 9.1 shows that cultural values determine rules of social behaviour and influence people's perceptions of each other, which, in turn, determine their social interaction and satisfaction or dissatisfaction with this interaction. The control variables such as demographic and socio-economic characteristics of the subjects, or length of stay, type of travel arrangements, and others are held constant in order to neutralize their effect.

It is hypothesized that the cultural differences in values, rules of social behaviour, and perceptions between international tourists and local hosts determine tourist-host interaction and satisfaction with this interaction.

The attributes of the model

The model shows that social interaction and satisfaction with this interaction is a cultural phenomenon, because it is influenced by cultural factors such as cultural values, rules of social relations, and perceptions. The variables of the model represent multidimensional and multifaceted concepts and should be analysed as part of a system rather than separately because of their mutual influence on each other and the nature of the specific relationships between them.

The study not only found significant differences in all measurement groups but also supported the existence of the relationships between cultural values, rules of social interaction, perceptions, social interaction, and satisfaction. The results of the study have been published in two consecutive articles titled 'Cultural Differences between Asian tourist markets and Australian hosts: Part 1 and Part 2' by Y. Reisinger and L. Turner and reprinted from the *Journal of Travel Research*, Vol. 40, No. 3, 2002, pp. 295–315, and Vol. 40, No. 4, 2002, pp. 374–384 with permission from Sage Publications. The study and its results are briefly presented below.

Importance of the Asian tourist market

Currently, the international tourism industry is faced with an increasing number of inbound travellers from Asia. The Asian tourist market stands to become the largest source of international tourists. The Japanese market is the largest single source but this will be challenged by China in the future. The Asian market has also shown the strongest annual growth in tourist arrivals to Australia. According to predictions, the Asian market will be the largest source of international tourists to Australia beyond the year 2000. Australia is the second most popular non-Asian destination after the United States of America for the Korean market (Prideaux, 1998). It is predicted that during the next five years China may become one of the prime sources of Asian outbound tourism due to its booming economy, emergence of an upper middle-upper class, and liberalization of border controls and currency regulations. The Singapore market will also grow and will provide a high number of repeat visitors. Australia's other Southeast Asian markets of Indonesia, Thailand and Malaysia will also continue to provide a steady source of tourists beyond the year 2000.

Consequently, tourist destinations will face the challenge of learning about the Asian tourist market and developing responsive and culture oriented marketing programs. Success in retaining and even increasing Asian market share in Australia will depend upon responding quickly to the needs of the distinct Asian markets. The Asian market niche with the greatest potential is the middle class from China, Malaysia, South Korea and Thailand (Crotts and Ryan, 1997), not the wealthy elite from Japan,

Hong Kong, Singapore, and Taiwan on which the tourism industry has traditionally concentrated. Thus, it will be important to understand the cultural orientation of these newly emerging markets for the purpose of marketing and the design of advertising campaigns (Mok and Armstrong, 1995). The ability to respond to each market's peculiarities and to adopt not just global marketing programs but regional programs will provide a challenge (McAllan, 1997).

Research objectives

The main research objectives of the study were:

1. To identify the key cultural differences between the Asian tourist markets and the Australian host population, as a representative of western culture
2. To determine the key dimensions of these differences, and their indicators
3. To find the main relationships between cultural differences and Asian tourist satisfaction
4. To develop cultural models that can provide insight into the factors influencing Asian tourist-Australian host interaction, and satisfaction with this interaction and
5. To identify major cultural themes that should be included in every promotional strategy aiming at the Asian tourist market.

In the research study, culture refers to a stable and dominant cultural character of a society shared by most of its individuals. Culture does not refer to the subcultures of many ethnic groups living in a society. The authors understand that individual Asian markets are heterogeneous with respect to socio-cultural characteristics. The authors also believe that any cultural grouping is heterogeneous at a particular scale, and that there are regional as well as individual differences in any culture, including Japan (Iverson, 1997). In this study all Asian samples except the Japanese one (100 per cent of Japanese tourists are from Japan) are represented by more than a single country. For instance, the Mandarin-speaking market is represented by tourists from Mainland China, Singapore, Taiwan, Hong Kong, and a very small percentage of tourists from Malaysia and Vietnam. The South Korean market is represented by 99.4 per cent of tourists from South Korea and 0.6 per cent from Japan. Similarly, the Thai market is represented by 98 per cent of tourists from

Thailand and 2 per cent from Japan and China. The Indonesian market is represented by 93.4 per cent of tourists from Indonesia and 6.6 per cent from Hong Kong and India. However, the issue of the regional differences is not analysed here. The aim of the study is to analyse various Asian cultures from a broad national perspective, as opposed to a regional or individual perspective, and to recognize a national dominant cultural character of the major Asian markets that distinguishes them from the Australian population. Similarly, the Australian sample is composed of hosts of different origins such as Britain and New Zealand, with 96 per cent of the Australian sample born in Australia, and 4 per cent born in the United Kingdom and New Zealand.

The two distinct groups, tourists and hosts, are chosen for the study because these groups are the major tourism players. Hosts in this study are nationals of the visited country who provide services to tourists (e.g., front office employees, bus drivers, shop assistants, waitresses, custom officials). They are employed in places most frequented by tourists, such as accommodation, restaurants, tourist attractions, etc. These places offer maximum opportunities for direct tourist-host contact. As a result, hosts represent the first contact points with tourists. Consequently, cross-cultural differences in the interpersonal interaction in the tourism context are most likely to be apparent in these two groups: tourists and hosts.

One may, of course, argue that the interaction between local providers and international tourists is itself impacted upon by business practices and tourism transactions that shape the nature of the tourist-host contact, thus the variations in this contact may not be necessarily attributed to the nature of cultural differences. However, the provider's business practices as well as the tourist's perceptions of these practices are by themselves culturally determined. Thus, the variations in their interpersonal interaction are attributed to the cultural differences in their perceptions of what constitutes socially and culturally appropriate service behaviour. This is supported by the literature review findings, which show that the cultural differences in interaction patterns between guests and service providers lead to different perceptions of the guests' treatment (Sheldon and Fox, 1988).

The research study hypothesizes that there are significant differences in Asian and Australian populations in the tourism context and that these differences can be grouped into dimensions of cultural differences between Asian tourists and Australian hosts.

Study methodology

The detailed study methodology used in the study is presented in the publisher's website at www.bh.com/companions/0750656689. A brief summary is presented below.

Sample

A sample of 618 Asian tourists (Indonesian, Japanese, South Korean, Mandarin and Thai) visiting the Gold Coast region, Australia's major tourist destination, were personally interviewed in their own language, alongside 250 Australian service providers who were randomly selected from a variety of sectors of the tourism and hospitality industry.

Instrument

Five measurement groups of cultural values, rules of social behaviour, perceptions of service, forms of interaction, and satisfaction with interaction were measured by a structured questionnaire. The responses were measured on a 6-point scale from least important (least satisfied) to most important (most satisfied). A section on personal characteristics included information on the sociodemographic profiles of respondents.

Procedure

The instrument originally translated into Asian languages and back translated to the English language, was pre-tested twice in two pilot studies. Professional native Asian-language-speaking interviewers collected data from 870 respondents: 250 Australian hosts and 618 Asian tourists from five language groups (106 Indonesian, 108 Japanese, 172 South Korean, 130 Mandarin-speaking, and 102 Thai).

Data analysis

Because of the smaller individual sample sizes there was a need to reduce the number of variables originally analysed. Thus, the analysis focused only on the variables that statistically differed between the Asian and Australian populations. The Mann-Whitney U-Test identified these differences. The basic dimensions of the cultural differences (the gap scores) were determined by Principal Components Analysis. Only the raw scores for those variables that differed were factor analysed, as from a marketing perspective the interest lay in what cultural aspects were different rather than similar. Although an analysis of the entire set of variables would be interesting, the required number of variables to case size would have been too large. R-type factor analysis was used (instead of Q-type) to analyse relationships among the variables (instead of cases) and to identify groups of variables forming latent dimensions (factors). Principal Components Analysis was chosen (instead of Common Factor Analysis) in order to minimize the number of factors needed to account for the maximum portion of the variance represented in the original set of variables, and to reduce the specific and error variance as a proportion of the total variance. Oblique rotation was chosen to obtain several theoretically meaningful interrelated factors, as opposed to orthogonal rotation, which reduces the number of variables to a smaller set of independent factors regardless of how meaningful the resulting factors are. Only the factors having latent roots (eigenvalues) greater than 1 and factor loadings greater than 0.6 were considered significant. Comrey in Hair *et al.* (1995) suggests that loadings in excess of 0.63 (40 per cent of overlapping variance) are very good and above 0.7 (50 per cent of overlapping variance) are excellent.[1]

Results of the Mann-Whitney U-test

The results of the Mann-Whitney U-test identified seventy-three out of 117 (62.4 per cent) significant differences between Asian tourists and Australian providers in all five measurement groups: cultural values, rules of behaviour, perceptions of service, forms of interaction, and satisfaction with interaction that may be obtained from the publisher's website.[2]

The Mann-Whitney U-test also identified significant differences in all measurement groups between the individual Asian language groups and the Australian sample. In terms of the individual language groups, the Japanese were the most distinct from the Australian hosts, followed by the South Korean, Indonesian, Thai, and Mandarin-speaking tourists. Out of 117 areas of measurement, eighty-three significant differences were found between Australian hosts and Japanese tourists, seventy-four between the South Korean sample, sixty-four between the Indonesian and Thai samples and fifty-three between the Mandarin sample (refer to the publisher's website).[3]

Results of the Principal Components Analysis

The identified differences were grouped in several cultural dimensions determined by Principal Components Analysis, separately in the total Asian sample and each Asian language group.

Total Asia

In the total Asian sample, five dimensions were identified: perceptions of communication, values of family/competence, interaction, rules of feeling display, and satisfaction. The dimension of *communication* reflects the tourists' need for adequate communication with hosts, the hosts' ability to be informative, give adequate explanations, listen to tourists, and anticipate and understand tourists' needs. The dimension of *family/competence* reflects the importance of family and cues that describe the person's capabilities to succeed such as being intellectual, independent, self-controlled, and polite. The dimension of *interaction* describes the preferences for forms of social interaction such as being invited home, or playing sport together. The dimension of *feeling display* indicates disclosing personal feelings in public such as criticizing in public, or showing respect. The dimension of *satisfaction* shows the components of satisfaction with social interaction between tourists and hosts (see Table 9.1).

Indonesia

In the Indonesian sample, four dimensions were identified: perceptions of responsiveness, perceptions of attention, interaction, and satisfaction. The dimension of *responsiveness* consists of variables that describe the hosts' capacity to respond to tourists' needs and provide required service, the cues associated with timing of service provision, physical appearance of service providers, and the hosts' ability to solve problems. The dimension of *attention* consists of variables that describe the hosts' ability to pay attention to tourists, anticipate and understand their needs, be concerned about tourists, and listen to them. The dimension of *interaction* describes the preferences for forms of social interaction. The dimension of *satisfaction* relates to satisfaction with the hosts' knowledge of Indonesian culture and language.

Japan

In the Japanese sample, five dimensions were identified: perceptions of helpfulness, values of competence, interaction, rules of greetings and satisfaction. The dimension of *helpfulness* consists of variables that describe the providers' ability to help tourists and respond to their needs including being punctual, accurate, able to solve problems, trustworthy, respectful, hospitable, polite, confident, communicative, informative, and professional. The dimension of *competence* consists of variables that describe the cues associated with accomplishment such as being intellectual, logical, obedient, self-respectful, wise, and independent. The dimension of *interaction* describes the preferences for social

Table 9.1   Results of the Principal Components Analysis in the total Asian sample for the variables that differed between Australian hosts and all Asian tourists (significant factor loadings only)

Factor	Loading	Variables included in the factor
Communication	0.75601	Give adequate explanations
	0.75519	Anticipate tourists' needs
	0.74292	Understand tourists' needs
	0.73079	Listen to tourists
	0.72124	Offer individualized attention
	0.67482	Keep tourists informed
Family/Competence	0.76365	Family security
	0.74741	Being intellectual
	0.70615	Being independent
	0.65336	Being self-controlled
	0.61418	Being polite
Interaction	0.85795	Have close relationship
	0.82800	Invite home
	0.82584	Take part in parties
	0.82131	Play sport together
	0.81233	Share a meal
	0.77885	Exchange gifts
Feeling display	0.76020	Criticize in public
	0.74455	Show respect
	0.72936	Ask personal questions
	0.72554	Conform to social status
	0.71870	Respect others' privacy
	0.71268	Address by first name
	0.66947	Show emotions
Satisfaction	0.75012	With time spent together
	0.65842	With each other
	0.63060	With knowledge of Asian language

interaction. The dimension of *greetings* is related to the way in which people greet each other such as addressing by first name, or shaking hands. The dimension of *satisfaction* relates to the satisfaction with friendship and time spent together.

South Korea

In the Korean sample, five dimensions were identified: perceptions of communication, rules of feeling display, perceptions of performance, interaction, and satisfaction. The dimension of *communication* reflects the tourists' needs for adequate information and explanations, to listen to them, hosts' ability to speak the Korean language, and have some knowledge of the Korean culture. The dimension of *feeling display* is related to rules of social behaviour and concerns disclosing personal feelings in public. The dimension of *performance* consists of variables that describe the cues associated with providing high quality service as perceived by the Korean tourists, that is, being responsive, respectful, punctual, and neatly dressed. The dimension of *interaction* describes the preferences for social interaction. The dimension of *satisfaction* relates to satisfaction with providers and friendship.

Mandarin-speaking

In the Mandarin sample, five dimensions were identified: perceptions of punctuality, interaction, perceptions of understanding, rules of feeling display, and satisfaction. The dimension of *punctuality* focuses on the timing and responsiveness of service. The dimension of *interaction* describes the preference for forms of social interaction. The dimension of *understanding* is related to the hosts' ability to anticipate and understand individual tourists' needs, pay attention to tourists, and ability to speak the Asian language. The dimension of *feeling display* concerns disclosing personal feelings in public. The dimension of *satisfaction* relates to satisfaction with providers and time spent together.

Thailand

In the Thai sample, five dimensions were identified: perceptions of communication courtesy, perceptions of understanding, rules of feeling display, satisfaction and interaction. The dimension of *communication courtesy* consists of variables that describe the hosts' ability to treat tourists as guests and behave towards tourists in a respectful and polite manner. It entails the need to be trustworthy, considerate, and friendly. The dimension of *understanding* consists of variables that describe the hosts' ability to understand and anticipate tourists' needs, pay attention to tourists, listen to them, and keep them informed. The dimension of *feeling display* reflects cues associated with disclosure of personal feelings in public. The dimension of *satisfaction* relates to satisfaction with conversation, providers, and friendship. The dimension of *interaction* describes the preferred forms of social interaction.[4]

Interpretation of the cultural dimensions

The interpretation of the identified dimensions in the total Asian sample is presented below.

Total Asia

Communication.   As high uncertainty avoidance cultures, no Asian markets tolerate ambiguity and taking risk. They are concerned about communication difficulties in Australia. Asian languages such as Japanese, Korean, or Mandarin have several different levels used by various social classes and genders. For example, DeMente (1991b) reported that there are different levels of the Korean language used by various social classes in a Korean hierarchical society: (1) extremely polite form used when addressing superiors, (2) an intimate form for addressing close friends or equals, and (3) a rough form used when speaking to people on a lower social level. Also, all Asian markets use indirect smoothing strategies to manage conflicts (Kim and Gudykunst, 1988). This is in contrast to Australians, who tolerate ambiguity and risk and do not avoid conflicts.

As members of high context cultures, Asian people communicate in an indirect, implicit way by using numerous non-verbal cues such as body language, facial expressions or eye gaze. Australians, who belong to a low uncertainty and low context culture, have only one language used by all social classes and genders. They communicate in a more direct, explicit way by emphasizing words and verbal expressions.

Family/competence.   Asians are very much family oriented. Family needs and security are the concern of all its members. The relationships between the family members are of a dependence nature. Each member of the family depends on the other for security and protection. In Australia, this type of dependency does not occur. Family ties are looser; people are taught to be self-reliant and independent. Also, in Asian high power distance cultures, societies have well-developed social hierarchy. Proper education and intellectual achievements are important in order to get a good job and belong to the 'right social class'. For example, in the masculine Japanese culture emphasis is placed on professional competence, intellectual achievements, and wisdom (Zimmerman, 1985). In Australian low power distance culture, education and intellectual achievements are not of such importance. Australian society regards education as a right instead of privilege, and often disregards social position. Society places more value on sport heroes and financially wealthy people than intellectualists. On the other hand, Thai people do not commit themselves seriously to hard work or education, which are essential for success (Komin, 1990). Australians have more sense of achievement and internal motivation to work hard, self-actualization and self-reliance.

Interaction. As members of collectivistic cultures, Asian people are oriented towards group interests and needs (Hsu, 1953). Social relations are perceived in terms of social usefulness (Hsu, 1971a) and are characterized by group activities, keeping up with 'in groups', sharing and doing things together, dependence on each other, group loyalty and consensus, inclusiveness, and collaterality. For example, Ahmed and Krohn (1992) identified characteristic elements in Japanese behaviour, including travelling in groups and taking group photos. Similarly, the Korean culture emphasizes group travel (Kim and Prideaux, 1996; Prideaux, 1998). Also, in Asian cultures an individualistic behaviour is regarded as an expense to others (Hsu, 1971b). In contrast, Australians, who belong to a more individualistic culture are concerned about the individual's needs and well-being. They place greater emphasis on egalitarian, exclusive relationships, and 'doing one's own things'. The concept of privacy is strong and relationships within groups looser. Solitude is perceived positively and other people's privacy is respected. Consequently, Australian society is seen as a selfish social phenomenon in which an individual person's gain is a loss for the whole group.

In addition, as members of high power distance cultures, Asian people are obedient and submissive to a group leader, authority, and elders. Superior-subordinate hierarchical relationships dictate respect to higher ranking authorities reflected in the forms of being loyal to them, obeying them, fulfilling their instructions, showing total respect, and gratitude. Since Australians belong to a low power distance culture the concepts of group loyalty and obedience to authority and seniority are extremely weak.

All Asian societies are also supposed to hold together and function harmoniously. For example, Komin (1990) noted that in Thailand, polite, cool and superficial relationships are preferred with strangers because they guarantee a harmonious society. All social relationships in Asian societies conform to formal rules of appropriate behaviour (Hsu, 1972) that cover every aspect of conduct, including eating, drinking, seating, entertaining, greeting, and apologizing. As a result of very strict forms of social behaviour, Mandarin speaking societies use a third party in personal dealings (DeMente, 1991c). This custom is not known in Australian society where the focus is on quick and direct face-to-face dealings.

Further, all Asian societies are very much family dependent and give precedence in all things to the family, for them being invited to a home is a honourable event. For example, Japanese appreciate being invited to restaurants and nightclubs (DeMente, 1991a). Since cuisine is regarded as an important element of the Korean holiday experience (Prideaux, 1998) Koreans also appreciate being invited to restaurants for a meal.

Moreover, an important aspect of social relations in the Japanese, Korean and Mandarin speaking societies is the tradition of gift giving and reciprocating. This tradition creates and nurtures relationships with people. Gifts are always tailored to hierarchical position, age and gender of the receiver and donor, and are given as expressions of apology, appreciation, gratitude, or remembrance. In Japan, gifts are purchased for those who stayed at home (Morsbach, 1977). Gifts are the tangible ways of saying 'thank you' (DeMente, 1991c). Brand names are important. There are various types of gifts. Small thank-you gifts for hospitality and gifts for honoured guests are common in Japan (DeMente, 1991a; Zimmerman, 1985). However, in Australia gift giving often seems to be inappropriate and the donor can be suspected of a bribe. Also, the Australian style of expressing gratitude verbally with a simple 'thank you', whether casual or emotional, is treated in Mandarin-speaking societies as insincere (DeMente, 1991c).

Feeling display. As members of high uncertainty avoidance and formal cultures, Asians do not display their feelings in public in order not to cause disagreement and conflict. They do not swear and do not ask personal questions. Komin (1990) noted that the Thai are reluctant to ask personal questions, if these could in any way imply a criticism and make others uncomfortable. However, questions regarding age and earnings, which are impolite to ask in Australia, are regarded as polite in Thailand because they offer a quick way of establishing a person's status (Komin, 1990). By complying with formal rules of social behaviour, keeping emotions under control, and being self-restrained and reserved they save own and other's face and maintain social harmony. The concept of 'saving face' prescribes using respectful language, being extremely polite, avoiding criticism and excessive complimenting, and not damaging one's own or others' reputation (DeMente, 1991b). Failure to keep emotions under control may mean loosing face, respect, status, and causing humiliation on both sides. Wei *et al.* (1989) noted that the Chinese are expected to possess dignity, reserve, patience, and sensitivity to customs. In order to behave properly in the Mandarin-speaking societies, the most common way is 'to do nothing' and 'say nothing' (DeMente, 1991c). Such practice is totally irrational and unacceptable from an Australian viewpoint. Australians, who belong to a low uncertainty and informal culture, are unrestrained in their behaviour and have less control over their verbal and non-verbal expressions. They openly disagree, criticize each other and swear in public. Rules of social behaviour play a minor role in their lives. They are not concerned about destroying someone else's reputation and saving one's own and other's face. The focus is on solving problems and conflicts rather than avoiding them. Australian people are also encouraged to ask questions and employ critical thinking to challenge and disagree.

Further, in Asian cultures people use smaller interpersonal distance than in Australia. Sitting and standing occurs in very close proximity. However, physical contact such as holding hands, leaning on shoulders, touching knees, or feet and linking arms are usually avoided in public. In contrast, Australians use larger interpersonal distance, touch less, and prefer to sit side-by-side less.

Satisfaction. Satisfaction with interpersonal relations in collectivistic Asian cultures depends on the development of an atmosphere of closeness and co-operation. Friendship for Asian people implies obligations. For example, Wei *et al.* (1989) reported that for Chinese friendship implies mutual obligations and reciprocation. In Thailand, the determination of friendship depends on who one is, whom one knows and one's wealth (Komin, 1990). Also, Asian people tend to 'fit' people they meet into a social hierarchy. In more individualistic Australia, the satisfying social relationships are exclusive and based on mutual interests and activities rather than social hierarchy. Australians tend to find out what a person is like. Social relationships do not imply any obligations on the parties involved. Australians regard friendship as being relatively superficial. Also, the development of satisfying social relationships in Asia takes a longer time than in Australia. For example, the Japanese require a long time to get to know people well, to develop an atmosphere of trust ('shinyo') (Ziff-Levine, 1990), comfort ('amae') (Nakane, 1973), and complete acceptance. In contrast, it is easier to develop relationships with Australians and get along well with them in a relatively short period of time.

In terms of satisfaction with service, service in Asia is of a higher standard, personalized, and more customer oriented. Although in Australia the service quality is high there is still much scope for improvement in order to match the Asian standard. For example, Koreans see the

Australian service providers as being too slow (Prideaux, 1998) and the local cuisine also has a poor image (Kim, 1997). Koreans do not regard Australians as friendly and welcoming (Kim, 1997). In fact, they have an image of Australia as a racist country (Prideaux, 1998).

Further, as members of high uncertainty avoidance cultures, Asian people are worried about the exposure to language difficulties when travelling overseas. Although their English language skills are improving they are unhappy about Australians' inability to communicate with Asian tourists. According to Indonesians and Koreans, the Australian hosts' knowledge of the guests' culture and language is imperative to be able to respond to the guests' standards of behaviour and needs. One of the major problems for Koreans visiting Australia is language difficulties and lack of appreciation of distinctive Korean culture (Prideaux, 1998). Thus, 'Koreans are dependent on tour guides to navigate them through a country which has no public signage in Korean and few tourism workers who speak the language' (Prideaux, 1998, p. 98). As a result, Australia has failed to provide a product that lives up to the promotional images of the country (Prideaux, 1998).

Although Thai people have a great sense of humour, they do not appreciate sarcasm, which is accepted in Australia. They also don't pay much attention to time constraints. In Thailand conversations between people are relaxed. However, they require conformity to rules of social conduct (Komin, 1990).

The analysis of the cultural dimensions identified in each Asian language group points to several characteristic dimensions in each group. These dimensions are briefly presented below.

Indonesia
In the Indonesian sample, two characteristic dimensions were identified: perceptions of service responsiveness and perceptions of attention. In terms of responsiveness, Indonesians believe that service may occur over an extended time period. Being in a hurry is an indication of impatience (Geertz, 1967). In contrast, in Australia, time commitments are more important and must be kept. There is more focus on punctuality and efficiency of service provision. Also, in Indonesia physical appearance and appropriate dress should reflect social position and age. This is in contrast to Australian culture, in which clothing style is more casual. With regard to attentiveness, Indonesians believe that people must pay

attention to correct behaviour and the nature and forms of obligations, which are specified by a system of social hierarchy. In contrast, Australian society is more egalitarian and people's behaviour depends less on social position and age.

Japan

In the Japanese sample, three characteristic dimensions were identified: perceptions of service helpfulness, values of competence, and rules of greetings. In Japan, helpfulness is seen in terms of being punctual, informative, trustworthy, respectful, and polite. Punctuality is regarded as a measure of professionalism and competence. Australian society regards punctuality as relative to the importance of the occasion. Also, the Japanese require precision and accuracy of information (Turcq and Usunier, 1985). In contrast, Australians are not concerned with detail to such a degree and are not worried if the problems aren't solved immediately. Further, in Japan, the concept of trustworthy service is relative and depends upon the social situations and time. The sincere and trustworthy person strives for harmony with surroundings and a group through self-restraint ('enryo') (Dace, 1995). Australians, in contrast, are more direct and open. They tend to 'lay all cards on the table'. In Japan, respect for others and one's self is shown through fulfilling work obligations and complying with the rules of social etiquette (Ahmed and Krohn, 1992). In Australia, where people value equality, respect is gained through individual achievements.

Japanese politeness is an expression of social etiquette rather than a feeling of kindness, or regard. It requires no damage to one's own and others' reputation, avoidance of conflict, and controlling of emotions (Lebra, 1976). For Australians, manners are less comprehensive. An essential element of the Japanese polite character is an apologetic and humble attitude, and consideration to the effects of one's own behaviour on others (Ziff-Levine, 1990). However, the Japanese apologize not only when they want to admit guilt, but to avoid friction and offence, and demonstrate humility and regret (DeMente, 1991a), which may often seem to be illogical to Australians. Also, in a Japanese culture confidence and loud behaviour are regarded with suspicion and as rude (Condon, 1978). In contrast, Australians regard confidence as a sign of strength. Moreover, the Japanese tend to listen to and obey orders without questioning them. This is again in contrast to Australians who are unfamiliar with the concepts of obedience and listening to superiors.

In Japan, competence is seen to be dependent on personal qualities such as being self-controlled, logical, obedient, and self-respectful. Self-controlled means being disciplined, emotionally restrained, and able to comply with rules of formal behaviour. In Australian culture no corresponding aspects of life seem to be related. Australians are not concerned about controlling their own behaviour and complying with rules of socially accepted behaviour. The Japanese way of logical thinking is intuitive and flexible. In contrast, the Australian way of thinking is objective and absolute. The Japanese way of being obedient is shown by willingness to comply with the social order and respect for others, and it does not have an equivalent in Australia either. Further, respecting oneself in the Japanese context requires saving one's own and others' face. In Australia, self-respect is gained by collecting financial wealth and standing against authority.

In Japan, individuals are addressed by second names, titles, or functions. The Japanese use first names only with family members and childhood friends and feel embarrassed when called by their first names (DeMente, 1991a). Australian informality of calling people by their first names is regarded as rude. In Japan, meishi cards (*name-cards*) are exchanged at the beginning of conversation to indicate the titles, positions, and ranks of the owners. The exchange of name-cards is followed by a bow. There are different kinds and grades of Japanese bows, depending on age, rank, and social position (DeMente, 1991a; Zimmerman, 1985). The Japanese do not practise shaking hands as favoured by many Australians. However, since the Japanese have recently become used to dealing with western businessmen they politely accept handshaking (DeMente, 1991a).

South Korea

In the South Korean sample, only one characteristic dimension was identified: perceptions of service performance. In a relatively feminine culture such as South Korea, society is committed to personal relations (Kim, Q., 1988), quality of life, and social harmony. However, South Koreans also believe in masculine values such as inequality among people (Kim, Q., 1988), performance, and intellectual achievements. Respect is gained through intellectual achievements and hard work. Punctuality is a measure of professionalism. South Koreans do not appreciate the waste of time that occurs if meal service is slow (Prideaux, 1998). In Australia, people are more money- and possession-oriented; more emphasis is on performance, growth, and assertiveness. However, Australians also support feminine values such as equality and welfare of others. Further, in South Korea, there are specific customs concerning appropriate dress and physical appearance, which are prescribed by law for different social classes. This is again in contrast to Australian culture, in which clothing style is more casual and depends less on social position or age.

Mandarin-speaking

In the Mandarin-speaking sample two characteristic dimensions were identified: perceptions of punctuality and perceptions of understanding. Mandarin-speaking societies expect people to adhere to a full, heavy schedule, and be on time, or early for meetings and appointments (DeMente, 1991c). Being late is regarded as lacking sincerity, concern for the other, and professionalism. This is in contrast to the Australian style of work, which is more relaxed, and in which delays can be justified. Also, the Chinese are socially and psychologically dependent on others (Hsu, 1953). The inherent need to care about foreign visitors in the Mandarin cultures results in a national responsibility for giving constant attention to and helping foreigners to cope with the different customs to a degree that may become annoying for western visitors (Wei *et al.,* 1989). Chinese escort their guests constantly in order to not only ensure that visitors do not have contact with Chinese, who may offer a different view of their political reality, but to fulfil all needs of the visitors (Wei *et al.,* 1989). In Australia, people know best what their needs are and how these needs can be satisfied.

Thailand

In the Thai sample two characteristic dimensions were identified: percep-tions of communication courtesy and perceptions of understanding. The Thai people are very attentive and try to please everyone. The Thai say whatever is required in order to conform to norms of respect and polite-ness, and avoid unpleasantness and conflict. For Australians, truth is absolute and does not depend on a situation. The Thai people rarely say 'please' or 'thank you' as the Thai words of politeness carry the 'please' element. As a result, in English the Thai may appear to be demanding something, whereas in Thai they make a polite request (Komin, 1990). Also, the Thai use the smile instead of polite words (Komin, 1990). In Australia, words such as 'please' and 'thank you' are used commonly. Further, in Thailand, respect is shown to all of higher status and age, and also to objects of everyday life such as books, hats, umbrellas, elephants, and rice, which are associated with knowledge, the head, royalty, religion, and life (Komin, 1990). In contrast, Australians are less respectful and they do not have as many sacred symbols.

Marketing and management implications of the Principal Components Analysis results

The cultural differences between Asian and Australian populations presented in the study point to the development of specific marketing strategies aimed at the Asian tourist market. Promotional advertising aiming at all Asian tourists should focus on the opportunity to develop close human relations between tourists and Australian people. Travel itineraries should be developed and structured around socializing with Australian people and other travellers. As a base for the development of social relations attention should be paid to: (a) the dependent nature of Asian social relations; (b) the hierarchical structure of Asian societies and the ability of the hosts to comply with authority and seniority; and (c) social etiquette which demands the providers treat Asian tourists according to their age, social positions, and ranking. For example, special care, respect, and courtesy should be shown to elders, and obedience to any higher-ranking superiors. Appropriate seating arrangements in buses and restaurants, and hotel room allocation should be made according to age and social ranking. Australian providers should identify their professional status by wearing formal work uniforms and badges with names and positions displayed. Preferably an older person should represent management, as this person would be seen as being of high social status and professional experience. Similarly, an older person is a better tour guide choice being seen as knowledgeable and experienced. The hotel management should welcome and bid farewell Asian tourists at the airport or hotel, creating an atmosphere of social order and indicating that the management has a sense of responsibility and respect.

The hierarchy and seniority system and the compliance with basic rules of social etiquette should be emphasized in advertising. All Asian tourists should be addressed by their titles and last names, except Thai tourists who should be called by their titles and first names. Tourists should wear badges with their names and titles. Although the Japanese and Korean tourists do not expect foreigners to know exactly how to bow, Australian providers should show some inclination to conform to their custom of bowing, instead of handshaking, to show their politeness and respect of tourists. In addition, exchanging business cards with

English text on one of the sides, indicating the social status of the person introduced, followed by a bow would fulfil the Japanese custom of introduction. The Thai tourists should be greeted with a smile instead of 'hello' and a handshake. Advertising to Japanese and Korean tourists should incorporate pictures of bowing. Advertising to Thai people should show people with a smile on their faces.

Marketers should emphasize the time spent in Australia as a means of developing social relations with Australians, and consider that the average Asian tourist values the importance of time spent on socializing and devoting personal time to other people. Conversations should comply with the rules of formal etiquette. Providers should not feel offended when asked about their age or salary earnings. In fact, they should ask tourists these questions to establish their social status. Ironic and sarcastic comments or jokes, common in Australia, should be avoided. The Australian relaxed, casual and slow pace lifestyle, which offers much time for socializing should be promoted, in particular to Indonesian and Thai tourists. The aspect of 'having a good time, fun and pleasure' should be the focus of promotional messages aiming at the Thai market.

Given the sensitivity and importance of face saving to all Asian tourists, caution has to be exercised in personal dealings with Asian tourists involving openly displaying feelings and expressing opinions, in order to prevent conflict and disagreement in interpersonal relations between providers and tourists. Special care should be taken not to insult and damage the reputation of the tourist, even if criticism is constructive and negative feelings justified. It is important not to offend any tourist and not to swear in front of them, not to criticize, or talk about sensitive issues. However, personal questions related to tourist social statuses are permitted. The providers should strive to be considerate and take into account the effects of one's own behaviour on the tourists' feelings. If there are any differences in opinions providers should find a suitable way of expressing their own views that does not offend and harm a tourist. Failure to do so will result in conflict and may cause humiliation, loss of dignity and social status on both sides. Consequently, providers should practise self-control, coolness of manners, non-assertiveness, and humility.

The promotional strategies aiming at the Japanese and South Korean markets should emphasize the educational and intellectual aspects of travel to Australia in order to enhance the tourists' intellectual and cul-

301

tural experiences. The value of knowledge and wisdom should be used as criteria for the enhancement of the Japanese and South Korean tourist's social status and their recognition among fellow nationals.

Commercial advertising should be directed towards Asian families so as to appeal to all its members rather than the individual tourist. Special offers for extended families should be proposed and large family tours organized. The advertising messages should promise the fulfilment of family needs including security. The safety of airlines, the high quality of Australian infrastructure and recreation facilities, low crime rate, clean and unpolluted environment can be highlighted in promotional brochures. The competence and professionalism of Australian service providers need to be stressed specifically to the Japanese market. Focus should be on the ability of the providers to fulfil professional obligations, being respectful, and obedient. By doing this the cultural predisposition of Asian tourists to avoid risk can be overcome, without loosing interest in travelling to Australia.

Marketing strategies aiming at Asian tourists should also focus on a team spirit and promote group activities such as group travelling, sightseeing, picnics, barbecues, or recreational activities. Individual activities may not be popular among Asian tourists who prefer to feel 'in-group'. Tours guides, front office, airline staff, and restaurateurs should never leave the Asian tourists on their own, as they demand constant attention. In particular, the Mandarin-speaking tourist groups should not be separated even for a short period of time because of the inherent need for support and dependence.

All Asian tourists would be particularly pleased when Australian hosts follow their custom of gift-giving. Small welcome and farewell gifts should be given to tourists on their arrival and departure as a means of showing an appreciation for coming to Australia. An appropriate gift should be given, such as a box of golf balls, and in Australia, a boomerang or koala toys. Every gift should be artistically wrapped as the Japanese and Koreans, in particular, value external presentation. Gifts should be given in order of seniority. In addition, a small gift in the form of Australian fruit or a bottle of wine should be available in each hotel room. A lot of discretionary time for purchasing gifts for each family member should be included in the travel itineraries for Asian tourists. Australian tour operators should organize special shopping tours.

Advertising aimed at all Asian tourists should focus on hosts performing acts of kindness that bind tourists and make them feel obliged (Lebra, 1976) such as gift-giving, experiencing a sporting game, sharing an interest in Asian art, food, or other elements of culture. The Asians appreciate being invited to a nightclub or out for dinner. Being invited home is regarded as an honourable and rare event, and it can shorten significantly the time necessary for the development of relations. This later aspect may be important for hosts dealing with visiting Asian tour operators.

Australian providers should be anxious to provide the best service they can, particularly to the Japanese. Those who provide services to the Japanese, South Korean and Mandarin-speaking tourists should be punctual. Of importance is the effective dissemination of information to passengers and corrective action during service break down (Laws, 1990). When the service cannot be delivered to tourists on time, providers should provide an explanation for the service delay, apologize politely and compensate for lack of promptness and efficiency, even if it is not their fault. Compensation in the form of a personal written apology or a small gift would be appropriate and eliminate the potential for offence and frictions in human interactions with Asian tourists. Any waiting time should be entertaining to give tourists a feeling of getting the most of every moment of their holiday. For example, the Japanese tourists, who value education and intellectual achievements, could be shown educational books or videotapes of Australia while waiting at the airport, or in the hotel lobby. Also, serving Japanese or Chinese tea before the meal would show the tourists that the order is being fulfilled and would give them a feeling of smooth service delivery. However, Australian providers should be less concerned about being punctual and delivering service on time to Indonesian and Thai tourists. Indonesian and Thai tourists should not be hurried. They require relaxed and flexible service.

Every promotional campaign aiming at the Asian tourist market should emphasize Australian genuine hospitality, concern for tourists, and the ability to anticipate and understand their needs. Promoting Australian hosts' commitment to personalized service would enhance the Asian tourist's interest in travelling to Australia.

Australian providers should learn some basic phrases and principles of the Asian languages to be used in different social situations with people of different social standing in order to be perceived as communicative and informative. Just a small ability in speaking Asian languages would help to greet and farewell tourists, enquire politely about their trip or health, make polite casual comments, and be able to respond to their queries. Australian providers should not expect all Asian tourists to speak the English language. The Japanese, South Korean and Mandarin-speaking tourists would be particularly grateful to hosts for having a degree of competence in their mother tongues, which would also enhance tourist satisfaction with Australian providers. Since the Japanese rely more on print media (Mihalik *et al.*, 1995), visitor guides, brochures, and magazines translated into Japanese should be made available to all Japanese and Australian travel agents, foreign and domestic libraries, public and private, and all other points of tourist information. The provision of multilingual signs and services would also assist all Asian tourists.

Learning the non-verbal aspects of communication including body language, gestures, or eye gazing should complement learning Asian languages. It would be advisable to understand the customs of Asian greeting, entertaining, gift-giving, and even eating and drinking habits. The different principles of truth and sincerity also need to be understood. Australian providers need to be alert for signals that reveal the true meanings of the Asian words and expressions. They should learn how to recognize what is unsaid, intentions behind the Asian words, and say only what has to be said to conform to rules of politeness, respect, and avoidance of conflict. Straightforwardness should be avoided as it might be regarded by Asian tourists as rude and wouldn't be reciprocated. Australian providers must be careful in interpretation of subjective assessment provided by Japanese tourists in the host country (Iverson, 1997) and not be complacent.

Special efforts need to be made to learn about the Asian guests' country of origin, its history, traditions, music, food, and everyday life. This is particularly important to Korean and Indonesian tourists. This would not only be an indication of the hosts' willingness to please Asian tourists, but also show an interest and appreciation of their culture and enhance the tourists' self-ego and pride.

Structural equation modelling analysis

The series of interdependent, multiple relationships between the identified dimensions and their key indicators were assessed by structural equation modelling (SEM) analysis using LISREL VII.2 (Joreskog and Sorbom, 1989a,b). The SEM is confirmatory factor analysis and aims to determine a relationship between the latent variables, that is, whether cultural differences between Asian tourists and their Australian hosts determine tourist interaction and satisfaction.

Theoretical models with defined relationships between latent constructs and their indicators were developed. Every model has several latent constructs, each measured by a set of manifest (observable/measurement) variables. The variables measuring each latent construct are presented in path diagrams with arrows. A straight arrow indicates a direct relationship from a construct to its indicators. A curved line connecting two constructs indicates just a correlation between the constructs. The variables involved in a diagram are: measurable x-variables $x_1...x_n$, latent exogenous variables $\xi_1...\xi_n$ measured by x-variables, and measurement errors $\delta_1...\delta_n$ in the indicators for exogenous x-variables. Since the study's aim is to measure the relationships between the latent constructs and their indicators the diagrams also involve y-variables $y_1...y_n$, latent endogenous variables $\eta_1...\eta_n$ measured by y-variables, measurement errors $\varepsilon_1...\varepsilon_n$ in the indicators for endogenous y-variables, and measurement errors in equations $\zeta_1...\zeta_n$ that indicate that the endogenous variables were not perfectly explained by the independent variables.

The correlation matrix was the preferred input data type because it allowed: (a) to explore the pattern and the strength of interrelationships between latent constructs and their indicators; (b) a comparison across different variables, and their correlations with the dimensions; (c) more conservative estimates of the significance of the coefficients than the co-variance matrix (Hair *et al.*, 1995); (d) easy interpretation of the results; and (e) possible direct comparisons of the coefficients within a model. The Pearson product-moment correlation was used to compute the correlations. The correlation matrix was computed using PRELIS (Joreskog and Sorbom, 1988).

The initial estimates were computed by the Two-Stage Least-Squares (TSLS) method and the final solution by the Maximum Likelihood Estimation (MLE) method. The MLE method was more suitable as it is an iterative procedure and minimizes a fit function by successively improving the parameter estimates. The MLE method is also robust against departures from normality and can be used in large samples (the largest sample was 618). The sample size required to ensure appropriate use of MLE is 100 to 200 (Hair *et al.*, 1995). This requirement was met by all the Asian samples ranging from 102 to 173 respondents.

The assessment of the models' fit was done on the basis of: (a) the ratios of Chi-square to the degrees of freedom; (b) sample sizes; (c) goodness-of-fit (GFI) values; (d) adjusted for the degrees of freedom goodness-of-fit measures (AGFI); and (e) root mean square residuals (RMSR) (average residuals correlation). Each of the indicators and constructs were also evaluated separately by examining: (1) squared multiple correlation coefficients (SMC) for both *x*- and *y*-variables; (2) the total coefficient of determination (TCD) (R^2) for all *x*- and *y*-variables jointly; (3) *t*-values for the paths; (4) correlations between the latent constructs (ϕ-values and *t*-values); (5) standard errors (SE) for each coefficient and construct; (6) fitted residuals (FR); and (7) standardized residuals (SR). In some instances modification to models was made by deleting or adding parameters, if it was theoretically justified. The modification indices (MI) were used to decide which parameters should be added or deleted, to reduce Chi-square and improve the fit of the models. For each dependent latent construct one path emanating from it was fixed to 1 (the only option available in LISREL 7) in order to set the measurement scale for this construct, that is, to make the latent metric identical to the metric inherent in the observed variable receiving the fixed path, and to achieve model identification. None of the paths emanating from independent latent constructs was fixed, as the purpose was to test the influence of *all* independent observed variables on the dependent variables.

Results of structural equation modelling

The results of the LISREL and all measures-of-fit suggested that the developed models for the total Asian market and each individual Asian market fitted the data well. The fit estimates for all models are shown in Table 9.2. The solution is standardized.

The Chi-square indices are small in relation to the degrees of freedom. Goodness-of-fit (GFI) values range between 0.92–0.96 and indicate acceptable fits. Adjusted for the degrees of freedom goodness-of-fit measures (AGFI) range between 0.86–0.93 and also indicate acceptable fits. Root mean square residuals (RMSR – average residuals correlation) have values below a marginal acceptance level of 0.08 and indicate strong correlations in the original correlation matrix.

Table 9.2 LISREL fit estimates for all groups

				Measures of fit			
	All Asian	Indonesian	Japanese	South Korean	Mandarin	Thai
Chi-square	101.79	23.40	45.82	38.14	34.63	58.83
Degrees of freedom	79	19	43	34	25	44
Probability	0.043	0.220	0.356	0.287	0.095	0.067
Goodness of Fit Index (GFI)	0.923	0.955	0.936	0.962	0.937	0.922
Adjusted Goodness of Fit Index (AGFI)	0.882	0.892	0.885	0.927	0.861	0.862
Root Mean Square Residuals (RMSR)	0.059	0.038	0.049	0.034	0.055	0.040
Total Coefficient of Determination (TCDx)	0.98	0.979	0.955	0.990	0.999	0.997
Total Coefficient of Determination (TCDy)	0.97	0.994	0.992	0.996	0.869	0.994

However, it is important to note that these statistics provide overall measures of fit of the models to the data (GFI, AGFI and RMSR) and do not express the quality of the models. It has been argued that the Chi-square should not be used as a valid assessment index (Joreskog and Sorbom, 1989b), particularly when there is data departure from multi-variate normality. Joreskog and Sorbom (1989b) suggested the use of other measures of fit assessment such as:

1. the squared multiple correlation coefficients (SMC) for the x- and y-variables, which represent reliabilities of the x- and y-variables (these are above 0.9 and indicate that the independent and dependent variables explain a very high amount of variance in their latent dimensions, and thus measure these dimensions very well);
2. the total coefficient of determination (TCD) (R^2) for all x- and y-variables (these are remarkably high, range between 0.95–0.99 and they indicate that all x- and y-variables *as a group* measure the latent constructs very well);
3. t-values for the paths (these were very large – larger than 2 – and pointed to the indicators' power to reliably predict their latent constructs, thus verifying the relationships among indicators and constructs);
4. the correlation coefficients between the latent constructs, according to the MLE method, are high and indicate that the latent constructs are significantly correlated with each other;
5. the standard errors for coefficients and constructs are small and indicate that the values of the parameters are estimated accurately. The standard errors of correlation between the latent constructs are also small. However, what is small or large depends on the units of measurement in latent constructs and the magnitude of the parameter estimate itself. Standard errors are robust against moderate departures from normality; thus, they should be interpreted with caution if the condition of normality does not hold. Therefore, t-values are used as independent units of measurement;
6. the fitted residuals which represent the differences between the observed and the fitted correlations; these are small relative to the size of the elements of the correlation matrices and indicate that the fit of the models is acceptable; and
7. the standardized residuals (SR), which are fitted residuals divided by their standard errors and are interpreted as standard normal deviations. There are numerous SR values exceeding the value of 2.58 in absolute terms and indicate specification and prediction error, for a

pair of indicators. However, their number is within the acceptable range, that is, one in twenty residuals exceeding 2.58 by chance.

These fit measures suggest that there are well-defined relationship paths in the models. They do not *precisely* indicate whether the models *are* or *are not* supported by the data, and what is wrong with the model (Joreskog and Sorbom, 1989b). Consequently, these measures could show even better fit, and be sounder if some paths were eliminated from the models, and the models run again. However, this was not done. According to Joreskog and Sorbom (1989b), the quality of the models should also be judged by external criteria such as theoretical grounding. In this regard, the choice of path structure and content has strong theoretical justification based upon an extensive literature review.

Analysis of the models

Total Asia

An assessment of the results suggest that differences in rules of behaviour (feeling display), followed by the differences in cultural values (family/competence) have an effect on satisfaction and that these two dimensions together determine Asian tourist satisfaction. The direct paths from cultural values and rules of behaviour to satisfaction are significant and indicate that differences in values and rules contribute directly and significantly to satisfaction. The three major differences in values that directly and significantly determine satisfaction, are differences in attaching importance to self-control, family security, and intellectualism. The three key differences in rules that directly and significantly determine satisfaction, are differences in addressing people, showing respect, and criticizing in public. On the other hand, the direct paths from values and rules to interaction are insignificant and indicate that differences in values and rules did not have a direct and significant effect on interaction.

Secondly, differences in perceptions (communication) do not have a direct effect on Asian tourist satisfaction. On the other hand, differences in perceptions have a direct effect on interaction. Although there is a correlation between the dimensions of values, rules and perceptions, the influence of differences in perceptions on satisfaction is indirect only and mediated through interaction. The three key differences in perceptions that have direct and significant influence on interaction and indirect influence on satisfaction are the differences in understanding and anticipating tourists' needs, and paying attention to the tourist.

Thirdly, interaction has a weak but significant effect on satisfaction. The key differences in interaction that have a direct effect on satisfaction are the differences in developing and maintaining close personal relationships, attitudes to being invited home, sharing a meal, and playing sport. An improvement in the model fit was achieved by using modification indices and allowing 'playing sport' to measure satisfaction. This relationship appears to be reasonable. Personal interviews with the tourists revealed the importance of playing golf for Asian tourist satisfaction. Finally, the two key indicators of satisfaction affected by the differences in interaction are differences in satisfaction with time spent together and satisfaction with knowledge of an Asian language.

Further, although differences in cultural values have a significant effect on satisfaction this effect is weak, while the path between cultural values and interaction is insignificant. This suggests that differences in cultural values do not determine preferences for social interaction and may have a significant effect on satisfaction. Overall, the greatest direct and significant effects on Asian tourist satisfaction are differences in rules of behaviour (feeling display) (see Figure 9.2).

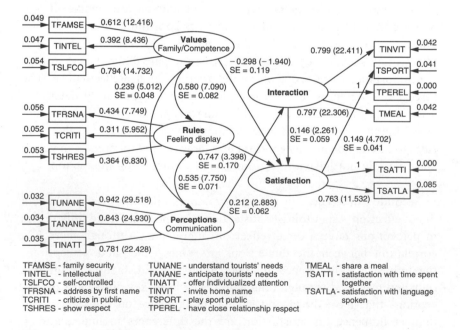

TFAMSE - family security
TINTEL - intellectual
TSLFCO - self-controlled
TFRSNA - address by first name
TCRITI - criticize in public
TSHRES - show respect

TUNANE - understand tourists' needs
TANANE - anticipate tourists' needs
TINATT - offer individualized attention
TINVIT - invite home name
TSPORT - play sport public
TPEREL - have close relationship respect

TMEAL - share a meal
TSATTI - satisfaction with time spent together
TSATLA - satisfaction with language spoken

Figure 9.2 Model for total Asia (significant paths only)

Japan

Differences in rules of social behaviour (greetings) have a significant positive but very weak influence on social interaction with the Japanese tourist. The two major differences in rules, which directly and significantly determine interaction with the Japanese tourist, are the differences in addressing and greeting people. Differences in perceptions of service (helpfulness) have a significant positive influence on Japanese tourist satisfaction. The two major differences in perceptions of helpfulness, which have a significant effect on tourist satisfaction, are differences in perceptions of the service providers being helpful and punctual. Neither differences in perceptions of helpfulness of service nor differences in cultural values of competence are significant determinants of interaction. Neither differences in cultural values of competence nor the differences in rules of greetings are significant determinants of satisfaction. However, it must be noted that the dimension of service perceptions (helpfulness) is significantly and positively correlated with the dimension of cultural values (competence) and the dimension of rules of behaviour (greetings). Also, social interaction only slightly, but significantly, influences satisfaction through the mediating effect of rules of behaviour. The three key differences in interaction, which affect satisfaction through the rules of behaviour, are differences in sharing recreation facilities, playing sport, and participating in a party. The two major indicators of satisfaction that are affected by the differences in interaction are differences in satisfaction with friendship and time spent together. An improvement in the model fit was achieved by using modification indices and allowing 'being obedient' to measure rules of social behaviour. This relationship appears to be reasonable (see Figure 9.3).

South Korea

Differences in rules of social behaviour (feeling display) and differences in perceptions of service (performance) exert a significant and positive influence on tourist satisfaction and these two dimensions determine Korean tourist satisfaction. The three major differences in rules of feeling display that significantly affect satisfaction are differences in displaying emotions, criticizing and swearing. The two major differences in perceptions of service providers' performance that significantly affect satisfaction are differences in perceptions of providers being punctual and respectful. The two major indicators of satisfaction influenced by the differences in rules of feeling display and differences in perceptions of the providers' performance are satisfaction with friendship and time spent together. The differences in rules of behaviour (feeling display) also have a significant but weaker

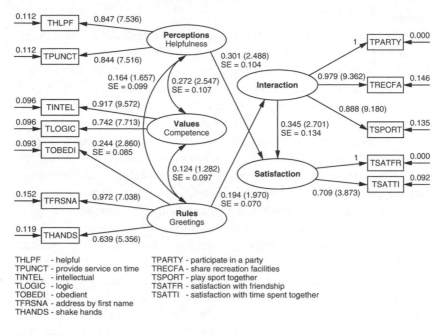

THLPF   - helpful
TPUNCT - provide service on time
TINTEL - intellectual
TLOGIC - logic
TOBEDI - obedient
TFRSNA - address by first name
THANDS - shake hands

TPARTY - participate in a party
TRECFA - share recreation facilities
TSPORT - play sport together
TSATFR - satisfaction with friendship
TSATTI - satisfaction with time spent together

Figure 9.3 Model for Japan (significant paths only)

indirect influence on satisfaction via interaction. Neither differences in perceptions of the providers' performance nor differences in perceptions of communication style are significant determinants of social interaction. Also, communication is not a significant determinant of satisfaction. However, it must be noted that all three dimensions of rules of behaviour, perceptions of communication and perceptions of service performance are significantly and positively correlated with each other. Although the direct influence of the differences in communication on interaction and satisfaction is positive, it failed to reach a statistically significant level. The interaction dimension only slightly, but significantly, influences satisfaction. The two major differences in interaction that exert influence on satisfaction are differences in playing sport and sharing a meal (see Figure 9.4).

Mandarin-speaking
Only the dimension of perceptions of understanding the tourist exerts a significant and positive, but weak, influence on social interaction and indirect influence on Mandarin tourist satisfaction via interaction. The two major differences in the perceptions of understanding that influence interaction and, indirectly, satisfaction are differences in understanding

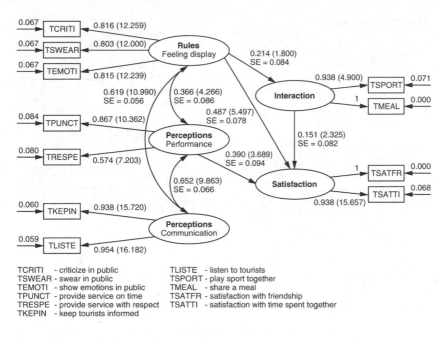

TCRITI   - criticize in public
TSWEAR - swear in public
TEMOTI   - show emotions in public
TPUNCT - provide service on time
TRESPE - provide service with respect
TKEPIN   - keep tourists informed

TLISTE   - listen to tourists
TSPORT - play sport together
TMEAL   - share a meal
TSATFR - satisfaction with friendship
TSATTI   - satisfaction with time spent together

Figure 9.4 Model for South Korea (significant paths only)

and anticipating the Mandarin-speaking tourist needs. Neither perceptions of service punctuality nor rules of feeling display determine interaction. Also, perceptions of service punctuality, perceptions of understanding, and rules of feeling display do not determine satisfaction. The dimensions of perceptions of punctuality and understanding are significantly and positively correlated with each other. Similarly, the dimensions of understanding and rules of feeling display are positively and significantly correlated with each other. The direct effect of social interaction on satisfaction is large and significant, indicating that interaction is a significant determinant of satisfaction. The two major differences in interaction that significantly influence satisfaction are differences in the preferences for participating in a party and sharing a meal. The two major differences in satisfaction influenced by the differences in interaction are differences in satisfaction with local providers and time spent together (see Figure 9.5).

Thailand

Differences in perceptions of understanding the tourist exert a significant positive influence on social interaction. The indirect influence of differ-

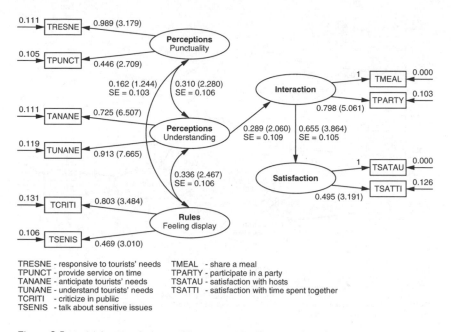

TRESNE - responsive to tourists' needs   TMEAL - share a meal
TPUNCT - provide service on time   TPARTY - participate in a party
TANANE - anticipate tourists' needs   TSATAU - satisfaction with hosts
TUNANE - understand tourists' needs   TSATTI - satisfaction with time spent together
TCRITI   - criticize in publiic
TSENIS   - talk about sensitive issues

Figure 9.5 Model for Mandarin-speaking group (significant paths only)

ences in perceptions of understanding on Thai tourist satisfaction via interaction is insignificant. The two major differences in perceptions of understanding that influence interaction are the differences in perceptions of the providers being able to anticipate and understand Thai tourist needs. The three major indicators of interaction influenced by the differences in understanding are being invited to a party and a home, and sharing a meal. Differences in perceptions of communication exert a positive and significant influence on satisfaction. The two major differences in perceptions of communication that influence satisfaction are differences in perceptions of the providers being able to provide the Thai tourist with accurate information and being trustworthy. The three major indicators of satisfaction influenced by the differences in communication are satisfaction with local providers, conversation, and friendship. Although, all three dimensions of rules of social behaviour (feeling display), perceptions of service communication and understanding are significantly and positively correlated with each other, rules of feeling display do not have any influence on interaction and satisfaction. The direct influence of rules of feeling display on interaction and satisfaction is positive, however, it failed to reach a statistically significant level. Also, interaction is not a significant determinant of satisfaction (see Figure 9. 6).

314

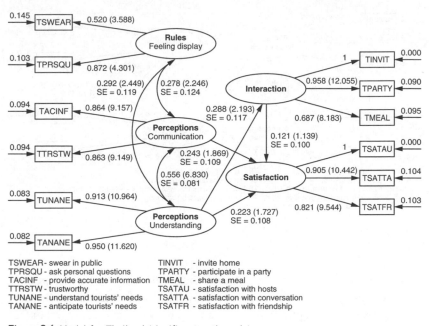

TSWEAR- swear in public
TPRSQU - ask personal questions
TACINF - provide accurate information
TTRSTW - trustworthy
TUNANE - understand tourists' needs
TANANE - anticipate tourists' needs

TINVIT - invite home
TPARTY - participate in a party
TMEAL - share a meal
TSATAU - satisfaction with hosts
TSATTA - satisfaction with conversation
TSATFR - satisfaction with friendship

Figure 9.6 Model for Thailand (significant paths only)

Indonesia

Neither differences in perceptions of service responsiveness nor differences in perceptions of service attentiveness have a significant influence on inter-action and Indonesian tourist satisfaction. However, it must be noted that perceptions of responsiveness and attentiveness are significantly and posi-tively correlated with each other. An improvement in the model fit was achieved by allowing the variable 'have close relationship' to measure satisfaction, and the variable 'satisfaction with the Indonesian language' to measure interaction. The personal interviews with tourists revealed the importance of personal relations for Indonesian tourist satisfaction and ability of the providers to communicate in the Indonesian language for interaction. These relationships appear to be reasonable. The interaction dimension does not determine satisfaction (see Figure 9. 7).

Marketing and management implications of the structural equation modelling analysis

An important implication of the study findings is that it becomes increas-ingly important for tourism marketers and managers to consider and use

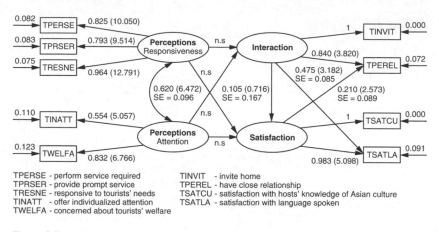

TPERSE - perform service required
TPRSER - provide prompt service
TRESNE - responsive to tourists' needs
TINATT - offer individualized attention
TWELFA - concerned about tourists' welfare

TINVIT - invite home
TPEREL - have close relationship
TSATCU - satisfaction with hosts' knowledge of Asian culture
TSATLA - satisfaction with language spoken

Figure 9.7 Model for Indonesia

knowledge of cultural differences and their influences on social interaction with international tourists. It is clear that tourism marketers cannot directly rely on perceptions of service to generate Asian tourist satisfaction, as tourist satisfaction can also be influenced by cultural values, rules of social behaviour, and social interaction. Tourism marketers can best directly influence Asian tourist satisfaction by emphasizing, in their promotional campaigns, the importance of values such as self-control, family security and intellectualism, and the rules of social behaviour such as proper address, respect, and avoidance of criticism. Perceptions of service and, in particular, perceptions of understanding, anticipative and attentive service are important indirect determinants of Asian tourist satisfaction, hence they indirectly influence tourist willingness to interact with Australian providers and, in turn, affect Asian tourist satisfaction.

For the Japanese tourist market, developing tourist perceptions of helpful and punctual service should directly influence Japanese tourist satisfaction. Rules of proper greeting such as the proper addressing of people should be used to directly influence the Japanese willingness to interact socially and to then indirectly generate satisfaction.

South Korean tourist satisfaction should be directly influenced by learning the appropriate cultural rules of displaying feelings and, in particular, not criticizing, swearing and showing emotions in public, and developing perceptions of punctual and respectful service. Further, understanding the appropriate rules of feelings displayed can directly influence the South Korean tourists' willingness to interact socially and then indirectly generate satisfaction.

Mandarin-speaking tourist satisfaction is indirectly influenced by the mediating effect of a proper understanding by the hosts of being able to understand and anticipate the Mandarin tourist needs, as these percep-tions directly determine social interaction with the Mandarin speaking tourist, and indirectly influence their satisfaction.

Thai tourist satisfaction is directly influenced by perceptions of a proper communication style, that is, providing the tourist with accurate and trustworthy information, and developing tourist perceptions of hosts as being able to understand and anticipate the Thai tourists' needs. Further, an understanding of the Thai tourist needs directly influences the willingness of Thai tourists to interact socially, and indirectly influ-ences their satisfaction.

Indonesian tourists' satisfaction and interaction are not influenced by either the providers' responsiveness (perform responsive, required and punctual service) or attentiveness (offer individualized attention, being concerned about tourists' welfare). This indicates that there are possibly other more clearly distinguishing variables this study failed to identify for the Indonesian sample.

Summary

Principal Components Analysis was used to identify the dimensions of cultural differences between Asian and Australian populations in tour-ism. The results of a structural equation modelling analysis deter-mined which cultural differences between Asian tourists and Australian providers determined their social interaction and satisfac-tion. Five cultural models for Indonesian-, Japanese-, South Korean-, Mandarin- and Thai-speaking groups were developed. The findings show that marketers cannot directly rely on perceptions of service to generate Asian tourist satisfaction but must also consider cultural values and rules of social behaviour. The implications of the results for tourism industry managers and marketers are presented.

Discussion points and questions

1. Explain the advantages of using a Principal Components Analysis in tourism research.
2. Identify the research issues that might be analysed using the PCA.
3. Explain the purpose of applying a structural equation modelling in tourism.

Endnotes

[1] Two statistical packages were used for data input, namely the SPSS for Windows Release 6.0 (Norusis, 1993) and the GB-STAT for Windows Version 5.0 (Friedman, 1994).

[2] Eighteen out of thirty-six areas of measurement showed significant differences in cultural values, twenty-two out of thirty-four in rules of social interaction, twenty-three out of twenty-nine in perceptions of service, seven out of eleven in forms of interaction, and three out of seven in satisfaction with interaction.

[3] The tables with the significant differences between the individual Asian language groups and the Australian sample are available from the researchers.

[4] The results of the Principal Components Analysis for each Asian language group are available from the researchers.

Further reading

Boshoff, C. and Mels, G. (1995) A causal model to evaluate the relationships among supervision, role stress, organizational commitment and internal service quality. *European Journal of Marketing* 29(2): 23–42.

Getty, J. and Thompson, K. (1994) The relationship between quality, satisfaction, and recommending behavior in lodging decisions. *Journal of Hospitality and Leisure Marketing* 2(3): 3–22.

Gundersen, M., Heide, M. and Olsson, U. (1996) Hotel guest satisfaction among business travelers: What are the important factors? *Cornell Hotel and Restaurant Administration Quarterly* 37(2): 72–84.

Homer, P. and Kahle, L. (1988) A structural equation test of the value-attitude-behavior hierarchy. *Journal of Personality and Social Psychology* 54: 638–646.

Reisinger, Y. and Turner, L. (1999) A cultural analysis of Japanese tourists: challenges for tourism marketers. *European Journal of Marketing* 33(11/12): 1203–1227.

Part 4

Conclusion

The significance of this book lies in suggesting a solution to the problem facing the international tourism industry of maintaining growth in inbound tourism. The book suggests that in order to respond better to the international tourist markets and avoid problems of negative perceptions and dissatisfaction with hosts, tourism industry officials should reassess their marketing practices and focus more on the cultural differences between tourists and hosts and the impact of these differences on the tourist cultural needs and experiences.

The book offers an explanation of the cultural influences on the interpersonal relations between culturally different tourists and hosts. It provides suggestions for improving marketing strategies that attempt to capture the culturally different tourist. By considering cultural differences international tourism industry operators could use a combination of cultural themes to capture the attention of the specific tourist markets. This book also offers research opportunities, which might be useful to other researchers working in related areas. More work is also required to verify the results demonstrated in this book.

Several important conclusions can be drawn from the previous chapters. The research presented in this book shows that cultural differences do exist between various populations in the tourism industry. Cultural differences between international tourists and the host community represent a very important assessment index of social interaction between tourists and hosts, and satisfaction with this interaction, in a cross-cultural tourism context. Cultural differences in values, rules of social interaction, and perceptions of service are very useful tourism constructs for explaining tourist-host social interaction and determining tourist satisfaction with this interaction. Cultural differences should form a foundation for the development of new hypotheses and theories about tourist holiday behaviour. Tourism marketers and managers should be concerned about the influence of cultural differences on tourist behaviour and work together to minimize their negative effects.

The conceptual model of the influence of cultural differences on tourist-host interaction and satisfaction with this interaction can be used in future tourist satisfaction research. This model is useful and effective because it is based on the findings of an extensive literature review. The model was tested using multivariate statistical techniques that are highly appropriate for investigating a complex concept such as culture and has proved to be very helpful in identifying cultural differences.

Knowledge of cultural differences should be used in identifying culturally different tourist markets and cultural differences should be used as very useful constructs for international tourist market segmentation, targeting, and positioning. The cultural backgrounds of international tourists help to identify cultural profiles of the market segment and determine promotional strategies that directly target a specific cultural market segment. Moreover, cultural differences should be used more often as segmentation criteria to complement the traditional segmentation criteria (geographic, socio-demographic, psychographic and behaviouristic) that seem to be insufficient for segmenting culturally different international tourist markets.

Among the cultural criteria, cultural values, rules of behaviour, perceptions, social interaction, and satisfaction appear to be very important. These variables are useful in identifying specific profiles of the Asian tourist market and for developing culture oriented marketing strategies. The key cultural themes that are of great importance to Asian tourists focus on developing close human relations with Asian tourists, proper communication that complies with Asian rules of social etiquette, face saving, avoiding direct and open expression of emotions and opinions, socializing and developing an atmosphere of closeness and respect related to a hierarchical social structure. In addition, of importance to Asian tourists are a team spirit and group activities, courtesy and responsiveness, competence, support for family, and proper greetings.

The book also identifies the need for multicultural education and training. Teaching cultural awareness is a professional obligation in the light of an internationalization of the tourism and hospitality industry and increased interaction of people from diverse cultures. As the tourism industry becomes more culturally diverse, future tourism and hospitality managers should understand their customers from different cultural backgrounds. All international holiday destinations catering for travellers from culturally different countries must recognize the need for multicultural awareness and skills training. Cross-cultural education is the only way to get ahead in the world today and should start at school and university institutions. Cross-cultural studies should be incorporated in academic curricula. Cultural awareness, communication, and interpersonal skills are necessary, not only to develop ability and knowledge for the provision of appropriate and culturally sensitive services to international tourists, but also to avoid and/or reduce tensions and build mutual understanding among international tourists and hosts with different cultural values. Cross-cultural studies are essential to prepare students to work in a multicultural environment. The tourism and hospitality industry is an international service industry that relies on the provision of services to culturally different customers. Although the number of tertiary students studying foreign languages and cultures is constantly increasing, there is a need for more subjects tailored to international tourism industry needs, including foreign cultures such as Asian, European or American cultures, cultural behaviours and expectations in host cultures, cross- and intercultural interactions and communication, and cultural confrontation. A variety of methods is available to teach cross-cultural skills such as culture assimilation programs, simulation games, subculture themes, critical incident methods, or case studies.

All tourism and hospitality industry employees should participate in compulsory cross-cultural training. Several training programs are available that teach appropriate interpersonal skills and cultural awareness skills. Jafari and Way (1994) suggested multicultural training that begins with language and cross-cultural communication training. They suggested a language training program that also includes culture, symbols, and understanding cultural expectations of foreign guests. Earley (1987) suggested intercultural communication training that develops the individual's self-awareness and the ability to recognize cultural differences in personal values and behaviour. Certo (1976) recommended the cross-cultural orientation programs that teach effective ways of interacting and avoiding interpersonal misunderstanding. Harris and Moran (1983) recommended action learning that teaches cross-cultural effectiveness in a host country and utilizes local trainers. Cross-cultural training programs

323

help to understand one's own culture, the culture of the tourist, appreciate the differences between cultures and, as a result, accept culturally different tourist markets. Generally speaking, such training teaches the provider to respect and communicate with culturally different tourists. As such, the international tourist would develop a feeling of the hosts' understanding of the tourists' cultural aspects and the willingness of hosts to cater for the tourist in a professional manner. Such training would help to guarantee every destination's success in the international tourist marketplace.

However, many training methods developed in the west might not be appropriate for other cultural groups. For example, role-playing, which is perceived as a highly effective method in developing interpersonal skills in the west, might not be effective in high risk avoidance cultures where members have difficulty agreeing to take up the roles assigned, and actively participate (Howe *et al.*, 1990). Therefore, cultural training should also be targeted at the cultural audience in a manner sensitive to particular cultural attitudes.

Additional web-based support material and references

The extensive referencing in this book has meant that the huge list of references needed for the reference list cannot be published with this book. Consequently, only a shortened list of major references is published and the remaining references are located on the publisher's website.

Other support material contained on the website includes:

■ a detailed chapter on hypothesis testing including recommended methods
■ a detailed set of tables for the Mann-Whitney U-test analysis used in Chapter 9
■ a glossary of terms relevant to the book.

References

(The list given below is for the major references cited within the book. A more comprehensive list of references can be found on our website: www.bh.com/companion/0750656689)

Adler, N. (1986) *International Dimensions of Organizational Behavior*. Boston, MA: Kent Publishing Company.

Adler, P. S. (1975) The transition experience: an alternative view of culture shock. *Journal of Humanistic Psychology* 15(4): 13–23.

Allport, G. W. (1954/1979) *The Nature of Prejudice*. New York: Doubleday Anchor; Reading, MA: Addison-Wesley Publishing.

Allport, G. W., Vernon, P. E. and Lindzey, G. (1951/1960) *A Study of Values: A Scale for Measuring the Dominant Interest in Personality*. Boston, MA: Houghton Mifflin Co.

Argyle, M. (1967/1978) *The Psychology of Interpersonal Behaviour*. Harmondsworth: Penguin Books Ltd.

Argyle, M. (1972) Nonverbal communication in human social interaction. In Hinde, R. (ed.) *Nonverbal Communication*. London: Royal Society and Cambridge University Press.

Argyle, M. (1975) *Bodily Communication*. London: Methuen.

Argyle, M. (1981) Intercultural communication. In Argyle, M. (ed.) *Social Skills and Work*. London: Methuen.

Argyle, M. (1982) Studies in cross-cultural interaction: intercultural communication. In Bochner, S. (ed.) *Cultures in Contact: Studies in Cross-Cultural Interaction*. Oxford: Pergamon Press.

Argyle, M. (1986) Rules for social relationships in four cultures. *Australian Journal of Psychology* 38(3): 309–318.

Argyle, M. and Cook, M. (1976) *Gaze and Mutual Gaze*. Cambridge, MA: Cambridge University Press.

Argyle, M. and Henderson, M. (1984) The rules of friendship. *Journal of Personal and Social Relationships* 1: 211–237.

Argyle, M. and Henderson, M. (1985a) *The Anatomy of Relationships: And the Rules and Skills Needed to Manage Them Successfully.* London: Heinemann.

Argyle, M. and Henderson, M. (1985b) The rules of relationships. In Duck, S. and Perlman, D. (eds) *Understanding Personal Relationships.* London and Beverly Hills, CA: Sage Publications, pp. 63–84.

Argyle, M., Furnham, A. and Graham, J. (1981) *Social Situations.* Cambridge: Cambridge University Press.

Argyle, M., Graham, J. and White, P. (1979) The rules of different situation. *New Zealand Psychologist* 8: 13–22.

Argyle, M., Henderson, M. and Furnham, A. (1985a). In Argyle, M. (1988) *Bodily Communication.* London: International Universities Press, pp. 184.

Argyle, M., Henderson, M. and Furnham, A. (1985b) The rules of social relationships. *British Journal of Social Psychology* 24: 125–139.

Argyle, M., Henderson, M., Bond, M. H., Iizuka, Y. and Contarello, A. (1986) Cross-cultural variations in relationship rules. *International Journal of Psychology* 21: 287–315.

Befu, H. (1971) *Japan: An Anthropological Introduction.* New York: Harper and Row.

Benedict, R. (1946/1967) *The Chrysanthemum and the Sword.* Boston, MA: Houghton Mifflin.

Benedict, R. (1974) *The Chrysanthemum and the Sword: Patterns of Japanese Culture.* Vermont and Tokyo: Charles E. Tuttle Company Inc. of Rutland.

Black, J. S. and Mendenhall, M. (1989) A practical but theory-based framework for selecting cross-cultural training methods. *Human Resource Management* 28(4): 511–539.

Bochner, S. (1982) *Cultures in Contact: Studies in Cross-Cultural Interaction.* Oxford; New York: Pergamon Press.

Bond, M. and Chinese Culture Connection (1987) Chinese values and the search for culture-free dimensions of culture. *Journal of Cross-Cultural Psychology* 18(2): 143–174.

Brislin, R. W. (1981) *Cross-Cultural Encounters: Face to Face Interaction.* New York: Pergamon Press.

Chinese Culture Connection (1987) Chinese values and the search for culture-free dimensions of culture. *Cross-Cultural Psychology* 18(2): 143–174.

Cole, M. and Scribner, S. (1974) *Culture and Thought*. New York: John Wiley and Sons.

Cook, M. (1979) *Perceiving Others*. London: Methuen.

Cook, S. W. (1962) The systematic analysis of socially significant events: a strategy for social research. *Journal of Social Issues* 18(2): 66–84.

Cook, S. W. and Sellitz, C. (1955) Some factors which influence the attitudinal outcomes of personal contact. *International Sociological Bulletin* 7: 51–58.

Cronen, V. and Shuter, R. (1983) Forming intercultural bonds. In Gudykunst, W. (ed.) *Intercultural Communication Theory: Current Perspectives*. Beverley Hills, CA: Sage Publications.

Damen, L. (1987) *Culture Learning: The Fifth Dimension in the Language Classroom*. Second Language Professional Library. Reading, MA: Addison-Wesley Publishing.

Dann, G. (1978) Tourist satisfaction: a highly complex variable. *Annals of Tourism Research* 5(4): 440–443.

Dodd, C. (1995/1998) *Dynamics of Intercultural Communication*. Boston, MA: McGraw-Hill.

Feather, N. T. (1980a) Similarity of values systems within the same nation: evidence from Australia and Papua New Guinea. *Australian Journal of Psychology* 32(1): 17–30.

Feather, N. T. (1980b) Value systems and social interaction: a field study in a newly independent nation. *Journal of Applied Social Psychology* 10 (1): 1–19

Feather, N. T. (1980c) The study of values. *Journal of Asia-Pacific and World Perspectives* 3: 3–13.

Feather, N. T. and Peay, E. R. (1975) The structure of terminal and instrumental values: dimensions and clusters. *Australian Journal of Psychology* 27: 151–164.

Forgas, J. P. (1985) *Interpersonal Behavior: The Psychology of Social Interaction*. Rusheutters Bay: Pergamon Press.

Furnham, A. and Bochner, S. (1986) *Culture Shock: Psychological Reactions to Unfamiliar Environments*. New York: Methuen.

Goodenough, W. H. (1957) Cultural anthropology and linguistics. In Keesing, R. M. (1981) *Cultural Anthropology-A Contemporary Perspective*. New York: Holt, Rinehart and Winston.

Goodenough, W. H. (1961) Comment on cultural evolution. *Daedalus* 90: 521–528.

Goodenough, W. H. (1971) *Culture, Language and Society*. Anthropology 7. Reading, MA: Addison-Wesley Publishing.

Gordon, L. V. (1960) *Survey of Interpersonal Values*. Chicago: Science Research Associates.

Gronroos, C. (1982) A service quality model and its marketing implications. *European Journal of Marketing* 18(4): 36–44.

Gudykunst, W. B. (1988) *Theories in Intercultural Communication*. Newbury Park, CA: Sage Publications.

Gudykunst, W. B. and Kim, Y. Y. (1984) *Communicating with Strangers: An Approach to Intercultural Communication*. Reading, MA: Addison-Wesley Publishing.

Gudykunst, W. B. and Kim, Y. Y. (1997) *Communicating with Strangers: An Approach to Intercultural Communication*. 3rd edn. Boston, MA; New York, NY: McGraw-Hill.

Gudykunst, W. B. and Ting-Toomey, S. (1988) *Culture and Interpersonal Communication*. Newbury Park, CA: Sage Publications.

Gullahorn, J. E. and Gullahorn, J. T. (1963) An extension of the U-curve hypothesis. *Journal of Social Issues* 19(3): 33–47.

Hall, E. T. (1959/1973) *The Silent Language*. Garden City, New York: Doubleday and Fawcett Company, Anchor Press.

Hall, E. T. (1965) *The Silent Language*. Greenwich, CT: Fawcett Company.

Hall, E. T. (1966) *The Hidden Dimension*. Garden City, New York: Doubleday and Fawcett Company.

Hall, E. T. (1976/1977) *Beyond Culture*. New York: Doubleday, Anchor Press.

Hall, E. T. (1983) *The Dance Of Life: The Other Dimensions of Time*. New York: Doubledy.

Hall, E. T. and Hall, M. R. (1987) *Hidden Differences: Doing Business with the Japanese*. Garden City, New York: Anchor Press/Doubleday.

Hampden-Turner, C. and Trompenaars, F. (1993) *Seven Cultures of Capitalism: Value Systems for Creating Wealth in the United States, Britain, Japan, Germany, France, Sweden and the Netherlands*. New York: Doubleday.

Hargie, O. (1986) *A Handbook of Communication Skills*. London: Routledge.

Harre, R. (1974) Some remarks on 'rule' as a scientific concept. In Mitschel, T. (ed.) *Understanding Other Persons*. Oxford: Blackwell.

Harre, R. and Secord, P. (1972) *The Explanation of Social Behavior*. Oxford: Basil Blackwell.

Harris, P. and Moran, R. (1979/1983/1996) *Managing Cultural Differences*. Houston, Texas: Gulf Publishing Company.

Hofstede, G. (1980) *Culture's Consequences: International Differences in Work-Related Values*. Beverly Hills, CA: Sage Publications.

Hofstede, G. (1984) *Culture's Consequences: International Differences in Work-related Values*. Abridged edition, Beverly Hills CA: Sage Publications.

Hofstede, G. (2001) *Culture's Consequences: Comparing Values, Behaviors, Institutions, and Organizations Across Nations*. 2nd ed. Thousand Oaks: Sage Publications.

Hughes, K. (1991) Tourist satisfaction: a guided cultural tour in North Queensland. *Australian Psychologist* 26(3): 166–171.

Hunt, H. K. (1991) Consumer satisfaction, dissatisfaction, and complaining behavior. *Journal of Social Issues* 47(1): 107–117.

Joreskog, K. and Sorbom, D. (1989a) *LISREL 7: User's Reference Guide*. Scientific Software Inc., Mooresville.

Joreskog, K. G. and Sorbom, D. (1989b) *LISREL 7: A Guide to the Program and Applications*. 2nd ed. Chicago Ill: SPSS Inc.

Kamal, A. A. and Maruyama, G. (1990) Cross-cultural contact and attitudes of Qatari students in the United States. *International Journal of Intercultural Relations* 14: 123–134.

Keesing, R. M. (1974) Theories of culture. *Annual Review of Anthropology* 3: 73–97.

Kim, Y. Y. (1988) *Communication and Cross-Cultural Adaptation: An Integrative Theory*. Intercommunication Series. Philadelphia: Multilingual Matters Ltd.

Kim, Y. Y. and Gudykunst, W. B. (1988) *Theories in Intercultural Communication*. International And Intercultural Communication Annual 12. Newbury Park, CA: Sage Publications.

Kluckhohn, C. (1944) *Mirror For Man*. New York: McGraw-Hill.

Kluckhohn, C. (1951a) The study of culture. In Lerner, D. and Lasswell, H. D. (eds) *The Policy Sciences*. Stanford, CA: Stanford University Press.

Kluckhohn, C. (1951b) Values and value orientations in the theory of action. In Parsons, T. and Shils, E. A. (eds) *Toward a General Theory of Action*. Cambridge, MA: Harvard University Press, pp. 388–433.

Kluckhohn, C. and Kelly, W. H. (1945) The concept of culture. In Linton, R. (ed.) *The Science of Man in the World of Crisis*. New York: Columbia University Press, pp. 78–106.

Kluckhohn, F. R. and Strodtbeck, F. L. (1961) *Variations in Value Orientations*. New York: Harper and Row.

Kroeber, A. and Kluckhohn, C. (1952) *Culture: A Critical Review of Concepts and Definition*. Papers of the Peabody Museum of American Archaeology and Ethnology, Harvard University Press 47(1): 223. New York: Random House.

Kroeber, A. and Kluckhohn, C. (1985) *Culture: A Critical Review of Concepts and Definitions*. New York: Random House.

Kroeber, A. L. and Parsons, T. (1958) The concepts of culture and of social system. *American Sociological Review* 23: 582–593.

Landis, D. and Brislin, R. W. (1983) *Handbook of Intercultural Training 2 and 3: Issues in Training Methodology*. New York: Pergamon Press.

Lehtinen, U. and Lehtinen, J. R. (1982) *Service Quality: A Study of Quality Dimensions*. Working Paper, Service Management, Institute Helsinki, Finland.

Lovelock, C. H. (1991) *Services Marketing*. 2nd ed. New Jersey: Prentice Hall.

Lustig, M. and Koester, J. (1993/1999) *Intercultural Competence: Interpersonal Communication Across Cultures*. New York: Harper Collins.

Maddox, R. N. (1985) Measuring satisfaction with tourism. *Journal of Travel Research* 23(3): 2–5.

Marsh, N. R. and Henshall, B. D. (1987) Planning better tourism: the strategic importance of tourist-resident expectations and interactions. *Tourism Recreation Research* 12(2): 47–54.

Maznewski, M. (1994) *Synergy and Performance in Multi-cultural Teams*. PhD thesis University of Western Ontario.

Morris, C. W. (1956) *Varieties of Human Value*. Chicago: University of Chicago Press.

Nakane, C. (1973) *Japanese Society*. New York: Penguin.

Oberg, K. (1960) Culture shock: adjustment to new cultural environments. *Practical Anthropology* 7: 177–182.

Olander, F. (1977) Consumer satisfaction – a sceptic's view. In Hunt, H. K. (ed) *Conceptualization and Measurement of Consumer Satisfaction and Dissatisfaction*. Cambridge, MA: Marketing Science Institute, pp. 409–452.

Parasuraman, A., Zeithaml, V. A. and Berry, L. L. (1985) A conceptual model of service quality and its implications for future research. *Journal of Marketing* 49: 41–50.

Parasuraman, A., Zeithaml, V. A. and Berry, L. L. (1986) *SERVQUAL: A Multiple-Scale Item for Measuring Consumer Perceptions of Service Quality*. Cambridge, MA: Marketing Institute.

Parasuraman, A., Zeithaml, V. and Berry, L. L. (1988) SERVQUAL: a multiple-scale item for measuring consumer perceptions of service quality. *Journal of Retailing* 64: 12–40.

Parasuraman, A., Zeithaml, V. and Berry, L. L. (1990) *An Empirical Examination of Relationships In an Extended Service Quality Model*. Cambridge, MA: Marketing Science Institute.

Parasuraman, A., Berry, L. L. and Zeithaml, V. (1991) Refinement and reassessment of the SERVQUAL scale. *Journal of Retailing* 67(1): 39–48.

Parsons, T. (1951) *The Social System*. Glencoe, Ill: Free Press.

Pearce, P. L. (1980a) Favorability-satisfaction model of tourists' evaluations. *Journal of Travel Research* 14(1): 13–17.

Pearce, P. L. (1980b) Tourism's human conflicts. *Annals of Tourism Research* 7(1): 21–134.

Pearce, P. L. (1982b) *The Social Psychology of Tourist Behaviour*. International Series in Experimental Social Psychology. Vol. 3. Oxford; New York: Pergamon Press.

Pearce, P. L. (1982c) Tourists and their hosts: some social and psychological effects of intercultural contact. In Bochner, S. (ed.) (1982) *Cultures in Contact: Studies in Cross-Cultural Interaction*. Oxford; New York: Pergamon Press.

Pearce, P. L. (1988) *The Ulysses Factor: Evaluating Visitors in Tourist Settings*. New York: Springer Verlag.

Pearce, P. and Bochner, S. (1982) Tourists and hosts: some social and psychological effects of intercultural contact. In Bochner, S. (ed) *Cultures in Contact: Studies in Cross-Cultural Interaction*. International Series Experimental Psychology Vol. 1. Oxford: Pergamon Press, pp. 199–221.

Pitts, R. and Woodside, A. (1986) Personal values and travel decisions. *Journal of Travel Research* 25(1): 20–25.

Pizam, A. and Calantone, R. (1987) Beyond psychographics – values as determinants of tourist behavior. *International Journal of Hospitality Management* 6(3): 177–181.

Porter, R. E. and Samovar, L. A. (1988) Approaching intercultural communication. In Samovar, L. A. and Porter, R. E. (eds) *Intercultural Communication: A Reader*. 5th ed. Belmont, CA: Wadsworth Publishing Company.

Reisinger, Y. (1992b) Tourist-host contact as a part of cultural tourism. *World Leisure and Recreation* 36(2): 24–28.

Reisinger, Y. and Turner, L. (1999c) Structural equation modelling with LISREL: application in tourism. *Tourism Management* 20(1): 71–88.

Reisinger, Y. and Turner, L. (2002a) Cultural differences between Asian tourist markets and Australian hosts Part 1. *Journal of Travel Research* 40(3): 295–315.

Reisinger, Y. and Turner, L. (2002b) Cultural differences between Asian tourist markets and Australian hosts Part 2. *Journal of Travel Research* 40(4): 374–384.

Robinson, G. L. N. and Nemetz, L. (1988) *Cross-Cultural Understanding.* UK: Prentice Hall International.

Robinson, J. and Preston, J. (1976) Equal status contact and modification of racial prejudice: re-examination of the contact hypothesis. *Social Forces* 54: 911–924.

Rokeach, M. (1968a) A theory of organization and change within value-attitude systems. *Journal of Social Issues* 24: 13–33.

Rokeach, M. (1968b) *Beliefs, Attitudes and Values.* San Francisco: Jossey-Bass.

Rokeach, M. (1973) *The Nature of Human Values.* New York: Free Press.

Rokeach, M. (1979) *Understanding Human Values: Individual and Societal.* New York: Free Press.

Samovar, L. A. and Porter, R. E. (1988) *Intercultural Communication: A Reader.* 5th ed. Belmont, CA: Wadsworth Publishing Company.

Samovar, L. A. and Porter, R. E. (1991) *Communication Between Cultures.* Belmont, CA: Wadsworth Publishing Company.

Samovar, L. A., Porter, R. E. and Jain, N. C. (1981) *Understanding Intercultural Communication.* Belmont, CA: Wadsworth Publishing Company.

Samovar, L., Porter, R. and Stefani, L. (1998) *Communication Between Cultures.* Belmont, CA: Wadsworth Publishing Company.

Schein, E. (1992) *Organizational Culture and Leadership.* 2nd ed. San Francisco, CA: Jossey-Bass Publishers.

Schneider, D. (1976) Notes toward a theory of culture. In Basso, K. and Selby, H. (eds) *Meaning in Anthropology.* Albuquerque, New Mexico: University of New Mexico Press, pp. 197–220.

Schneider, S. and Barsoux, J.-L. (1997) *Managing Across Cultures.* New York: Prentice Hall.

Scollon, R. and Scollon, S. (1995) *Intercultural Communication: A Discourse Approach.* Cambridge, MA: Blackwell.

Shostack, G. L. (1985) Planning the service encounter. In Czepiel, J. A. Solomon, M. R. and Surprenant, C. F. (eds) *The Service Encounter.* Lexington, MA: Lexington Books, pp. 243–254.

Smith, V. L. (1978) *Hosts and Guests.* Oxford: Blackwell.

Smith, V. L. (1989) *Hosts and Guests: The Anthropology of Tourism.* 2nd ed. Philadelphia: University of Pennsylvania Press.

Sutton, W. A. (1967) Travel and understanding: notes on the social structure of touring. *International Journal of Comparative Sociology* 8(2): 218–223.

Swan, J. E. and Mercer, A. A. (1981) *Consumer Satisfaction as a Function of Equity and Disconfirmation*. Unpublished Paper, University of Alabama in Birmingham, Alabama.

Taft, R. (1977) Coping with unfamiliar cultures. In Warren, N. (ed.) *Studies in Cross-Cultural Psychology 1*. London: Academic Press.

Taft, R. (1979) Effect of a planned intercultural experience on the attitudes and behavior of the participants. *International Journal of Intercultural Relations* 3(2): 187–197.

Tajfel, H. (1969) Social and cultural factors in perception. In Lindzey, G. and Aronson, E. (eds) *The Handbook of Social Psychology*. Reading, MA: Addison-Wesley Publishing.

Triandis, H. C. (1972) *The Analysis of Subjective Culture*. New York: Wiley-Interscience.

Triandis, H. C. (1977a) Subjective culture and interpersonal relations across cultures. In Loeb-Adler, L. (ed.) Issues in Cross-Cultural Research. *Annals of the New York Academy of Sciences* 285: 418–434.

Triandis, H. C. (1977b) *Interpersonal Behavior*. Monterey, CA: Brooks/Cole Publishing Company.

Triandis, H. C. (1994) *Culture and Social Behavior*. New York: McGraw-Hill.

Triandis, H. C. (1995) *Individualism and Collectivism: New Directions in Social Psychology*. Boulder, CO: Westview Press.

Triandis, H. C. and Triandis, L. M. (1960) Race, social class, religion, and nationality as determinants of social distance. *Journal of Abnormal and Social Psychology* 61: 110–118.

Triandis, H. C. and Vassiliou, V. A. (1967) Frequency of contact and stereotyping. *Journal of Personality and Social Psychology* 7: 316–328.

Triandis, H. C., Vassiliou, V., Vassiliou, G., Tanaka, Y. and Shanmugam, A. V. (1972b) *The Analysis of Subjective Culture*. New York: John Wiley and Sons.

Trompenaars, F. (1984) *The Organisation of Meaning and the Meaning of Organisation a comparative study on the conceptions and organisational structure in different cultures*. PhD thesis, University of Pennsylvania.

Trompenaars, F. (1993/1997) *Riding the Waves of Culture: Understanding Cultural Diversity in Business*. London: Brealey.

Turner, L. and Reisinger, Y. (1999) Importance and expectations of destination attributes for Japanese tourists to Hawaii and the Gold Coast compared. *Asia Pacific Journal of Tourism Research* 4(2): 1–18.

Valle, V. A. and Wallendorf, M. (1977) Consumers' attributions of the causes of their product satisfaction and dissatisfaction. In Day, R. L. (ed.) *Consumer Satisfaction, Dissatisfaction and Complaining Behaviour*. Bloomington: Indiana.

Van Raaij, W. F. and Francken, D. A. (1984) Vacation decisions, activities, and satisfaction. *Annals of Tourism Research* 11(1): 101–112.

Vassiliou, V., Triandis, H. C., Vassiliou, G. and McGuire, H. (1972) Interpersonal contact and stereotyping. In Triandis, H. C. and Vassiliou, V., Vassiliou, G., Tanaka, Y. and Shanmugam, A. V. (eds) *The Analysis of Subjective Culture*. New York: John Wiley and Sons.

Wei, L., Crompton, J. L. and Reid, L. M. (1989) Cultural conflicts: experiences of US visitors to China. *Tourism Management* 10(4): 322–332.

Whorf, B. L. (1956) *Language, Thought, and Reality, Selected Writings*. Cambridge, MA, Cambridge Technology Press of Massachusetts Institute of Technology.

Zavalloni, M. (1980) Values. In Triandis, H. C. and Brislin, R. W. (eds) *Handbook of Cross-Cultural Psychology: Social Psychology 5*. Boston, MA: Allyn and Bacon.

Index